Transformation Theology

Transformation Theology is the first book in a series which presents new work in the area of theological engagement with and for the world. This orientation takes as its point of departure fundamental reflection upon revelation – understood as a presently dynamic and transforming reality in space and time – as well as the intersection of theology with current issues in public life. The Transformation Theology series aims to provide a new forum for constructive and critical thinking on the interaction of revelation, church, society and world.

Planned titles include:

The Command of Grace

Spirit and Letter

Religion and the Act of Reading

The Christian Text: Theology, Language and World

Revelation, Politics and Law

Transformation Theology

Church in the World

Oliver Davies

Paul D. Janz

Clemens Sedmak

t&t clark

Published by T&T Clark International
The Tower Building, 11 York Road, London SE1 7NX
80 Maiden Lane, Suite 704, New York, NY 10038

www.continuumbooks.com

First published 2007

British Library Cataloguing-in-Publication Data
A catalogue record for this book is available from the British Library

Typeset by YHT Ltd, London
Printed on acid-free paper in Great Britain by Cromwell Press Ltd, Trowbridge, Wiltshire

ISBN-10: HB: 0-567-03246-9
        PB: 0-567-03247-7
ISBN-13: HB: 978-0-567-03246-1
        PB: 978-0-567-03247-8

Contents

Prologue: Transformation Theology

At the heart of the Christian gospel and church confession is the claim that God took on flesh for us in Jesus Christ and entered into our world of space and time. It is therefore the claim that God became real for us in the only way in which he can truly be real for us: as a fellow human being, who experiences as we do and shares our mortal fate. But our claim is also that he lived differently from us, for his death was also a being raised into life and the bringing of a new kind of life for us into the world.

The claim to the reality of the incarnation is not a simple one. It is not for instance the claim that Jesus had only historical, though perhaps paradigmatic, existence and is now dead, or his ultimate fate unknown. It is rather the claim that he is really risen and, as we say in the creeds, that he is now seated at the right hand of the Father in heaven. The Christian confession is that he still lives, therefore. True humanity and true divinity are *still* truly one in him, today no less than in the days of his mortal flesh, and he is still truly alive.

But how realistic is this claim? Or with what theological intelligibility can it be affirmed today? Or to put it another way, what do we mean when we confess that Jesus still lives? After all, for the incarnate Son of God to be alive – if his being alive is to have any significance for us at all – must be for him to be embodied. If he is not embodied, in some humanly meaningful sense of this term, then our human nature – to which embodiment definitively belongs – cannot be any longer expressed in him. Historically the Church resisted the notion that Christ's humanity has been absorbed into his divinity following the resurrection, just as it resisted the notion that his humanity after his resurrection is wholly other than our own. The way that the pre-modern Church envisaged this was in terms of a heavenly scene in which Jesus, risen, ascended and glorified, was seated at the right hand of the Father in heaven. This requires a certain kind of cosmology, however – one very alien to our own – and so we find ourselves confronted today in much more difficult ways with the questions concerning Jesus' continuing humanity and embodiment, and with what it is that we mean when we proclaim that he is still truly alive. We have struggled to make sense of the Christian claim not only that the body of Jesus is risen, but

1

also and particularly that his body is now ascended and glorified, even though these are, according to scriptural and creedal tradition, the current and living transformations of Jesus' embodied life. The world order of which Christians are no less a part than anyone else has developed accounts of matter and the material which seem to be deeply at odds with the transformation which is implied in Jesus' ongoing embodiment.

In relation to our doctrinal inheritance, therefore, there appears today to be a kind of loss or deficit in theology, a sense of interruption in the continuing living reality of the incarnate Jesus Christ. For we may indeed be able to make the foundational claim that the self-revelation of God in the man Jesus of Nazareth some two millennia ago was indeed a *real* self-revelation in flesh and blood. But we have ceased to know how to be able to affirm that this *very same* real world of sensible human embodiment in space and time into which Jesus came should even today continue to be the site of God's real self-revelation in Jesus Christ just as it was then. We are thus apt, along with Karl Barth, to understand theology today as needing to exercise itself as a discipline 'between the times' of what is seen as the two specific and definitive 'realities' of God's self-revelation: a past reality in the incarnation of Jesus Christ in a human body, and a future reality in the final judgement. What has occurred as a consequence of such a view is that the reality of theological reference and authority has come to be located everywhere but in the present: in the reality of a distant past, in the reality of an extreme future, or in the utterly intangible 'reality' of a radical beyond.

It is our common view, therefore, that contemporary theology has been deeply shaped by a 'fundamental loss to incarnational revelation' and finds itself, often even at its very deepest levels, in a broad retreat from the real world of space and time as the ongoing site of God's self-revelation today, and thus as the site of its own subject matter. It has instead increasingly allowed its focus to come to rest entirely within the sensibly abstracted, or strictly linguistic and grammatical domains of text, kerygma, narrative, hermeneutics, dialectic and so on, as *end-stations* for theological authority and endeavour. This observation should in no way be understood as intending to diminish the vital necessity of any of these as essential components in the very fabric of theological reflection and exchange. It is only to say that, insofar as these have indeed been allowed to become ends in themselves, theology has thereby lost its connection to its own indispensable incarnational ground at the centre of embodied life, and has ceased to be meaningful there.

But now it is precisely for this reason that we must also speak of another kind of theological deficit or interruption, in addition to the one separating much of contemporary theology from its own doctrinal heritage on these matters. This second interruption or lacuna concerns what is often a deep separation which can exist today between academic theology and the Church. For while it is true that the theological restriction of the self-revelation of God to sensibly abstracted domains does indeed make the *theological* task itself much easier, nevertheless such a view of revelation can have no real meaning or resonance for the real Church in the world today. That is, it can have no resonance or meaning for the living community of faith, where the present reality of Jesus Christ for real embodied human beings is affirmed unhesitatingly and daily, by confession and practice, as the indispensable ground of the Church's own dynamism and being. Of course theology speaks a great deal *about* the Church in the form of descriptive ecclesiologies. But all too seldom does it address itself in fundamental ways *to* and *for* the Church and in the service of the Church.

We cannot conceal the sense, therefore, that the mistrust and even suspicion under which academic theology is often held today by the Church is rooted precisely in the fact that much of contemporary theology has lost its way with regard to the critical issue of the reality of the incarnation for us today. As the following chapters will show, there are several crucial historical reasons for this loss, and the loss is indeed a very deep one. And while what is offered in this volume under the title of *Transformation Theology* is not yet an ecclesiology, it nonetheless seeks to provide a groundwork for bridging the gulf that often exists between academic theology and the community of faith, by providing a rigorous *theological* account of the present reality of Jesus Christ in the world today, as this is already affirmed in living faith within the Church.

Why then 'Transformation Theology' exactly? Or what precisely is the intended significance of this term? It may already be clear from the foregoing that Transformation Theology is not meant to be understood *firstly* or most fundamentally as denoting a transformation in the *life of the believer*, or in the praxis and self-understanding of the believer in the world. It is of course also this, and indeed very importantly and indispensably so, but only derivatively. (This is one of the transformational aspects addressed by Clemens Sedmak in the third pair of chapters below, under the theme of ethics.) Likewise, Transformation Theology should not be understood as denoting *firstly* a transformation in *theological procedure* or method, even though it will again also importantly demand this as well, and this indeed in truly fundamental and far-reaching ways, but again only derivatively. (This is the aspect addressed by Paul Janz in the second pair of chapters.) Transformation Theology is rather to be understood firstly as a form of reflection which acknowledges in faith the irreversible transformation that has taken place in the body of Jesus Christ himself by the divine power, in the living and present reality of his resurrection and Ascension. It is this body, to which Transformation Theology points, with and on behalf of the Church, that must always remain its primary ground. It is concerning the theological and doctrinal imperatives and possibilities of this fundamental transformation, which – through new creation – has profound implications also for the transformation of the world which 'hosts' the transformed and transforming body, that Oliver Davies writes in the initial pair of chapters. When taken together, therefore, the 'transformation' pointed to, spoken of and called for in this enterprise is theologically comprehensive, and it falls into three different yet inextricably related emphases: firstly, doctrinal and creedal, or in terms of theological content; secondly, methodological, or in terms of theological procedure; and thirdly, ethical, or in terms of what the first two taken together must mean in Christian life and praxis, and indeed for ethics itself as a discipline.

Or, to sum this up somewhat more fully, what draws these focuses together, and what thereby identifies Transformation Theology in its initial formulation in this book, is something essentially threefold, corresponding to the three pairings of chapters by Oliver Davies, Paul Janz and Clemens Sedmak. Firstly, it is an affirmation of the continuing fullness and reality of the incarnation today with a view to the transformation which is encountered in the body of the incarnate Jesus Christ himself in the present reality of his resurrection and Ascension. But such a reaffirmation of Jesus Christ as presently real then also requires, secondly, a fundamental transformation in theological procedure or method, and especially a transformation in original modes of theological attentiveness. Most essentially, this second transformation involves the redis-covery of the real world of embodied sensible human experience in space and time as the ongoing and indispensable site of God's self-revelation today, and therefore as a primary and indispensable source of theological authority today. Thirdly, and on the basis of these first two, it addresses in a new way the transformation which is demanded in Christian life and praxis, and indeed thereby in ethics itself as a discipline for theology, resulting finally in a transformation of the world itself. In all of these respects, therefore, Transfor-mation Theology at its heart is resolutely and uncompromisingly a *theology in the world*. And what this means most essentially is that in any of its modes – doctrinal/creedal, methodological, ethical/practical – it is an endeavour which finds its points of theological reference never anywhere else but in and through the world, which is to say always incarnationally, just as the ongoing and living present reality of the incarnate Christ himself demands.

But it is vital now to emphasize something further. And this is to say that, despite its uncompromising orientation in and to the world, what will be presented here will be no less rigorously a genuine *theo*-logy. In other words, Transformation Theology takes with full seriousness the Barthian challenge – and the immense value of Barth's contribution on this point for present-day theology should never be underestimated – that theology's rightful and defining focus can and must be thoroughly and fundamentally on 'the Godness of God'. It thereby agrees also fully with the corresponding affirmation of the 'infinite qualitative distinction' between God and the world, or between this life and the next. It objects, however, along with Bonhoeffer, Rahner and others, to the further Barthian development of this (which has also become the generally prevalent view today), that theological engagement with the Godness of God can only be assured by directing theological attention *away* from the real world of sensible embodiment and into essentially mental domains, rather than focusing its attention in and through this world precisely as the indispensable locus of theological authority.

It is for this same reason that Transformation Theology is to be distinguished all the more from the current radical approaches to orthodoxy, which seek to regain a 'public' legitimacy for theology by isolating theology entirely within philological, literary or other essentially theoretical domains. Indeed, such approaches radicalize precisely the aspects of the Barthian enterprise that this book seeks to limit and correct. It cannot be denied that the 'public' legitimacy gained in such ventures is indeed a grammatically self-guaranteeing and thus a supremely impregnable 'legitimacy', in virtue of which every kind of theological triumphalism can be claimed. But by sequestering itself entirely within the grammatical confines of theory, whether philological, literary or social, it can have no real bearing on the pressing question with which the real Church in the world finds itself constantly confronted: namely that of the present reality of Jesus Christ at the centre of sensibly embodied human life.

Far from orienting itself to self-guaranteeing theoretical resolutions within theology, therefore, Transformation Theology in fact does precisely the opposite. It orients itself most fundamentally not to the *resolutions* which can be provided within theory and grammar, but rather most fundamentally to the inexorable *resistances* with which thinking unavoidably finds itself confronted in embodied reality. In other words, the primary thrust of reason in this theological project is *critical* and not 'holistic' as it is frequently treated in theology today. It is an orientation, as such, which seeks neither to exclude nor to soften the difficulty for theology of the questions about real embodiment, or the questions about the sensible reality within which embodiment is defined. It seeks rather to bring these questions to their full sharpness in order to restore sensible embodied reality to its proper place as the indispensable site of God's self-revelation in the world, within which incarnational revelation will be found to confront theology with what Paul Janz calls an intractable 'finality of *non-resolution*' for any of its fundamental questioning.

In other words, Transformation Theology wishes to resist any easy circumvention of the difficult demands of space and time by the infinitely varied and sophisticated strategies of the human mind, which – for all their richness – have often become oriented almost entirely to structures of meaning and conception to the exclusion of what must remain the more primary *reception* of causally embodied reality through sensibility. Yet by thus reinstating the vitality of sensible embodiment as an indispensable source of attention for theology, the intention is by no means to revert to an opposing error by overemphasizing the sensible at the expense of the rational (as if it were somehow possible to split these apart anyway, whether anthropologically or incarnationally), or to espouse a new kind of neo-Romantic, anti-rational vitalism. Far from this, it is, rather, precisely through the recovery of the authority of sensible reality as *incarnational reality* for theological reflection, to raise reason within faith to the very highest levels of its critical capacity and integrity, by ensuring that it always remains properly responsive and attentive to the sensible embodiment within which human reason has its origin and ground, and from within which the incarnate Christ comes to meet us as God's reality for us in the world.

The reality of incarnational revelation as new creation and transformation, which is bound up with the empirical here and now, communicated to us

through the Spirit in the actuality of our sensible living, demands of us a new
openness, therefore. Indeed, its primary function is to make the world for us a
place of openness and unthought-of 'possibility' which is inestimable and
unfathomable in its depth and extent, since all is now received in the light of
the impossible abundance of divine creativity. This is not something to be fully
ordered and possessed by theological reflection. It is, rather, encountered
theologically in the immediacy of our own sensible existence, where the shared
reality of 'world' as causal actuality and causal possibility comes to meet us with
the greatest immediacy and resistance. The openness which is the divine
creativity made present to us through the incarnation of Christ is a continuing
challenge to us to live through the senses in the presence of the generative
power of God: calling us back, time and again, to a proper engagement with the
world, to a proper life in the fullness of Spirit and to a proper place as Church in
the unfolding of God's creation.

In Chapter 1, Oliver Davies sets out the doctrinal grounds for the continuing
embodiment of Jesus Christ, who is both in the world as identifiable (cf. Acts 9)
through his humanity and is the body which contains the world (cf. Col. 1)
according to his divinity. At the centre of this chapter is an account of the
cosmological contexts for the Christian doctrine of the Ascension in the pre-
modern period, and an argument is given for the view that it was a change in
those cosmological contexts, principally from the sixteenth century, which led
to a reformulation of belief concerning the ascended Christ. What had been a
critical doctrine at the centre of the Church's understanding of its own future
destiny with God, its universal mission on earth and the character of its
'sacramental' life, now became, in the post-Reformation period, virtually an
irrelevance. Oliver Davies will argue that this 'slippage' in Christian doctrine is
not confessionally defined and is apparent across the range of Christian traditions in the contemporary world and that it calls into question also significant
aspects of our understanding of the role of the Holy Spirit.

In Chapter 2, Davies sets out an alternative account of the Ascension, based
upon a close reading of the sole instance of an encounter with the risen *and*
ascended Christ in the New Testament. St Paul's Damascus road experience is
read as a paradigm for the reality of the ascended body, and for the role of the
Holy Spirit with respect to it. It is on the basis of this text that Davies advances
a new Christological reading of the body of Jesus and gives an account of the
Holy Spirit as the Spirit of Christ's body, who sets Christians into a sensible
continuity of relation with the continuing or living body of Jesus, into whom
we are baptized. Thus Christian existence entails a change in our sensibility, so
that the life of our senses is brought into conformity with the transformation of
the world, which now contains the ascended body of Jesus and is conformed to
it. It is argued that ecclesial existence is a sensible living in and through the
Spirit which is ordered to the glorified body of Jesus and which looks towards
the new creation as the new order made real in him.

Paul Janz in the second pair of chapters then addresses a basic transformation
in theological questioning and procedure itself which is required by the

affirmation of the present reality in the world of the risen and ascended Jesus Christ. The focus here will be especially on a recovery of the real world of sensible human embodiment as the ongoing and indispensable site of God's self-revelation today, and therefore a recovery also of the real world as a primary and indispensable source of theological authority. As Chapter 3 will discuss, one of the most important aspects of the restoration of sensible attentiveness will be the recovery also of vital modes of relationality which have become forgotten or lost as sensibility has faded from view, especially under the influence of a certain 'spirit of idealism' which still predominates today in both theology and the human sciences. This will be seen to have especially far-reaching implications for the apprehension of revelation itself, which is reintroduced here as demanding to be encountered not originally as a mental communication exclusively within 'ratio', as it is predominantly viewed today, but as a fundamentally and originally *causal* divine communication to embodied human beings in the real world of space and time (which is in fact the predominating view traditionally).

The re-establishment of revelation as a divinely causal communication then becomes the motivating ground for Chapter 4, which is structured around three interrelating themes. It begins by asking what it is exactly that is disclosed in the revelation or gospel of Jesus Christ, even in the foundational events themselves, i.e., in the real empirical history of Jesus' incarnation and human embodiment. It finds that the scriptures answer this consistently and unmistakably in the overarching Pauline theme that 'in the gospel *a righteousness from God* is revealed, a righteousness that is by faith from first to last' (Rom. 1.17). The 'content' of revelation therefore is found to be given ultimately always as the transforming 're-entry' of the divine righteousness into the real world of embodied human life in Jesus Christ. This recognition then necessitates a further basic theological reorientation to the divine transcendence itself, and there are two sides to this. First, as the advent of the divine righteousness, God's transcendence is found to announce itself in revelation not in the fundamentally 'alterative' and distancing terms of the 'Wholly Other', or the absolutely remote, which stands radically 'over-against' creation. Rather, as the re-entry of the original divine righteousness, incarnational revelation will be found to announce itself at its origin in the *ex nihilo generative* terms of 'the Wholly New', a divine generativity which expresses itself from within the self-same created world in which we find ourselves bodily and sensibly alive. At its generative origin *ex nihilo*, therefore, the new or the new creation resists secondly any theological apprehension of it as a representational 'referent' for our thinking consciousness. Rather, as the re-entry of the divine righteousness, it confronts theological questioning originally with the authority of a *demand* on our practical consciousness. Indeed, grace itself will be found to announce itself with the authority not merely of a 'referent' but with the authority of a command, the 'command of grace', which needs to come to expression as pneumatology.

In the final pairing of chapters, Clemens Sedmak works through the important implications that Transformation Theology has for Christian ethics as well. Ethics is being done in the world under non-ideal conditions. Doing ethics under non-ideal conditions means that we do not start from a *tabula rasa*. Ethics is undertaken in the midst of tragedies, tragedies that deny human beings even the right to act morally, the right to choose among alternatives, the right to justify one's course of action. A tragedy like world hunger points to the limits of ethics – the limits of moral resources available for people and the impact this has on the limits of ethical reasoning. World hunger is not a technical problem that can be solved, but a tragedy that disrupts our categories, theories and classifications. It generates a 'wound of knowledge' that forces us to recognize the unfinished quality of ethical conversations and their commitment to causal transformation. Twenty-four thousand people die every day from hunger and from the consequences of undernourishment. Transformation Theology calls for the translation of ethics from a conceptual into a causal dimension, calls for a self-transformation of the ethicist and a transformative commitment to the world. This is only possible if the disruptive power of tragedies like world hunger, refugees or chronic pain is recognized. This recognition of constant disruption does not render us helpless and unable to move, however. It is, rather, an engine for transformation, for entering commitments, for transforming one's way of being in the world in the recognition of how Jesus Christ himself is real in the world. It is in this sense that the ultimate force of transformation is identified as the divine causality of love, not as a sentimental feeling, but as a powerful and dynamic presence and also as a fundamental orientation towards life, exemplified by the fundamental praxis of Jesus, who urged us to feed the hungry and to multiply the bread.

Through the focused combination and intersection of these three trajectories – doctrinal, methodological and ethical – we are seeking not only to identify the problem before us in its full depth, but also to begin what may be a longer process of rectifying it in terms of generating theology which can recalibrate basic aspects of Christian thinking in the light of the continuing incarnation of Jesus Christ, which is to say in the light of his place at the heart of the created order, as the transformed and transforming body of God. We have no doubt that there will be other ways of returning to the full incarnational force of Christian doctrine and our hope is that this book will both provoke new thinking and point the way to further stages in a project which calls both for an *aggiornomento*, by 'bringing theology up to date', and an *ad fontes* or return to the primary sources of Christianity which, in this respect at least, we have ceased to read responsibly.

DOCTRINE

1

Lost Heaven

Oliver Davies

The claim that God is real for us in Jesus Christ is one that concerns both faith and world. Christian belief will inevitably be shaped by our understanding of world therefore, though frequently in ways which go unnoticed. Part of the argument given in this chapter is that it was a new understanding of cosmology and materiality which subtly, though fundamentally, influenced the development of theology at a critical period during the development of the Reformation, though with effects which would make themselves felt over time across the spectrum of Western Christianity. One of those effects was to loosen the relation between the domain of sensibility (the life of the senses) and the actuality of faith. The 'modern' conception of matter and of the universe suggested that the reality of God for us in Jesus Christ should be sought in the spirit, not in the world, in human interiority and subjectivity, and subsequently in narrativity, rather than in the sensible as such. The sensible domain, it seemed, was a universal field that was better left to the scientist and empiricist. So deep were the changes brought by the new cosmology, over a period of centuries, that much of Christian theology has come to depart, often in profound ways, from the sensible emphases which characterized the classical tradition, from scriptural Christianity to the theology of the early Reformers. There are of course outstanding modern theologians such as Karl Rahner and Dietrich Bonhoeffer for whom sensibility and the material – the 'givenness' of everyday embodied life – retained a critical role in the reception of faith, but overwhelmingly the trajectory has been and continues to be one which leads *away* from the material as such.[1] Most particularly, what we have seen is the eclipse of a properly *doctrinal-referential* account of the 'world' as the place in which God became real for us in Jesus Christ and where he continues to be real for us as incarnate Word. Not having such an account of 'world', we have also lacked a properly theological account of what it is for us to be *in* the world as God's world.[2]

No appeal for a return to a pre-modern cosmology, in any of its forms, plays any part in this book. But at the same time it is impossible not to be aware today of the extent to which the cosmology which displaced the traditional Christian-Aristotelian one was in itself deeply flawed. The quantum universe of the modern age, with its infinity of *depth*, offers a horizon within which it is at least meaningful to speculate of invisible realities at the heart of the empirical or classical level of perception and experience. If Newtonian physics, with its emphasis upon space as extension and upon matter as the play of forces, seemed outrightly to reject a Christian cosmology (except in terms of divine authority and origination), then quantum mechanics is indeed more hospitable to it. But it is so only to the extent that it does not in principle rule out some of the cosmological possibilities which follow from belief in the incarnation. It would be wrong to take this as indicating scientific support for Christian doctrine: allowing for the possibility of a framework within which such phenomena could take place and supporting the view that such phenomena have taken and are taking place are two quite different things. But nevertheless, there is the sense that there are new possibilities for dialogue between theology and scientific cosmology with our present state of knowledge.[3]

But neither quantum theory, nor secular notions of world current today, can return us to that which has been forgotten. The language of 'world' is in itself problematic, for it tends to slip between the interstices of theological reflection. If world is not merely the *saeculum*, which is to say the uncertain, un-graced domain which forever stands in need of the gospel's proclamation, then we make use of it in one or more of its secular forms. Thus 'world' becomes 'environment', which is to say that it is the increasingly fragile object of our corporate actions. Or 'world' becomes the economic activity of our advanced social organization, in which – amongst other things – new technologies are ceaselessly produced, as human knowledge enters ever more deeply into and more extensively shapes our everyday reality. Or there again, 'world' is the community of peoples, who are more closely linked through global networks, gaining in knowledge of each other and interacting more with each other as communications increase in quality and extent ('one world'). But if we use the outrightly theological term 'creation', then we seem to move away altogether from the ordinary world of space and time: the ordinary, everyday, negotiated, empirical reality which must always be for us the place where the world most immediately 'happens'.

Indeed, if we reflect for a moment, we can see that there is in fact something intrinsically paradoxical in thinking the concept 'world'. How can we con-ceptualize something which is in effect a totality: the totality of all that is and can ever come to be? Is that not an idea which is simply too big? To objectify 'world' as a concept is to forget that subjectivity, our own and others' sub-jectivity, is itself an integral part of world which itself can never be objectified.[4] When we speak of 'world' as a totality, we are surely effectively speaking of something other than the present sensible reality of which we are ourselves intrinsically a part. We are applying a totalizing idea then which cannot but do violence in some important sense to the *actuality* of world.[5]

And yet, despite all the difficulties of concept and terminology, 'world' is an idea to which Christian theology is bound, since in faith we proclaim a God who creates and enters the world, through incarnation, reconciling 'all things visible and invisible' (Col. 1.16) and inaugurating the new creation. Like

Judaism and Islam, its sister 'Creator' religions, Christianity lays claim to 'world' though only under the conditions of revelation which means, in the case of Christianity, under the condition of the continuing or living body of Jesus, to which we make reference when we recite the creed.

1. The Classical Paradigm

The extent to which the scriptural authors and then the early Christians conceived of the world in Christological terms can still surprise us. The strong account of creation, as creation from nothing, which became the characteristic Christian reading of Genesis, presupposed the unity of all things by virtue of their common status as *created*. This was a universal unity which derived from the common relation of all that exists to the one Creator, to whom all things owe their existence. The unity of the creation was specifically linked with the Word of God, 'through whom all things were made' (Jn 1.3), in whom 'all things in heaven and earth were created', in whom 'all things hold together' and through whom 'God was able to reconcile all things, on earth or in heaven' (Col. 1.16–20).[6] It was not a closed or totalizing unity, however, since the relation between creature and God was a dynamic one which would lead to resolution in an ultimate and eschatological unity.

The Israelites believed in a three-part cosmos, of heaven or heavens above the earth and *sheol* (or the underworld) below it.[7] This is the 'world' of all that is, in the sense of 'the heavens and the earth' described at Gen. 1.1.[8] They further subdivided 'heaven' into three parts. The first was the air in which the birds fly.[9] The second was the firmament or sky in which the stars can be seen.[10] And the 'third' or 'highest heaven' is the dwelling place of God, where his throne was or which, according to some traditions, was identical with his throne.[11] It is not true to say that Yahweh was *confined* to the highest heaven, however, since there are traditions which suggest that the glory of God extends or can extend throughout heaven and earth.[12] The very height of heaven creates the possibility that God's glory will overflow, extending throughout the earth, as in Ps. 57.5, where we read, 'Be exalted, O God, above the heavens. Let your glory be over all the earth'[13], or at Isa. 6.3, where the angels around his throne in heaven declare: 'the whole earth is full of his glory'.[14] Passages such as Isa. 11.9–10, Rom. 8.18–21 and Rev. 21.1–4 show the eschatological depth of this thematic.[15]

It is important to note, however, that even though the highest heaven as the dwelling place of God exhibited all the properties of the glorious otherness of the divine Creator, it still existed within the same world structure. The occasional references to human figures such as Enoch[16] and Elijah[17] (or in later tradition St Paul[18]) journeying or being taken 'up' to heaven, or indeed to humans suddenly 'seeing' heaven from earth, such as Elisha's servant,[19] or Micaiah,[20] or Jacob seeing 'the angels of God ... ascending and descending' in his dream at Bethel,[21] reminds us of the extent to which a potential continuity between heaven (where God is) and earth (where human beings are) could at any point become a reality. It was movement in the other direction, from heaven to earth, which proved more influential, however. Yahweh's own – equally unpredictable – descents to earth, as his glory resides with the Israelites wandering in the desert or, in later tradition, the descent of his glorious presence upon the mercy seat in the Temple, itself a reconstruction on earth of the Temple in heaven, provided the foundation of Israelite cultic religion.[22] Nor was the possibility of the realization of heavenly glory on earth confined to the Temple, but, as we have seen, could also be extended to all the earth. As the Letter to the Hebrews shows, it is these kinds of ideas which formed the background to Jesus' own ministry on earth and his returning ascent or entry 'into heaven itself, now to appear in the presence of God on our behalf'.[23]

But it was not only the Jewish people who understood the heavens to be the 'home of the gods' or at least the place where the divine was present in a particular way. Like most other ancient Mediterranean and Middle Eastern peoples (who were blessed with clear skies by day and night), the Greeks had developed a fascination with the movement of the heavenly bodies. This concern took natural scientific expression in Ptolemaic astronomy which conceived of the sky as containing a series of revolving invisible crystalline rings, whose revolutions determined the motions of the planets. This model supported the idea that planets were living intelligences which had the power to influence and to order events on earth, processes which could be mapped through astrology. The principle of continuity between earth below and the heavens above was therefore a feature of this system too, although it also had a series of more philosophical ramifications gathered under the metaphysical term 'participation', with its 'essences' and 'natures'. If the expansion of early Christianity away from its Jewish roots into the Hellenic mainstream marked its evolution into a world religion, then one of the greatest challenges facing Christian theologians in the early centuries was the reconciliation of the Ptolemaic cosmos with the model of the world as described in the opening verses of Genesis. Two fourth-century authors, the Pseudo-Clementine and Basil the Great, wrote highly influential accounts of the cosmos which combined Greek astronomy with the creation of 'heaven and earth', as depicted in Gen. 1.1–19.[24] The Christian natural scientists experienced the same difficulty that had appeared in Israelite cosmology in that the incorporeality of God the Creator seemed in tension with the principle of locality. Much discussion turned on this problematic, with some thinkers locating heaven (or the Empyrean as the Christians called it, borrowing a term from the Neoplatonists) as the dwelling place of God, together with the blessed within the furthest crystalline sphere, while others, such as Albert the Great, placed God beyond the Empyrean in a yet further sphere.[25] But within all the variations, one factor remained constant, as indeed it had in the Jewish cosmology. However conceived, heaven, where God dwelt and the saints with him, was always where it had to be: at the very highest point of all. Exaltation and physical height were deeply connected ideas in premodern cosmology.[26] And however strange this paradigm may seem to us today, it secured the possibility of a direct continuity between the heavenly above and the earthly below, albeit under exceptional conditions, through the principle of superabundance or overflow.

The change when it came was massive and, like all such changes, it is difficult to trace. There are no more foundational concepts than cosmological ones. But by their nature they manifest more indirectly than directly. The significance of classical cosmology for pre-modern culture extended far beyond the reach of the finely drawn maps of the Ptolemaic world. Somewhat surprisingly to the modern mind, one of the primary places in which we can see its effects on Christian theology is in the doctrine of the Ascension, and, no less surprisingly to us today, in the liturgical theology and sacramentalism of early Christianity, which bore a close theological relation to it. We need to note these effects firstly, therefore, before proceeding to examine the ways in which the theology of the Ascension itself, and the apprehension of 'sensibility' and 'world' which closely accompanied it, began to undergo significant changes in the aftermath of, or in parallel to, the far-reaching transformations in cosmological understanding which first properly appeared in the sixteenth century.

The Ascension, and subsequent 'session' of Jesus at the right hand of the Father, are described or referred to on numerous occasions in the New Testament.[27] Luke and Acts narrate the event itself.[28] The Gospel of John reflects upon the meaning of the Ascension as a forthcoming event, linking it with the coming of the Paraclete and the ultimate destiny of Christians with God in heaven.[29] We can identify a typological function, where NT usage picks up the first verse of Ps. 110: 'The Lord says to my lord, "Sit at my right hand until I make your enemies your footstool"'. This passage had messianic resonances for the early church.[30] At Mt. 26.64 ('From now on you will see the Son of Man seated at the right hand of Power and coming on the clouds of heaven'), it appears to be combined with the messianic Son of Man passage from Dan. 7.13 ('I saw one like a human being coming with the clouds of heaven'). The Ascension and session (or feast of Christ's 'royal enthronement' as Jean Danielou calls it[31]) represents the exaltation and glory of Christ throughout the Pauline literature. Eph. 4.7–13, for instance, draws out the cosmological significance of the Ascension, by linking it with the pre-existent Christ, or Word, who 'came down' from heaven and who enjoys cosmic functions in Christian tradition (as the one through whom all things were created, through whom all things are held in existence and in whom all things are reconciled[32]). According to the Ephesians tradition, which still draws upon the dynamic of height, these functions seem to transfer to the ascended Christ: 'He who descended is the same one who ascended far above all the heavens, so that he might fill all things' (Eph. 4.10). Christ's ascension into heaven therefore is grounded in a prior descent, recalling the Old Testament theme of God's glory filling the earth, and it marks what later tradition would call the ubiquity of his glorified body. Moreover, in the Letter to the Hebrews, it is Christ's presence within the heavenly tabernacle which guarantees his eternal priesthood exercised on our behalf before God.[33] Only because Christ has entered into the immediate presence of God can he perform the mediatorial functions on behalf of the humanity whose nature he assumed and which remains present in him. Similarly, it is the Ascension and the session which ground the mission of the Church, as Jean Danielou has shown in his study of the earliest theological and liturgical use of Pss. 24, 68 and 110.[34] The final entry of the faithful into the presence of God and their restoration to wholeness through the resurrection of the body at the end of time are also functions of Christ's own ascent in his human body to the Father, and of the ultimate transformation of the world by analogy with the transformation of his glorified body.[35]

A particular passage from the Gospel of John appears to contain an allusion to this principle of glorious descent-ascent, in combination with what may be early references to the practice and meaning of the Eucharist. The Johannine Christ identifies himself as 'the living bread that came down from heaven' (Jn 6.51) and states: 'Those who eat my flesh and drink my blood have eternal life, and I will raise them up on the last day: for my flesh is true food and my blood is true drink' (Jn 6.54–5). In the narrative this strong identification of Jesus' flesh and blood with bread and wine perplexes the disciples, evoking Jesus' response: 'Does this offend you? Then what if you were to see the Son of Man ascending to where he was before?' (Jn 6.62). This line has been taken to allude to the visible authority which Jesus will possess when he is seen to ascend to heaven, like the 'Son of Man' figure glimpsed by Daniel, to whom 'dominion and glory and kingship' are given (Dan. 7.13–14). But the passage concludes, again with eschatological resonance: 'It is the Spirit that gives life; the flesh is useless' (Jn 6.63). The reference to Spirit here may in fact signal a theological link between Eucharistic, or sacramental, piety and the Ascension itself.[36] Jn 6.62 might reflect the Old Testament and Ephesians theme that the earth is filled with the glory of God on account of God's own ascension or elevation. Jesus who is 'the living bread who came down from heaven' returns to heaven and thus, by implication, fills the world with his glory. The evocation of the role of the Spirit of Pentecost points to the discernment of the divine nature of Jesus, as the universal Word through whom all things were made, who is the true meaning of both Eucharist and incarnation.

A link between Ascension and the sacraments, which is to say between the ascended and glorified body of Jesus in heaven and our own bodily experience here on earth, comes unequivocally into view in Augustine's account of sacraments, and particularly in his critique of the Donatists. In *On Baptism: Against the Donatists*, Augustine developed his case for what is generally known as the efficacious or instrumental nature of the sacramental sign. The Donatists had questioned the validity of baptism received from a priest who had lapsed during the recent persecutions; they are thus set on establishing a rigorist, schismatic Church. Augustine's response is the formulation of what was to become a classical principle of Catholic sacramentalism, which is that the sacrament belongs to Christ himself of which he is its true minister. Its efficacy, which results from the sacrament performed, is not determined by the moral state of the human minister therefore but is determined by the reality of Christ as Head of the Church. When making this argument for the objectivity of the sacrament in *Answer to Petilian*, Augustine stresses that he is speaking of Christ who 'is alive, sitting at the right hand of the Father'.[37] He states that 'Christ also Himself washes, Himself purifies with the selfsame washing of water by the word, wherein the ministers are seen to do their work in the body'.[38] More generally, Augustine makes the case that it is through the Ascension that Christ is the Head of the Church and that we who are his Body are in union with him: 'whole Christ is "Head and Body" [...] let the members of Christ understand, and Christ in his members understand, and the members of Christ in Christ understand: because Head and Members are one Christ. The Head was in heaven, and was saying, "Why dost thou persecute me?" We with him are in heaven through hope, Himself is with us on earth through love.'[39] It is not the case therefore that the material signs in the sacrament are being 'commandeered' (to use a later vocabulary) by divine power but rather that the divine agency of Christ, risen and ascended, is one which is exercised both from heaven above and *from within* the material world. For Jesus to sit on the right hand of the Father is for Jesus to be glorified, and is thus for him to return in his human nature to the cosmic inclusivity which his divine nature had enjoyed since 'before the world was', since 'in respect of his Godhead all things were made by Himself, and in him were created all things in heaven and earth, visible and invisible'.[40] The instrumentality of the sign is neither a property of the autonomy of the material therefore, nor is it the result of an extraordinary divine command, but it is rather a function of Christ's glorified presence throughout the world, through the power of his truth and glory. This power is an eschatological one, which is both established in us and discerned by us through the power of the Spirit of Pentecost, which is the Spirit of the end times, given to us after the withdrawal of his human body from our eyes.[41]

Almost 1,000 years after Augustine's discussion of the sacrament, Thomas Aquinas set out the same paradigm with clarity and precision. Unlike the polemical Johannine passage (which may have been anti-docetic) and Augustine's writings (which were at least in part anti-Donatist), Thomas is concerned to ask general questions about the ontology or nature of the Eucharistic body of Jesus. He affirms that the body of Christ is not 'locally' present in the Eucharist, since it is 'locally' present only in heaven, but it is nevertheless 'sacramentally' present. This means that the 'substance' of Christ's body is made present through the material 'quantities' of the elements which remain following their consecration.[42] Thomas was continuing, and effectively concluding, a medieval discussion on the *nature* of the Eucharistic body which had begun in the ninth century with the literalist Eucharistic account of Paschasius, leading in the Berengarian controversy of the eleventh century to a confrontation between those who advocated respectively spiritualist, literalist and sacramental readings of the nature of Christ's presence in the Eucharist.[43]

In what we have reviewed, the following picture emerges. The Christian sacramental system, for which material signs were instrumental forms of supernatural grace, was not as such the product of a pre-modern geocentric conception of the universe (since it was generated by theological and incarna-tional reasonings, with their roots deep in the Jewish experience of a Creator and covenantal God), but it was significantly supported by it. That cosmology tolerated a strong sense of the universality of Jesus' presence, while also allowing him to continue to exist 'locally' in human form in heaven, where he is occu-pying *a place*. He was still in embodied form (however complex and challenging that glorified body now was) and was thus in continuity with the material order of creation itself. As a consequence, he remained in continuity with our own embodied sensibility, not exactly as he had been when he lived among us, but nevertheless in a way that was meaningful to the countless numbers of Chris-tians who believed that they experienced him in the liturgy and who believed quite literally that the liturgy itself had real cosmic meanings.

We can see something of the pervasive power of this – now vanished – Christology, in Dante's classic *Divine Comedy*. That work combines liturgy and cosmology, following very precisely the liturgical order of the Church's year and current maps of the known universe. It therefore begins with an account of how early in the morning of Good Friday the figure of Dante walked out of the world into limbo and then stumbled down into the depths of the underworld. From there he began the arduous climb of Mount Purgatory and finally ascended the heights of heaven. Heaven is where the Trinity dwells. The Trini-tarian light spreads through the universe and the Trinitarian love is the power that 'moves the sun and the other stars' – which is to say, it is the power which ultimately drives the Ptolemaic universe.[44] And yet, we should note, Dante is careful to preserve the presence of the ascended human body of Jesus in heaven, since he discerns something in the Trinity which he calls *nostra effige*,[45] or 'our image', and believes that he sees there the distinctly material phenomenon of a smile: 'O eternal light, existing in yourself alone, Alone knowing yourself; and who, known to yourself And knowing, love and smile upon yourself!'[46] Within the classical paradigm set out by Dante, the ascended body of Jesus is the promise that we too can in principle enter heaven and come before God in our human nature and bodies; and it is this which Dante is consciously exploiting in the – naturally fictional – account of his own pilgrimage through the known universe. It is an account, however, which has at its core an idea of height that is at once cosmological and astronomical, philosophical and theological, and which ties together divinity and humanity, heaven and earth.[47]

When the nature of the Eucharistic body became again a central question, as it did during the early years of the Reformation, it was already apparent that the understanding of the world was undergoing fundamental change. The new heliocentric cosmology was only set out by Copernicus in his *De revolutionibus* of 1543, but it had already become known in the first two decades of the sixteenth century, and Lutherans were among his closest companions.[48] Copernicus' work also looked back to developments in natural science and astronomy which were already evident as early as the fourteenth century, just as the account of matter and the material which his findings implied resonated strongly with nomin-alism and humanism, the origins of which also lie in the High Middle Ages.[49]

The fact that debates about the Eucharist and the ascended body of Christ played such a central role in the early stages of the Reformation has caused some surprise to commentators.[50] And yet, in the context of its day, it was surely a very natural thing. Not only was this an obvious point of contention with Roman Catholic tradition, since it was a central pillar of the priestly office and of the Catholic sacramental order, but the conjunction of divine causality and materiality (that is to say, material, natural or created causality), which is implicit in Eucharistic and sacramental theology, made it inevitably an area of acute debate at a time when deep changes in the understanding of both causality and materiality were under way. In other words, the centrality of Eucharistic debates in the very earliest stage of the Reformation, to which Brian Gerrish draws our attention, was the result not only of Catholic-Reformed polemic but also, and more deeply, offered the first occasion in which the Christian mind had to engage with what were unfolding as revolutionary changes in our most basic conceptions of materiality, world and our place in it. These changes, generated by natural science, and destined to refigure immeasurably our understanding of matter and the world, held unforeseeable threats to the very ground of Christianity, as an *incarnational* religion, which confesses that God himself has taken on human flesh and has himself entered the material order.

Zwingli, the humanist-trained Reformer, first addressed the Eucharist in one of his earliest reforming texts, the 'First Disputation' of January 1523, in which he set out a critique of its sacrificial character.[51] Later in the same year, in his 'Exposition of the Articles of the First Disputation', he contested Luther's description of the Mass as a 'testament', preferring the term 'memorial'.[52] And then, in a letter of 1524, Zwingli defined the word 'is' in the words of institution 'This is my Body' as meaning 'signifies', or 'calls to mind', and thus set himself in clear opposition to the Catholic – and Lutheran – understanding of the real presence of the body and blood of Christ in the Eucharist.[53] In 1527 Zwingli added to his denial of the instrumental nature of the sacramental sign the argument that since the body of Jesus was in heaven it could not simultaneously be in the Eucharist.[54] Not until 1526 did Luther write specifically against Zwingli's teaching. In *The Sacrament of the Body and Blood of Christ – Against the Fanatics* Luther argued for the view that Christ could be in the bread and wine as well as in heaven with an appeal to the glorified body of Christ and to the principle articulated in Ephesians: 'Moreover we believe that Christ, according to his human nature is put over all creatures (Eph. 1.22) and fills all things, as Paul says in Eph. 4.10. Not only according to his divine nature, but also according to his human nature, he is a lord of all things, has all things in his hand, and is present everywhere.'[55] Luther pointed to the way in which preaching can create the sense for us that Christ is in our hearts and adds:

> Christ still sits on the right hand of the Father, and also in your heart, the one Christ who fills heaven and earth. I preach that he sits on the right hand of God and rules over all creatures [. . .]; if you believe this, you already have him in your heart. Therefore your heart is in heaven, not in an apparition or dream, but truly. For

where he is, there you are also. So he dwells and sits in your heart, yet he does not fall from the right hand of God. Christians experience and feel this clearly.[56]

Luther's appeal was to a very traditional conception of heaven, therefore, and he based his 'ubiquity theory' on the presence in heaven of Jesus' human body, again following tradition, specifically Eph. 4.9–10, and upon his own experience of the sacrament. Calvin likewise evoked his experience of the sacrament,[57] but his view differed from that of Luther with respect to ubiquity. Calvin strongly agreed with Zwingli that the human body of Jesus must occupy a place and could not therefore be 'locally' present both in heaven and in the bread on the altar.[58] But he differed from Zwingli in his insistence that the Eucharist does genuinely allow us to feed upon the saving body of Jesus *as he exists in heaven*. Calvin's view was that the flesh of Christ is in heaven, and not in the Eucharist, but that we truly feed upon that flesh through the sacrament of the Lord's Supper which attests to and represents the otherwise mysterious embodied and living relation of the faithful with Christ outside the sacrament.[59] The *sursum corda* played an important role in Calvin's Eucharistic theology therefore, as we are urged to turn our thoughts and hearts upwards, in gratitude, to where Christ feeds us with his body from heaven through the Holy Spirit.[60] A further key area in which Calvin agreed with Luther against Zwingli was in his commitment to the instrumental character of the sign, based, as with the Luther, upon the characteristically Reformation emphasis of belief in the fidelity of God's Word in the sacrament.[61]

A number of points of great importance come into view in these inner-Reformation exchanges. The first group are fundamentally doctrinal in kind and they focus on the question of the nature of the presence of the body of Jesus Christ in the Eucharist. A strong version of real presence will depend upon some account of the instrumental nature of the sacramental sign. This in turn depends upon the view that the glorified body of Jesus, which remains a real body, still penetrates the whole world from heaven, through glory, power and Spirit. Thus in a sacramental hermeneutics, matter is in some sense internal to the divine power, and can be instrumental to it.

The second group of questions concerns not doctrine but astronomy and cosmology which had, until now, supported the traditional doctrinal positions. Luther, for instance, appeared to be aware of Copernicus' work, for there is a reference to him as being 'a fool who wants to turn the whole art of astronomy upside down'.[62] Anticipating later debates, Luther countered the new theory by stating that 'Joshua commanded the sun to stand still and not the earth' (Josh. 10.12–13).[63] Calvin, on the other hand, seemed less certain. He unequivocally affirmed the real and continuing embodiment of Jesus Christ:

For what does all Scripture more clearly teach than that Christ, as he took our true flesh when he was born of the virgin and suffered in our true flesh when he made satisfaction for us, so also received that same true flesh in his resurrection, and bore it up to heaven? For we have this hope of our resurrection and of our ascension into heaven: that Christ rose again and ascended, and, as Tertullian says, bore the guarantee of our resurrection with him to heaven.[64]

And yet he also appears unsure as to where that body now is:

> When Christ is said to be in heaven, we must not view him as dwelling among the spheres and numbering the stars. Heaven denotes a place higher than all the spheres, which was assigned to the Son of God after his resurrection. Not that it is literally a place beyond the world, but we cannot speak of the Kingdom of God without using our ordinary language. Others, again, considering that the expressions, *above the heavens,* and *ascension into heaven*, are of the same import, conclude that Christ is not separated from us by distance of place. But one point they have overlooked. When Christ is placed above the heavens, or in the heavens, all that surrounds the earth – all that lies beneath the sun and stars, beneath the whole frame of the visible world – is excluded.[65]

Calvin therefore wished strongly to maintain that Jesus' body retains physicality, in accordance with his humanity, but at the same time he wished to keep heaven out of the existing – Ptolemaic – universe. Heaven is *a place*, as it needs to be if the body is to rest there, but the fact that it is a place is more important to him than where that place is (although it is still important to him that it should be 'above', a sublime height to which we lift our hearts in the *sursum corda*). In other words, Calvin wished the ascended body of Jesus to have locality, in order to preserve its properly human character, but he tacitly recognized that the scheme of the universe within which he was obliged to work was not as hospitable to these ideas as had once been the case.

2. The Modern Paradigm

It is critical that we become aware of what exactly the changes were that took place from the sixteenth century onwards and which, whatever their origins and speed of dissemination, came to exercise a profound influence throughout the Christian Church, across its confessional boundaries. In the first place, pre-modern cosmology addressed the challenge of maintaining a relation between 'the heavenly' and, most specifically, the ascended body of Jesus through a topography of *extension*. The pre-modern universe of space and time is finite and the heavenly is distinguished from the earthly by the dimension of *height*. To be up above, above even the clouds and where the birds fly, is to be to all intents and purposes out of reach (for pre-modern technologies). And yet, there still remains a connection between the heavenly and the earthly since the principle of extension guarantees the possibility of continuity (which is precisely what Dante exploits in his *Divine Comedy*). In the pre-modern debates about the ascended body of Jesus, including the debate between Luther and Zwingli, all insisted as a matter of priority that the ascended body has 'local' existence, which means to say that it occupies space: otherwise it could not legitimately be said to be a real body. The loss of the sense of heaven as a *place*, therefore, which for all its otherness was still in extended relation with all other places, removed the cosmological *Sitz im Leben* for the ascended body of Jesus.

What were the consequences of this? In the first place we must recall that it was to this body that the Church looked in the classical period – down to and including Calvin – to see the realization of its own anticipated future in the presence of God in heaven. The human body of Jesus in heaven was the guarantee of our own possible ultimate destiny in the presence of God as creatures. Leo the Great spoke for patristic tradition when he stated:

> There was great and indescribable cause for rejoicing when, in the sight of the holy multitude, above the dignity of all heavenly creatures, the nature of the human race went up, to surpass the ranks of Angels and to rise beyond the heights of the Archangels, to have its being uplifted limited by no sublimity until, received to sit with the eternal Father, it was associated on the throne of His glory, to whose nature it was joined in the Son. Since, therefore, Christ's Ascension is our uplifting, and the hope also of the Body is raised to where the glory of the Head has preceded it, let us exult, dearly beloved, with worthy joy, and be glad in a pious thanksgiving.[66]

This was a personal, eschatological crisis, therefore, which touched on the very possibility of a future eternal life in the presence of God. We are reminded here also of Thomas Aquinas' conviction that it is the Ascension which is the 'cause of our salvation' since it is Christ's entry into heaven in his humanity which makes possible our own subsequent entry into heaven and it is his presence at the side of the Father which makes his intercession on our behalf effective.[67]

The second moment of this crisis was that it was God's place in heaven *above*, or that of the glorified Jesus, which helped people to believe that the divine glory would naturally overflow and fill the earth, which is to say pervade even the realm of sensibility (through liturgy, if not in other more exceptional ways). The calling into question of 'heaven above' (which had been so fundamental to the format of Eph. 4.7–13, for instance) brought in its train a cosmological crisis therefore as materiality itself became detached from 'the heavenly'. The period from the publication of Copernicus' *De revolutionibus* (1543) to Newton's *Philosophia naturalis principa mathematica* (1687) marked a very fundamental shift in cosmological awareness. This was heralded by the new Copernican model, as it was later by the work of Kepler and Galileo, when the new astronomical paradigms imposed themselves as irreversible and authoritative accounts of the world rather than mere speculative hypotheses. As Hans Blumenberg had remarked, there was something about the astronomical debates which triggered change.[68] But the change was far-reaching in that it led to the 'quantification' of matter and the re-conceptualization of matter as fields of forces and thus as efficient causality. This did not exclude God, who remained strong in many of the systems of seventeenth-century philosophy as Divine Author of all things, but it did change the nature of the relation between world and divinity.[69] Something of the gulf that divides the pre-modern from the early modern world can be gauged from Augustine's casual remark about the unquestioned universality and strength of belief in the Ascension of Christ in his own times.[70] It can also be seen in the fact that pre-modern Christians believed that the ascended body still existed in the very same universe in which they too lived. Indeed, they could point to its location in heaven on any decent map of the world. However challenging it may be for us to penetrate the detail of pre-modern sensibility and thought, it is not at all difficult to see that their sophisticated but deeply erroneous cosmology allowed them easily to conceive of the ascended body of Jesus as still *real*. With a strong sense of the ascended body and of the nature of heaven in which it rests, there came a robust conceptualization of the real relation between heaven and the world of ordinary human experience. This led in turn to a much stronger sense than we have of the extent to which the world of space and time, and therefore the bodily senses, are at their root open to and engaged by Christ, risen and ascended.

3. Spirit and Matter

The profoundly radical changes in cosmology which took place during the sixteenth and seventeenth centuries had the most immediate effect upon the Reformed churches since, as new churches, they were struggling to define themselves within and against Christian tradition. We need to look more closely therefore at the two quite different paradigms which emerged from this period, as important pointers to the kinds of strategies which would become characteristic of modern Christianity, down to our own day. In both cases the understanding of the Holy Spirit played a key role, and pneumatology will need to be at the forefront of our discussion in both the present chapter and the chapter to follow (as it is in Paul Janz's Chapter 4). As the possibly anti-docetic passages of Jn 6 and the anti-Donatist writings of Augustine show, understandings of the living body of Christ, of the Holy Spirit and the nature of matter come together in a particularly intensive way in the Eucharist, in which material signs are held to signify spiritual, which is to say immaterial, realities. It was precisely this issue of *causality*, in a time of deep scientific and cultural change, which informed the Reformers' Eucharistic debates, and which – for all the efforts to achieve agreement at the Marburg Colloquy of 1529 – remained the cause of quite fundamental division. [71]

Of all the reformers, Martin Luther remained closest to his Catholic inheritance in this as in other theological areas. In his polemic with the Zwinglians, Luther showed a commitment to the necessary, though in itself insufficient, role of materiality within faith, or what Luther termed the 'order of salvation'.[72] This pointed to the role of the incarnation, and of the body of Christ, as a given within history. In sacramental theology, Luther continued the Catholic understanding of the objective character of the Eucharist, although he did so in terms and with insights which were proper to the Reformation and which excluded both the traditional language of transsubstantiation and any possibility of a mechanistic reading of sacramental materiality. Luther replaced the 'efficacious sign' of Catholic tradition with the 'certain sign' of God's promise.[73] Luther also thought through the relation between Eucharist and incarnation in new ways, seeing both as instances of God's presence in hidden form, which is to say the human nature on the one hand and the bread and wine on the other. Luther appealed to the faithfulness of God, as made present to us through the Holy Spirit, as the guarantor that God's divinity was truly present *within* the concealing materiality. It is in Martin Luther also that human subjectivity appeared in a new and intensified form. His classical accounts of inner conflict and of the mind in dispute with itself, which played such an important part in the formation of his theology, allowed the emergence of a new depth of reflection on and experience of the Holy Spirit. It is the Holy Spirit who makes Christ real to us within the conflicted human spirit, and thus makes possible our reception of the 'alien righteousness' of Christ given for us. But there is never any confusion between the Holy Spirit and the human spirit itself in Luther, since it is the Holy Spirit likewise who animates the materiality of the signs for us, making the preaching of the Word and the reception of the Lord's Supper genuinely sacramental instruments of divine grace. In his debate with the Zwinglians, Luther is clear that materiality – in the case of both the incarnation and the sacraments of the Lord's Supper and baptism – does not 'trap' grace and thus make it open to human manipulation. The Holy Spirit remains sovereign and free. Indeed, in 'This is my Body' he states regarding his opponents: 'they think that nothing spiritual can be present where there is anything material and physical, and assert that the flesh is of no avail. Actually the opposite is true. The Spirit cannot be with us except in material and physical things such as the Word, water, and Christ's body and in his saints on earth.'[74] The 'order of salvation' is such that the Word needs first to be preached, the bread and wine offered, and God needs first to come to meet us in the historical reality of Jesus Christ, before the Spirit can work through and in us, through and in external signs, in such a way that we are truly nourished and established in faith through grace. The dynamic at work here has been well expressed by one Lutheran scholar in the words: 'The activity within the realm of the Spirit is not man's activity before God but his participation in God's activity in the world.'[75] Luther does not set up an opposition between Holy Spirit and the world, therefore. Rather, his account of sacramental theology is a realist one in that it is predicated upon the real existence of Christ within history who is made real *to us now* through the agency of the Holy Spirit who both indwells us (who is 'in our hearts') and indwells the material signs of Word and sacrament.

Although Luther himself held to a pre-Copernican understanding of the universe, it would soon become more difficult to resist the Copernican change. The acute tension became evident with the persecution in Wittenberg of the Lutheran scientist Johannes Kepler, who discovered the elliptical nature of the revolution of the planets, for denying the ubiquity of Christ's body.[76] During the sixteenth and seventeenth centuries Lutheran exegesis would be dominated by the problematics posed for biblical truth by advances in the natural sciences. Nevertheless, the basic structure of Lutheran sacramental theology would remain intact. No longer dependent upon, or at least supported by, a particular cosmology, sacramental theology would itself provide the ground for continuing belief in the real presence of Christ within the world, and therefore – however impaired by modern materialism – for the inclusion of the world within the economy of Christian revelation. Paradoxically, therefore, despite the wide-ranging critique of Catholicism that we find in Luther and his extensive development of new Reformation categories and terms, Luther's own position on the Eucharist served also to anticipate Roman Catholic sacramentalism of modern times. Real Presence in its modern versions is less a function of scriptural cosmology than something that is supported and sustained through the tradition and traditional practices of the Church. For us today sacramentalism is an important potential witness to the presence of Christ *in the spatio-temporal world*, beyond the sacramental spaces; although we may suspect that the sacramental presence itself is all too often seen solely as the unique communication of Christ to his Church, his own body, rather than also as a window upon divine presence in the world of space and time.[77]

The account of the Eucharist developed by Zwingli was quite different in kind from that of either Luther or the Catholics, as it was from Calvin's Eucharistic theology. As we have seen, the Eucharistic debate incorporated issues to do with the nature of the body of Christ, which were fundamentally of a *doctrinal* kind, as well as issues to do with the place of heaven, which ultimately had a *cosmological* character, and understandings of, or presuppositions about, the nature of material signs in the communication of spiritual realities. This latter theme necessarily opened out into imponderable issues to do with the nature of matter itself and, above all, the relation between spirit (human) or Spirit (divine) and the material order. Thus the very nature of the human body as material entity also came into view. In other words, the nature of cosmology is that it is virtually unlimited in its potential influence on human thought, self-understanding and conceptualization – and hence also experience – of the world we live in. The Reformers were constructing their new theology, then, at the very moment in which one of the most dramatic changes in cosmology that the Western world had ever experienced was taking place. Moreover, the character of cosmological change is, while revolutionary, also slow and subtle. Nor can we make precise divisions between the purely scientific aspects of that change and the cultural or even social analogues which accompany it. For instance, Copernicus' *De revolutionibus* belongs as much to a history of the rise of natural science that grew out of nominalism and humanism as it does to the history of formal astronomy, just as, in our own day, Einstein's theories of 'general' and 'particular relativity' and Heisenberg's 'uncertainty principle' resonate deeply with the 'turn to the subject' and 'perspectivalism' which are so fundamental to modern thought. For those, therefore, who live in the midst of such cosmological change, the influence of that change is incalculable.

Zwingli set out a position on the Eucharist which was quite distinct from that of the Catholics, as it was also from that of Luther. It is a position which was significantly different also from that of Calvin. Zwingli's position was distinctive in that he denied the efficacious nature of the Eucharistic sign and argued instead that the sacrament had a memorial function, serving to remind us of Christ's atoning death for us and thus prompting us to praise and thanksgiving.

Zwingli's argument for his Eucharistic theology contains two elements, which are, however, closely related. In the first place, he stressed that Jesus cannot be locally present in two places at once; since he is present in heaven, seated at the right hand of the Father, he cannot also be in the bread and wine. Zwingli's belief that the 'local' character of Christ's body in heaven precludes the possibility of his 'local' presence in the bread and wine recalls Thomas Aquinas' view that the sacramental presence of Jesus in the Eucharist is 'substantial' though not 'local' on account of the fact that Jesus is *in loco* only in heaven. Calvin likewise denies the possibility of the 'local' presence of Christ in the Eucharist (while arguing that God's promise in the Eucharist allows us to feed upon his 'local' body in heaven[78]). Luther too accepts that Jesus has a 'local' existence in heaven, which is the presence and power of God in 'the humanity of Christ'.[79] But he strongly contests the view that the character of this 'local presence' is such as to prohibit any possibility of Christ's 'real presence' elsewhere.[80] As incarnate God, whose power extends throughout the universe, Christ can be present how and where he will. Luther's claim that there can be nothing extraordinary in the real presence of Christ in the Eucharist, attested by the scriptural words of institution, is based upon the fact that the Creator's power is 'essentially present' within his creation.[81] Against Zwingli he writes:

> [I]t must be essentially present at all places. Even in the tiniest leaf. The reason is this: It is God who creates, effects and preserves all things through his almighty power and right hand, as our Creed confesses [. . .] If he is to create or preserve it, however, he must be present and must make and preserve his creation both to its innermost and outermost aspects.

Luther then focuses upon God's presence within the human body:

> For it is he who makes the skin and it is he who makes the bones; it is he who makes the hair on the skin, and it is he who makes the marrow in the bones; it is he who makes every bit of the hair, it is he who makes every bit of the marrow. Indeed, he must make everything, both the parts and the whole. Surely, then, *his hand which makes all this must be present* [my italics]; that cannot be lacking.

And Luther concludes with the classic scriptural quotations from Old and New Testaments which emphasize God's glory throughout the world, filling both heaven and earth. He finally asserts that the presence and power of the Creator within the creation is so undeniable and rich that the issue of the simultaneous existence of Christ's body and blood in heaven and the Eucharist is 'a trivial matter'.[82]

It cannot be the 'local' character of the body of Jesus in heaven as such, therefore, which prompted Zwingli to deny his presence and accessibility in or through the Eucharist; it has to be something else. If Luther argued for the ubiquity of Christ's body on the grounds of the Christology of Ephesians and Ps. 110 ('God's right hand'), then Zwingli likewise turns to doctrine, though his reading of the scriptural texts is based on a prior understanding of the properties of a 'body'. A body is necessarily 'circumscribed, limited and particular'.[83] Zwingli insisted that although divinity and humanity are one in Jesus Christ, having a body is solely a property of the human nature, while ubiquity is solely a property of the divine nature. Zwingli does not shy away from the corollary that the divinity of Jesus, which is everywhere, *has no body*.[84] A further corollary is that the body of Jesus, which is purely a human body, is indistinguishable from our own bodies. We would be wrong to think of it as possessing extraordinary properties or as being capable of doing extraordinary things, therefore: after all, if we cannot be in two places at once, then how can he? Indeed, Zwingli paints a memorable picture for us of the resurrected and ascended body of Jesus sitting beside the Father in heaven, in an entirely 'untransformed' state, until the Last Days.[85]

Any scriptural expressions which suggest that the humanity has properties of the divinity (cf. Jn, 'I shall be with you always') must be taken as a manner of speaking and be properly attributed to the divinity, and vice versa. Though we may speak of the two natures in terms of the other, there can properly speaking be no *communicatio* or exchange between them, even in heaven. The body of Jesus remains throughout only human and thus entirely ordinary. Moreover, Zwingli suggests that any alternative to this view – any attempt to conceive of Christ's presence in the Eucharist as a 'spiritual body', for instance – can only entail a denial of the true humanity of Christ on the cross, which is a view he attributes to the early heretic Marcion.[86]

Zwingli's argument is notable for its selective reading of scripture (is the pre-resurrection body of Jesus which undergoes transfiguration, or the resurrected body which passes through walls and disappears, really so ordinary?) and for its insistence that no other reading can fail to be heretical. The logic of a divine impassibility and the logic of a transformation and glorification (in the terminology of the Fourth Gospel) of Jesus' human embodiment through the resurrection and Ascension are not contradictions, any more than the belief that Christ is present in a spiritual body in the Eucharist would be a denial of his true humanity on the cross. These are fanciful, theological non sequiturs.

And yet, anyone reading Zwingli today, regardless of their own beliefs, will surely recognize that there is much in Zwingli's theological worldview which is profoundly representative of the modern. Even if he leaves us with the image of Christ, patiently seated at the right hand of the Father, and quietly ageing (is that not the implication?), we may well feel that Zwingli in this debate, more than Luther or Calvin, points towards the future. And this follows, I would suggest, from his distinctively 'modern' account of the material as such. In the case of the Catholics, Luther or indeed Calvin, their strong account of sacramental theology (whether on metaphysical grounds, as with the Catholics, or through the authority of God's Word, for the Reformers), cohered with their understanding of Christ's body as being susceptible to transformation and glorification while still remaining a material human embodiment, 'locally' present in heaven. In other words, what we see here is a continuous account of the material as such which understood the material order, under certain specific conditions, to be open to divine intervention and transformation. Zwingli's point, on the other hand, is that the body of Jesus simply cannot be other than limited, occupying a particular place, or his human nature will be compromised. Indeed, it *must* be 'untransformed'; otherwise faith in the true humanity of Christ is compromised. This seems in effect to be a theological rereading of scripture (indeed in many respects one which is against scripture) in the light of a certain non-negotiable account of what it is to be material. And it is this that we can recognize as being what we term 'materialist', or perhaps 'common-sensical'. The view that matter is *not* transformable has been widespread in the modern period; it has been and continues to be pervasive even in those Christian traditions which hold to a continuing sacramentalism and to the glorious nature of the body of Christ.

The sense that we can already see in Zwingli a configuration which became deeply characteristic of the modern worldview, and which took primary expression in an opposition between human and divine s/Spirit on the one hand and body and materiality on the other, is only increased when we take into consideration remarks he makes about the relation between Spirit and matter. The text of Jn 6.63 ('It is the Spirit that gives life; the flesh is useless') played an important part in Zwingli's work.[87] The original meaning of this phrase is akin to the Pauline opposition of 'spirit' and 'flesh' as anthropological categories. The former represents our capacity or potential to live a virtuous life in accordance with divine grace, while the latter represents our refusal or inability to do so. It is thus a position which Augustine was later to characterize as the issue of whether we love the lesser good (things in the world) or the greater good (the loving Creator of the world). But what is clear (as Luther pointed out at length[88]) is that Zwingli used the *ethical* character of 'spirit' and 'flesh' to designate *ontological* categories. Indeed, in his discussion of the Eucharist from 1524, Zwingli effectively used the anthropocentric 'spirit–flesh' opposition of St Paul to refigure the ontological relation between the Holy Spirit and the material world. Spirit is not something that acts in the world, transforming the materiality of the signs into sacramental realities, as for Luther, but is now something that is set up over and against materiality as such. If Christ 'leads us away from sensible realities to internal and spiritual ones' as Zwingli states, then the Spirit offers paths of access to the divine which do not lead through the material world.[89] Zwingli's account of the structure of the Eucharist is predicated upon the primacy of a 'spiritualized', which is to say disembodied, self, and a 'spiritualized' Holy Spirit, which is to say a Holy Spirit whose sphere of action is now primarily the human spirit itself, fostering an ontology of either non-relation or indeed opposition between s/Spirit on the one hand and the materiality of the external world on the other.

Like Luther before him and Calvin after him, Zwingli lived in a transitional age, between two worlds. The one suggested a literal interpretation of the Bible with respect in particular to heaven and traditional cosmology, while the other suggested a view of matter which was already 'materialist', and thus of a very different cosmological kind. Reconstructions of the deep motivations underlying the specific conceptualities of thinkers living in a time of cosmological change will always be speculative, but it is difficult not to see these thinkers, each of whom is seminal for the development of modern Christianity, as responding to this transition, each in his own way. Thus Luther rejects Copernicus, while Calvin perhaps takes account of him but holds to the 'local' body of Christ, without a fixed 'heaven', and to the transformative power of God's Word. Zwingli, however, combines a commitment to a literal reading of the scriptural heaven, with a materialist account of matter which alone feels to him to be true to this world (or real). Between these two fixed poles of a pre-Copernican heaven and a post-Copernican materiality, Zwingli makes the necessary doctrinal compensations. These will establish Spirit, which is the activity and power of God, as something which is at odds with the material order, and it will begin to make a far-reaching alignment between human spirit and divine Spirit, both conceived in opposition to the material and to material causality. Thus *escape* from the material will replace *transformation* of the material as the primary Christian, or Christological, dynamic. A further underlying issue, therefore, and it is one which will deeply shape the intellectual landscapes of the centuries to come since it has existential force for those who ask it, is the question of human freedom: how it is to be thought and where it is to be found?

4. Living the Loss

It is easier for us to see today than it was then that pre-modern Christian teaching on the ascended and glorified body of Jesus reflected both a series of scriptural affirmations about the nature of the Word and its intimate relation to the created order, and a certain kind of cosmology, in combination. The latter also seemed to have scriptural warrant but was superseded over a period of time by alternative and better accounts of the nature of the world we live in. A significant consequence of this cosmological transition was the loss of heaven itself as 'a place', which is to say as an identifiable region of the universe where the material order was conjoined – and thus in continuity with – the spiritual or intelligible order. A further development in this period was the loss of an understanding of matter as being open to the Creator's power in such a way and to such an extent that it could undergo fundamental transformation. It is these convictions about heaven and the transformative possibilities of matter which found graphic expression in the image of the ascended and glorified body of Christ which, according to scriptural and creedal tradition, is really 'seated' at the right hand of the Father in heaven.

Nothing that has been said so far should be taken as disapproval of the great advances in natural science that took place over the sixteenth and seventeenth centuries, and which continue today. These were both necessary and positive. The rise of the historical-critical method in biblical studies was likewise a natural and positive development: not the end of theological exegesis but something that theological exegesis would now need to be in dialogue with. But what this discussion is doing is raising pointed questions about how proper it is from a theological point of view that the Christian community should have allowed itself to become so alienated from the ascension tradition in the light of what were, in the final analysis, purely secular advances in scientific under-standing of the structure of the material world. After all, the theological rationale for the Ascension and glorification of Christ rested primarily upon the belief that the ascended and glorified body manifested the truth that Christ was indeed the incarnate Word who was 'in the beginning with God' (Jn 1.2), through whom and for whom 'all things have been created' (Col. 1.16) and in whom 'God was reconciling the world to himself' (2 Cor. 5.19). It is important therefore not to confuse the extent to which the Ptolemaic universe supported the scriptural cosmological paradigm, in the light of its identification of heaven with height, with the doctrinal content which was being communicated *through* that cosmological system. The doctrinal content can in principle legitimately survive the former's demise.

It is important also to recall the full breadth of doctrinal resonance with which the ascended body of Jesus was associated in the early Church. The Gospel of John unequivocally presents the departure of the body of Jesus as a necessary condition for the coming of the Paraclete. The so-called 'session' of Christ, together with the coming of the Holy Spirit of Pentecost, grounds the Church as a missionary movement, with an obligation to evangelize the world. Christ seated in heaven represents the fullness of his divine power and thus his mandate over the whole of the earth. In the same way, as we have seen, the Letter to the Hebrews makes the session a condition of Christ's eternal and perfect priesthood and mediatorship. Moreover, the concept of heaven itself is closely bound up with these divine functions of the embodied Word. Heaven, in classical tradition, is a place: an extraordinary one in many ways but nevertheless a place in which the glorified body of Jesus could have 'local' existence. The loss of heaven for us had perhaps one clear consequence above all others. It removed the link between our own earthly reality and the transformed materiality of the glorified body. Heaven in its traditional form offered an ideal possibility of how the world could be, might be, under the conditions of that body. Without heaven as the real site of that body, in continuity with our own world of ordinary space and time, a gulf opened up between the glorified body of the Word incarnate and our own reality of space and time, the immensity of which no act of religious reasoning nor indeed of authentic imagining could bridge.

Notes

1 Feminist thematization of the body has played an important role in offering resistance to forms of theological abstraction, of course. However, 'body' carries many complex nuances with respect to policy, privacy and individuation for us today, and the tendency in Transformation Theology is to speak rather of sensibility, or 'the life of the senses': that is, 'body' as it opens into 'world'. See Nicholas Lash, *Easter in Ordinary* (London: SCM Press, 1988), for a persuasive attempt to resist the abstraction of doctrine.

2 It is of course the case that countless numbers of ordinary Christians continue to experience Jesus Christ as a reality and continue to ground their faith in the 'sensible real' of their everyday lives. That is not in question. The critical points made here concern the theological thematizations of world, incarnation and faith, and thus concern the churches' reflexive understanding of the content and practice of faith. Of course, any identifiable deficit in the churches' exposition of the formal content of faith as doctrine must be of concern with respect to the lived community of faith.

3 On this theme, see for instance John Polkinghorne, *Quantum Physics and Theology: An Unexpected Kinship* (London: SPCK, 2007).

4 Immanuel Kant, *The Critique of Pure Reason*, A297/B353–A298/B354. See below, p. 100.

5 This does not imply, of course, that past and future are not part of the present, as memory and hope, or future orientation, nor that the immediacy of the 'here and now' is unmediated, or untouched, by culture. But such a focus on the actuality or immediacy of experience in the 'here and now' does suggest something of Levinas' critique of Heidegger and 'ontology' (Emmanuel Levinas, *Totality and Infinity*, trans. Alphonso Lingis, Dordrecht: Kluwer Academic Publishers, 1991, pp. 35–40), which argues against a totalizing conception. The particular form of this critique in Transformation Theology becomes more evident in Paul Janz's notion of the role of the sensible in what he calls 'finality of non-resolution' and in the appeal to 'newness' rather than 'otherness'. This is a different kind of critique from that of Levinas. See pp. 94–107.

6 For the cosmological functions of the pre-existent Christ, see also 1 Cor. 8.6; 2 Cor. 5.17; Heb. 1.2–4. For the earlier role of the divine 'wisdom' in the creation, which is an important model at this point, see Ps. 136.5, Prov. 3.19, Jer. 10.12.

7 'Creation from nothing' is a concept which emerges relatively late on in Jewish tradition (see 2 Macc. 7.28–9), but the view that the world was Yahweh's creation, whether from nothing or from chaos, is a pervasive idea among early Christian thinkers, where it is linked with providence. See Gerhard May, *Creatio Ex Nihilo* (Edinburgh: T&T Clark, 1994), pp. 148–78.

8 See also Jer. 23.24 and Acts 17.24.

9 Gen. 2.19; 7.3, 23; Ps. 8.8 (the Hebrew phrase used in all these cases is 'birds of heaven').

10 Deut. 17.3; Jer. 8.2; Mt. 24.29. This corresponds to the raqia' or 'firmament' of Gen. 1.6.

11 This is literally the 'heaven of heavens'. According to 1 Kgs 8.30, it is God's 'dwelling place'. See also Deut. 10.14; Ps. 115.16. For the third and highest heaven as the site of God's throne, see 1 Sam. 4.4; Ps. 11.4. At Isa. 66.1, heaven is identical with God's throne (cf. Mt. 5.34). For the 'three heavens', see J. Edward Wright, *The Early History of Heaven* (New York: Oxford University Press, 1999, pp. 52–97). On early understandings of heaven, see also Colleen McDannell and Bernard Lang, eds, *Heaven: A History* (2nd edn, New Haven: Yale University Press, 2001) and Jan Swango Emerson and Hugo Feiss, *Imagining Heaven in the Middle Ages: A Body of Essays* (New York and London: Garland Publishing, 2000).

12 When Solomon dedicates his temple, for instance, he asks: 'But will God indeed dwell on the earth? Even heaven and the highest heaven cannot contain you, much less this house that I have built!' (1 Kgs 8.27; see also Pss. 57.5, 19 and 72).

13 See also Ps. 108.5.

14 See also Pss. 19.1 and 29.1. There may also be some parallel with the sun here, whose rays fill all the earth (cf. Eccl. 1.9, 'under the sun').

15 e.g. Isa. 11.9–10: 'They will not hurt or destroy on all my holy mountain; for the earth will be full of the knowledge of the Lord as the waters cover the sea. On that day the root of Jesse shall stand as a signal to the peoples; the nations shall inquire of him, and his dwelling shall be glorious.'

16 Gen. 5.24.

17 2 Kgs 2.1–11.

18 2 Cor. 12.2.

19 2 Kgs 6.17.

20 1 Kgs 22.19.

21 Gen. 28.12 and 17.

22 See G. A. Anderson, *Sacrifices and Offerings in Ancient Israel* (Scholars Press, 1987), Bruce Chilton, *Redeeming Time* (Hendrickson 2002) and R. E. Clements, *God and Temple* (Oxford: Oxford University Press, 1965). See also Marie E. Isaacs. *Sacred Space: An Approach to the Theology of the Epistle to the Hebrews* (Sheffield: JSOT Press, Supplement Series 73, 1992).

23 Heb. 9.24. See also Heb. 4.14.

24 See *Die Pseudoklementinen, II. Rekognitionen in Rufins Übersetzung*, ed. Bernhard Rehm (Berlin: Akademie-Verlag, 1965) and *Basil's Homilies on the Hexaemeron*. These texts are discussed in W. G. L. Randles, *The Unmaking of the Medieval Christian Cosmos, 1500–1760* (Aldershot: Ashgate, 1999, pp. 1–8). For a comprehensive survey of the pre-modern cosmos, see Edward Grant, *Planets, Stars and Orbs: The Medieval Cosmos, 1200–1687* (Cambridge: Cambridge University Press, 1996). I have summarized some of this material in Oliver Davies, *The Creativity of God. World, Eucharist, Reason* (Cambridge: Cambridge University Press, 2004, pp. 16–21).

25 Augustine already asks questions about the relation between the Third Heaven, earth and sensibility in the context of Paul's vision recounted at 2 Cor. 12.2–4 in his *Literal Commentary on Genesis*, XII (see also VIII, 1). See also the discussion of the resurrected body in *City of God*, XXII, 29. Gregory of Nyssa also suggests that heaven is the meeting place of material and noetic or intelligible realities (Hexaemeron, Migne, PG, 44, col. 81C). I am grateful to Robin Orton for drawing my attention to this passage.

26 Thomas Aquinas sums up this traditional belief in his *Summa Theologiae*, paras 3, q. 57, art. 4 and 5, where he argues that the ascended body of Jesus must be above all creatures both physically and spiritually.

27 Douglas Farrow in his study records 35 in all (*Ascension and Ecclesia*; Edinburgh: T&T Clark, 1999, pp. 275–80).

28 We find the statement at Mk 16.19 (in the uncertain longer ending): 'So then the Lord Jesus, after he had spoken to them, was taken up into heaven and sat down at the right hand of God.' The Lukan account simple records that Jesus 'left them' (Lk. 24.51; see also 9.51), while Acts has: 'When he had said this, as they were watching, he was taken up out of their sight' (Acts 1.9). In addition to the Ascension material in Chapter 14, John includes the encounter with Mary Magdalene in the garden at 20.17: noli me tangere.

29 Jn 14.

30 This line is actually quoted in the New Testament itself, at Acts 2.30–5; cf. Rom. 8.34, 1 Cor. 15.25–6 and Heb. 10.12–13. David Hays surveys the place of Ps. 110 in his *Glory at the Right Hand: Psalm 110 in Early Christianity* (SBL Monograph Series, Society of Biblical Literature, 1989). He understands the session in Christological terms to be expressing 'supreme exaltation without calling into question the glory and sovereignty of God the Father' (p. 159), but he doesn't place the use of Ps. 110 within the human context of identifying our ultimate post-mortem destiny in the presence of the Father through the body of the Son.

31 Jean Danielou, SJ, *The Bible and the Liturgy* (2nd edn, Indiana: University of Notre Dame Press and London: SPCK, 1960, p. 303).

32 See note 6 for references to the cosmological functions of the Word.

33 The central importance of the Ascension as representing the cosmic nature of the incarnation,

and as opening up the possibility of a new future for humanity in eternal life, is also reflected in the early liturgical traditions of the Church. As P. Jounel points out, the tendency in the earliest period was for the different elements of Easter to be combined in a single 50-day period. Only later, from the late fourth to early fifth centuries, did the celebration of the Ascension, for instance, take on the character of a distinct Feast. The spread of the feast probably owed much to the influence of Gregory of Nyssa, while the two sermons on the Ascension by Leo the Great on the occasion of its introduction in Rome set out the theological meaning of the new liturgical focus (A. G. Martimort, I. H. Dalmais and P. Jounel, *The Liturgy and Time: Vol. IV – The Church at Prayer*, London: Geoffrey Chapman, trans. M. J. O'Connell, pp. 57–64. The texts of the two sermons can be found in Leo the Great, Tractate 73, 4, CCL 138A:453). J. G. Davies has pointed out the extent to which Ascension and incarnation were combined in the thinking of the early church, with respect to Egeria's account of the celebration of the Ascension at Bethlehem, rather than Jerusalem, on the occasion of her visit there between 381 and 384. See J. G. Davies, 'The peregrinatio Egeriae and the Ascension', in *Vigiliae Christianae*, 8 (Amsterdam, 1954, pp. 93–101), and John Wilkinson, *Egeria's Travels to the Holy Land* (London: SPCK, rev. edn, 1981, pp. 77–8 and 141).

34 Danielou, SJ, *The Bible and the Liturgy*, pp. 304–18. He discusses Ps. 23 (24) ('Lift up the gates of heaven, let them open and the king of glory shall enter in', 24.17), Ps. 109 (110) ('The Lord says to my lord, "Sit at my right hand until I make your enemies your footstool"', 110.1), and Ps. 67 (68) ('Ascending on high, he led away captives; he gave gifts to men', 68.18). Danielou points to the sequence 'ascension, session, mission' and draws out how Ps. 110, in particular, with its language of exaltation and subjugation, underpins the 'evangelisation of the world' (pp. 310–11). See also Mk 16.19, Eph. 1.22, 4.10–11, and Acts 2.33.

35 e.g. Rom. 8.9–11, 18–39.

36 For a discussion on this, see Raymond E. Brown, *The Gospel according to John* (i–xii) (New York: Doubleday and Co., 1966, pp. 299–303). Compare Irenaeus' comments on how experience of the Eucharist shapes our Christological beliefs (*Against Heresies*, Book 4, Chapter 18, §5).

37 *Answer to Petilian*, Book 2, Chapter 7, §15–16 (*Nicene and Post-Nicene Fathers: St Augustine, Vol. 4*, Edinburgh: T&T Clark, repr. 1989, p. 532).

38 *Answer to Petilian*, Book 3, Chapter 49, §59 (p. 621).

39 Commentary on Psalms LV, 3 (*Nicene and Post-Nicene Fathers: St Augustine, Vol. 8*, Edinburgh: T&T Clark, repr. 1983, p. 210). See also *On the Trinity*, XV, xix, 33 and Commentary on the Psalms CXXII, 1 and LIV, 3.

40 *Tractate on the Gospel of John*, 105, 2 and 5. Augustine is quoting Col. 1.16 (*Nicene and Post-Nicene Fathers: St Augustine, Vol. 7*, Edinburgh:T&T Clark, repr. 1991, p. 396).

41 Augustine stresses the importance of the ascended body of Jesus for Christian faith and existence in Sermons 246.4, 270.2 and 264.4, as well as the important passage in Sermon 93 from the *Sermons on New Testament Lessons*. In passages from the *Homilies on the Gospel of John*, Augustine stresses that Christ's majesty remains in the world despite the withdrawal of his body (Tractate 50.4), as does his glory (Tractate 50.13). While his ascended body 'can be only in one place', Christ's truth 'is everywhere' (Tractate 30.1). See also Sermons 93–103 on John 16. We shall return to the incarnational logic of this position in the following chapter.

42 ST III, q. 76, art. 5.

43 Gary Macy, *The Theologies of the Eucharist in the Early Scholastic Period* (Oxford: Clarendon Press, 1984).

44 'L'amor che move il sole e l'altre stelle' (*Paradiso* XXXIII, l.145) (ET from *Dante: The Divine Comedy*, trans. C. H. Cisson; Oxford: Oxford University Press, 1993, p. 499).

45 *Paradiso* XXXIII, 132

46 'O luce etterna, che sola in te sidi,/ sola t'intendi, e da te intelletta/ e intendente te ami e arridi!' (*Paradiso* XXXIII, 124–6).

47 In terms of medieval theology, Dante's one act of poetic licence was the fact that he goes in a pre-mortem body to where others have only gone in a post-mortem body. On Dante, body and heaven, see Gary P. Cestaro, *Dante and the Grammar of the Nursing Body* (Notre Dame, IN: University of Notre Dame Press, 2002).

48 An earlier version may have been in circulation by 1530 and a preliminary account had appeared in the *Commentariolus* in the first decade of the century (Brian Gerrish, 'The Reformation and the Rise of Modern Science', in *id.*, *The Old Protestantism and the New: Essays on the Reformation Heritage*, Chicago: University of Chicago Press and Edinburgh: T&T Clark, 1982, pp. 163–78; here p. 165). See also Dorothy Stimson, *The Gradual Acceptance of the Copernican Theory of the Universe* (New York: Baker and Taylor, 1917).

49 On Copernicus and his system, see Alexander Koyré, *The Astronomical Revolution*, trans. R. E. W. Maddison (Paris: Hermann, 1973, pp. 13–116).

50 Brian Gerrish has argued in fact that 'Calvinism actually began its existence in the Reformation era as a distinct variety of sacramental theology, more particularly as a distinct interpretation of the central Christian mystery of the Eucharist' (*Grace and Gratitude: The Eucharistic Theology of John Calvin*, Edinburgh: T&T Clark, 1993, p. 2). Much the same could be said of the theology of Ulrich Zwingli (see following note).

51 The 18th Article asserts that the Mass is not a sacrifice but is a 'memorial' of the sacrifice (*Huldrich Zwinglis Sämtliche Werke, 1*, Zürich: Theologischer Verlag Zürich, 1982. *Corpus Reformatorum, 88*, p. 460).

52 *Huldrich Zwinglis Sämtliche Werke, 2*, Zürich: Theologischer Verlag Zürich, 1982. *Corpus Reformatorum, 89*, pp. 137–8.

53 'Ad Mattheum Alberum de coena dominica epistola', *Zwinglis Werke, 3*, Zürich: Theologischer Verlag Zürich, 1982. *Corpus Reformatorum, 90*, pp. 335–54; see especially p. 345. Here Zwingli is borrowing from the treatise on the Eucharist by the Dutch humanist Cornelis Hoen which he countered earlier in 1524.

54 'Antwort über Straussens Büchlein, das Nachtmahl Christi betreffend', *Huldrich Zwinglis Sämtliche Werke, 4*, Zürich: Theologischer Verlag Zürich, 1982. *Corpus Reformatorum, 91*, especially pp. 827–41. Again, this point had appeared in the treatise by Cornelis Hoen.

55 *Luther's Works, 36, Word and Sacrament 2* (Philadelphia: Muhlenberg Press, 1959, p. 342).

56 *Luther's Works, 36*, p. 340.

57 *Institutes of the Christian Religion*, 1559, 4.17.32. I am indebted to B. A. Gerrish's work for much that follows in this discussion of Calvin.

58 *Institutes of the Christian Religion*, 1559, 4.17.29. This had also been Thomas Aquinas' view, of course, and it was the traditional opinion.

59 'But as this mystery of the secret union of Christ with believers is incomprehensible by nature, he exhibits its figure and image in visible signs adapted to our capacity ...' in *Institutes of the Christian Religion*, 4.17.1 (*Institutes of the Christian Religion*, trans. Henry Beveridge, London: James Clarke, 1949, Vol. 2, p. 557). See also John Calvin, 'Commentary on John', *Ioannis Calvini opera quae supersunt omnia*, 25, pp. 144–56 (*Corpus Reformatorum, 47*); 'Short Treatise on the Supper of our Lord', *Selected Works of John Calvin*, ed. Henry Beveridge and Jules Bonnet, Grand Rapids, MI: Baker Book House, repr. 1983, 2, pp. 165–70. Gerrish has a valuable discussion on these themes in *Grace and Gratitude*, pp. 127–33.

60 *Institutes of the Christian Religion*, 1559, 4.17.18.

61 *Institutes of the Christian Religion*, 1559, 4.17.10. See also 4.17.1 where Calvin opposes Zwingli on the nature of Eucharist as gift, rather than the memorial of a gift.

62 *Weimar Ausgabe. Tischreden*, 1.419.16ff. (no. 855). Gerrish, who gives this quotation, queries the use of the word 'fool' in the light of Lauterbach's alternative version (Gerrish, 'The Reformation and the Rise of Natural Science', p. 168).

63 However, Bornkamm makes the valid point that we should be wary of reading from this a considered rejection of the Copernican system (Heinrich Bornkamm, 'Kopernikus im Urteil der Reformatoren', *Archiv für Reformationsgeschichte 40*, 1943, pp. 171–83; repr. in *id.*, *Das Jahrhundert der Reformation*, Göttingen, 1961, pp. 177–85).

64 *Institutes of the Christian Religion*, 1559, 4.17.29 (*Library of Christian Classics*, Philadelphia: Westminster Press, 1960, ed. J. T. McNeill, trans. Ford Lewis Battles, 2:1399–1400). The reference is to Tertullian, *On the Resurrection of the Flesh*, lines 2–3 (*Anti-Nicene Fathers, Vol. 3*, Edinburgh: T&T Clark, repr. 1986, p. 584). Calvin also denies the heresy of assuming that the human flesh of Christ 'was swallowed up by his divinity', which he attributes to Servetus (4.17.29; *Library of Christian Classics*, 2:1398).

65 *Calvin's Commentaries on the Epistles of Paul to the Galatians and Ephesians*, trans. Rev. William Pringle, Edinburgh: Calvin Translation Society, 1854, pp. 275–6 (Eph. 4.10). See also the commentary on Heb. 9.24, where there is a reference to 'the glorious kingdom of God which is above all the heavens' and which is contrasted with 'the heaven which we see, and in which the stars shine' (*Calvin's Commentaries on the Epistles of Paul to the Galatians and Ephesians*, trans. Rev. John Owen, Edinburgh: Calvin Translation Society, 1853, p. 216).

66 'On the Lord's Ascension'. Sermon 73, §4. Translation from W. A. Jurgens, *The Faith of the Early Fathers*, Vol. 3 (Collegeville, Minnesota: The Liturgical Press, 1979, p. 279).

67 ST III, q.57, art. 6.

68 Hans Blumenberg, *The Genesis of the Copernican World* (Cambridge, MA: MIT Press, 1987, pp. 8–21).

69 Amos Funkenstein, *Theology and the Scientific Imagination* (Princeton: Princeton University Press, 1986, pp. 3–57).

70 *City of God*, Book 22, Chapter 8, §1. Augustine replies to those who doubt the veracity of miracles by pointing to the more fundamental belief in the Ascension: 'How is it then that Christ is everywhere celebrated with such firm belief in His Bodily Ascension into Heaven …?'

71 The clash between scripture and humanism at Marburg is reflected in Luther's protest to his opponents, who contest his reiteration of 'hoc est corpus meum', that 'reason, philosophy and mathematics have no place here' ('vernunft, philosophia und mathematica gehören hierher nicht', in Gerhard May, ed., *Das Marburger Religionsgespräch 1529* (Gütersloh: Gütersloher Verlagshaus Gerd Mohn, 1970, p. 54.).

72 See Regin Prenter, *Spiritus Creator: Luther's Concept of the Holy Spirit* (Philadelphia: Muhlenberg Press, 1953, pp. 252–5), with references.

73 *Spiritus Creator*, pp. 259–66.

74 *That These Words of Christ, 'This is my Body', etc., Still Stand Firm against the Fanatics* of 1527, *Luther's Works*, 37, *Word and Sacrament 3* (Philadelphia: Muhlenberg Press, 1961, p. 95).

75 *Spiritus Creator*, p. 250.

76 Werner Elert, *The Structure of Lutheranism*, Vol. 1 (Saint Louis: Concordia Publishing House, 1962, pp. 427–8). This is an instance which shows how scientific disputation about the possibility of God's omnipresence within the material universe could conflict with Luther's scriptural arguments for the ubiquity of the body of Christ. See note 69 above for Funkenstein's discussion of challenges to the notion of world as 'God's body' in the light of scientific change during the late sixteenth and early seventeenth centuries.

77 The Roman Catholic Church was much slower to accept the cosmological changes, and the traditional, pre-Copernican cosmology was still prominent in Catholic writing from the mid-seventeenth century. See for instance Gabriel Henao, *Empyreologia seu philosophia christiana de empyreo caelo* (1652).

78 See notes 58 and 59.

79 *Luther's Works*, 37, p. 69.

80 *Luther's Works*, 37, pp. 55–6.

81 *Luther's Works*, 37, p. 57.

82 *Luther's Works*, 37, pp. 57–9.

83 'Über D. Martin Luthers Buch, Bekenntnis gennant', *Huldrich Zwinglis Sämtliche Werke, 8*, Zürich: Theologischer Verlag Zürich, 1982. *Corpus Reformatorum, 93*, pp. 167 ('Die ist ein lyb, ein umbzyleter, umbfasseter, umpryßner lyb'). This work dates from August 1528, and is a response to Luther's piece of March 1528.

84 'Antwort über Straussens Büchlein, das Nachtmahl Christi betreffend', *Zwinglis Werke, 4*, pp. 828–9.

85 'Antwort über Straussens Büchlein, das Nachtmahl Christi betreffend', *Zwinglis Werke, 4*, pp. 834–41 (especially p. 841: 'so man offenlich sicht, das wir den verstand des essens sines fleischs zum teil dahar messend, daß er an der grechten götlicher maiestet *unverwandelt* sitzt biß an'n jungsten tag, und demnach ewklich' [my italics]).

86 'Antwort über Straussens Büchlein, das Nachtmahl Christi betreffend', *Zwinglis Werke, 4*, pp. 835–8.

87 'Ad Mattheum Alberum de coena dominica epistola', *Zwinglis Werke, 3*, pp. 336–7.

88 This accusation forms a substantial part of *That These Words of Christ, 'This is my Body', etc., Still Stand Firm against the Fanatics* of 1527 (*Luther's Works*, 37, *Word and Sacrament 3* (Philadelphia: Muhlenberg Press, 1961, pp. 13–155), and it returns in *Confession Concerning Christ's Supper* of 1528 (*Luther's Works*, 37, see for instance pp. 96–100 and pp. 287–8). See also Gerhard, May, ed., *Marburger Religionsgespräch*, pp. 52–3.

89 'Ad Mattheum Alberum de coena dominica epistola', *Zwinglis Werke, 3*, p. 337. In his comments on Luther's dispute with Zwingli, Paul Althaus uses the phrase 'Spirit has an effect only on spirit' to describe the position of Luther's opponents (*The Theology of Martin Luther*, Philadelphia: Fortress Press, 1966, p. 395).

2

The Interrupted Body

Oliver Davies

In the previous chapter it was argued that the statement Christ 'sits at the right hand of the Father in heaven' was not in its original setting a metaphorical one. The metaphorization of such a central theological theme, which had previously been held to be literal, inevitably had profound effects. The roots of a distinctively modern kind of metaphorization can already be seen in the interpretative strategies associated with Josh. 10.12–13, which states that at Joshua's command the sun 'stopped in mid-heaven, and did not hurry to set for about a whole day'. This became a topos of vigorous debate among Lutheran theologians during the seventeenth century, which led to the development of the very reasonable exegetical principle of 'accommodation' in order to overcome the failure of literal reference at this point, in the light of a heliocentric understanding of the universe. 'Accommodation' was the belief that exegetes might prioritize what they understood to be the intention of the author rather than simply the content of the text.[1] We have to see this particular debate as a critical point in the gradual detaching, or relativization, of literal reference in the Bible, through not only the advent of new scientific data and understandings but also, increasingly from the eighteenth century onwards, the evolution of new understandings of the historical nature of scripture itself, which viewed it as a product of its own time rather than as a text which had universal literal or straightforwardly referential meaning. One of the key ways in which this developed, as Hans Frei has recorded, was in the emergence of a double history, whereby early modern Lutheran exegetes came to understand themselves to be embedded in North European historical narratives and identities which were quite different from those represented in the Bible.[2] Under the pressure of the relativization of the literal meaning of key passages of scripture, in the light of the new cosmology, and of an increased understanding of the provenance and form of scripture, it became inevitable that the Bible as a whole might come to be seen as having little relation to historical reality, and thus as no longer having any real relevance to faith. It was the turn to hermeneutics, which had been heralded in the early Romantic period, and which came to the fore during the later nineteenth and twentieth centuries, which seemed to offer a way out of this cul-de-sac. The rise of narrative and language-centred theologies is comprehensible only within the context of the demise of the text of the Bible as reliable historical source, giving us a realist account of salvation history. The new contemporary emphasis upon the Word as story and language allowed the re-emergence of scripture as authoritative text on the grounds of a revaluing of textuality as such, and of the text of scripture in particular. But the movement now was a different one. Rather than pointing reliably to the world, George Lindbeck could now say of scripture, for instance, that it is 'the text which absorbs the world rather than the world the text'.[3] This text saved human beings by virtue of its intrinsic power as text, bearing the saving narrative, rather than through its capacity to yield an accurate and reliable description of efficacious divine action in human history, as that which is external to the text. The text thus became an *alternative* world of sacred immediacy and saving meaning. And within that context, the real world of space and time, within which the living reader is reading the text, became a function of the textual one, to be redeemed in its irreducible non-textuality by the power of the sacred text as world-bearing text of origins and ends. Thus the field of the reader's sensible and embodied real, in which the sacred text itself is being read, became lost to view.

Metaphorization is in play also in our recitation or praying of the creeds. The statement that Christ was 'condemned by Pontius Pilate, was crucified, died and on the third day rose again' is past reference, as the statement that 'he will come again to judge the living and the dead' is reference to a future event. But if we take 'sits at the right hand of the Father' as metaphor, then the creeds seem to have no *present* reference. And yet, if the Christian claim is precisely that Christ really entered human history and that he lives, as fully human and fully divine, then it is indeed ironic that the referential function of creedal doctrine appears not to apply to the timescale in which it is most normally and most directly to be found. Reference, at its most direct, is to objects within the domain of our own present spatial-temporal reality. In reference, language 'points to' its objects: those people, things and states of affairs which form part of the common reality of speaker and addressee. Christian referential language, however, seems to point back, to historical fact, which is to say to a possible communal memory, and forward, to a possible communal eschatological hope, but it does not, it appears, 'point to' Jesus Christ, the Word made flesh, as current reality within the spatial-temporal framework of our lived experience.

Metaphor undoubtedly has an important place in many aspects of human language and experience. Philosophers such as Hans Blumenberg and Paul Ricoeur have given extensive accounts of the richness and creativity of the metaphorical in human thought and culture.[4] Metaphor has a particular role to play in Christian theology and texts, not least in scriptural texts themselves, which abound in metaphorical formulations. But this is not at all the same thing as when a phrase, which was for over 1,500 years a literal reference in the creed whereby the church community pointed to the reality of Christ in the present world, is now appropriated as a metaphor. By analogy with 'accommodation', the metaphorization of this literal reference is, of course, the way in which the church community continues to make sense of the 'session' for itself.

What we have to recognize, therefore, is that the metaphorization of the phrase 'seated at the right hand of the Father' inevitably means that what was previously reference to the reality of Christ in the present world, has now become an affirmation, the meaning of which is dependent upon the firmer affirmations about the past and future Christ which surround it. In other words, the phrase 'seated at the right hand of the Father' no longer points out to the world but points rather back to the mind of the church community itself, as it has struggled to make sense of the phrase in a world in which heaven can no longer envisaged as a place in which the real body of Jesus can be. In Christological terms we can thus begin to speak of 'Event Christology', whereby the Christian faith becomes the subjective reception in the present of the benefits of a past objective salvific event: the saving death and resurrection of Christ. The question as to the current reality of Christ as God incarnate is translated into a reception of the meaning of an event from the past and a reception of the *Spirit* in present time. Christ is present in another form: as Spirit (or in Catholic tradition, as Church and Spirit). Thus what is undoubtedly an entirely fundamental relation between Spirit and Son, and Church and Son, is changed from being a relation of Trinitarian *mediation* to one of simple substitution.

There has to be a sense, then, in which theology has failed to serve the Christian community in its affirmation of Christ's continuing reality which is at the heart of the Church's traditional faith. The change in cosmology did not and does not invalidate the doctrinal principle of a continuing and full incarnation. Christian faith does not entail any kind of belief in a heaven that is 'beyond the stars'. But it does commit us to a belief that Jesus has risen from the dead, that he lives and is still fully human. And being fully human, as well as fully divine, Jesus must still in some sense have 'local' existence and thus be in continuity with our own space-time reality today. The alternative to this possibility is either that the incarnation has ceased (Christ is no longer properly alive, or properly human) or that the humanity of Christ has been absorbed into his divinity: a possibility which the early church specifically rejected.

The metaphorization of heaven and of Christ's current state (that is, his 'continuing incarnation') cannot but represent a very profound shift in Christian theological sensibility. We can see it at work for instance when we speak of divinity and the sacred, which is to say 'the heavenly', in terms of *the metaphor of height*. To this extent the metaphor is supported by other metaphorical turns of phrase such as 'looking up to', 'being above', 'raising the mind', 'rising above', as well as those which understand height as 'commanding' and as 'the seat of power'. These ways of thinking are deeply embedded in our ordinary religious language. The power of a new metaphor, or what is sometimes called a 'live' metaphor, is that it gives us the opportunity to see something in a new way. As such, it is a linguistically generated reality. But the metaphor of heaven as height is in no sense a new metaphor. It is rather a 'dead' or 'frozen' metaphor in that it has become so embedded in our language that it no longer has the capacity to shock us into a new way of seeing things; if it ever did.

The question which inevitably follows is this: what does it mean for us today that we should use this particular metaphor so extensively? Does it really matter that we do so? And if so, how and to what extent? As a way of engaging with these questions, I want to offer a brief analysis of passages in which T. F. Torrance, one of the foremost theologians of the modern period, addressed the cosmological issue in his magisterial study *Space, Time and Incarnation*. A central theme in this work indeed is what he calls 'verticality', a term which, while not reducible to the metaphor of height in this context, is a particularly intensive application of it.

Torrance is concerned in particular to contest what he rightly perceives to be a disturbing dualism at work in our thinking of the relation between the secular and the theological order. In his view these too often seem to exist as alternatives, without intersecting at any point. In fact, Torrance strongly defends in principle Luther's affirmation of *hoc est corpus meum* against Zwingli's *hoc significat*, as a way precisely of maintaining contact between these two orders.[5] But he equally strongly repudiates Luther's cosmology of finite space as being Aristotelian and therefore not properly Christian.[6] For Torrance, the divine intersects 'like an axis' with the created order of space and time through the incarnation, and he proposes that this can be thought of as 'a vertical dimension' of divine intervention mediated by the Holy Spirit which intersects with 'two horizontal dimensions' of 'space and time'. The incarnation thus becomes 'a moving and creative centre' within space and time.[7]

Torrance takes the incarnation to be 'the place where the vertical and horizontal dimensions intersect, the place where human being is opened out to a transcendent ground in God and where the infinite Being of God penetrates into our existence and creates room for Himself within the horizontal dimensions of finite being in space and time'.[8] It is important therefore that Jesus Christ 'cannot be thought of simply as fitting into the patterns of space and time formed by other agencies, but as organizing them around Himself and giving them transcendental references to God in and through Himself'.[9] But at the same time, Torrance seeks the 'rejection of radical dualism' and 'the rejection of a deistic dualism', which is to say that he is denying both the theory that there is no point of contact at all between human and divine accounts of the world, and the theory that 'natural theology' is concerned with the world while 'positive or revelatory theology' reflects God's incarnation in it.[10] Quoting the parallel of geometry and physics, Torrance rightly argues that 'natural theology' needs in fact to be 'made *natural* to the proper subject-matter of theology', so that the gap between reflection on the natural world order and doctrinal reflection on God's redemptive action in the world can be closed.[11] For all his emphasis upon transcendence, Torrance also wishes to maintain the integrity, value and creatureliness of space–time. He summarizes his 'theological geometry' in a fine passage, where he argues that the intersection of the vertical and horizontal dimensions establishes that the incarnation is 'to be understood as the chosen path of God's rationality in which He interacts with the world and establishes such a relation between creaturely being and Himself that He will not allow it to slip away from Him into futility or nothingness, but upholds and confirms it as that which He has made and come to redeem'. He continues:

> Thus while the Incarnation does not mean that God is limited by space and time, it asserts the reality of space and time for God in the actuality of his relations with us, and at the same time *binds us to space and time in all relations with Him* [my italics]. We can no more contract out of space and time than we can contract out of the creature–Creator relationship and God 'can' no more contract out of space and time than he 'can' go back on the Incarnation of His Son or retreat from the love in which He made the world, with which He loves it, through which He redeems it, and by which He is pledged to uphold it – pledged, that is, by the very love that God Himself is and which He has once and for all embodied in our existence in the person and being of Jesus Christ.[12]

We could not hope for a clearer statement of the non-negotiable character of space–time for our real mortal existence and for our relation with God, who incarnates in our world, or for the unequivocal love of God for his world, and for us *within* it. Quite explicitly, T. F. Torrance is contesting the world-denying trend in Christian theology by insisting upon the foundational integrity of space–time within the theological order. Torrance is perceptively and judiciously addressing what might be termed the 'cosmological problem', therefore, which, since it turns on God's relation to the world, can be described as the most foundational question of contemporary theology.

And yet, there seems to be a single fundamental contradiction running throughout Torrance's approach, which follows from his determination to conceptualize a place for the world of space and time in incarnational revelation, from within the metaphor of *height*. This has far-reaching consequences. Both the 'horizontal' and the 'vertical' are of course physical dimensions of space and time. But, for his paradigm, Torrance allocates 'two horizontal dimensions' to the three dimensionality of 'space and time' and 'one vertical dimension' to the 'relation to God through His Spirit'.[13] From one perspective this might appear to enclose God's activity within the physical universe, and to mark a return to the pre-modern concept of God in the 'highest of the heavens', above the clouds, and thus in some kind of continuous relation with the earth. But of course that would be to read literally what is meant metaphorically. And so let us return to the metaphor.

To use language metaphorically is to speak of one thing in terms of another. In the case of the modern use of the material language of height for heaven and the heavenly, we wish to say that heaven, which for us stands outside all material dimensionality, can nevertheless be represented in spatial terms. When we use this kind of language (which now has *metaphorical* where once it had *literal* meaning), then we do so because the language of elevation has a privileged position in the tradition and is metaphorically expressive of God's real otherness, power and authority. When T. F. Torrance attributes 'verticality' to the divine in its relation to the 'horizontals' of space and time, then the reader understands that he does so because he wishes to set up an 'axial' paradigm of divinity and humanity – or createdness – in the incarnation such that the divine truly enters the created order but does so without compromising its own infinite freedom. In his own words, he wishes to exclude the possibility of 'resolving divine transcendence into this-worldly transcendence or any merging of the divine reality and this-worldly reality in the same horizontal level'.[14] He continues:

> In Jesus Christ the divine reality intersects this-worldly reality like an axis, so that if our language about God who cannot be observed and our language about the world which can be observed, must not be confused, it is because they intersect at decisive points, and not because they are merely the obverse of each other or because they are merely parallel to one another.[15]

Torrance's argument at this point rests critically upon geometry and the metaphorical application of an axis of 90 degrees: it is guided by it, or thought *within* it.

But the metaphor of dimensionality – in this case height – is not a metaphor like any other. Height is an indexical category, which means to say that it is a relational category which is predicated upon the human body. Something is only ever 'high' with respect to someone or something at a particular place and time. It can only have meaning when we know with respect to whom or what something is being described as 'high'. The indexicals of space ('above', 'below', 'in front', 'behind', etc.) are only meaningful if we know with respect to whom or what something is or was spacially located. In the same way, the indexicals of time ('now', 'yesterday', 'tomorrow', etc.) only have meaning if we know *when* they were uttered (my 'yesterday', as I write this, is not your 'yesterday' as you read it). Thus, as an indexical category, height, or 'verticality' to use Torrance's adaptation of it, is embedded in the deep structure of my real, embodied existence in the world of space and time.

If it is the case that Torrance's primary interest with his 'vertical'–'horizontal' distinction is to set up an opposition between the Creator–creation relation (or what he calls the 'relation to God through His Spirit'[16]) on the one hand and all created relations on the other hand (so that the former can be represented as being at 90 degrees to the three dimensionality of space and time, as intersecting with it), then it is also the case that there is nothing here to which the 'vertical' can properly be said to refer. We cannot properly refer, or point, to what is deemed *not* to be within space and time. And yet Torrance himself has rightly insisted that God can only communicate with us, or relate to us, from within space and time, since this is the character of our createdness.

By removing the Creator–creature relation from space and time, through opposing this relation (as verticality) to all spatio-temporal relations (as horizontality), T. F. Torrance has allowed his theology to be shaped by a metaphor and to become itself metaphorical, in the area of incarnation which – of all theological areas – ought to lay claim to real reference. Despite his declared wish to uphold 'the reality of space and time for God' in relation to us as the place to which God 'binds' us 'in all relations with Him'[17], he has turned that relation firstly into a 'geometrical' one, which is to abstract it *from* space and time, and then has rendered its 'geometry' metaphorical by defining the axis of 90 degrees as that which extends between space and time and what is outside space and time. This angle of 90 degrees thus cannot point to what is in space and time but only to what is 'outside' space and time. But does this matter?

It does and it doesn't. Indexical reference to what is not in space and time is not reference at all, and thus, by implication, can have no real meaning. And yet there are two elements to the significance of this metaphor of 'heavenly' or 'spiritual' height. The first is that to which it points, which is not spatio–temporal. But then there is the act of pointing itself, which clearly is in space and time (since that is where we are). And height is fundamental to our embodiment, to our being human. We know what it is for something to be above us. If the object pointed to is not in fact in space and time, and has no referential existence, then what we are left with is the act of pointing itself: the act of pointing *away*. Whereas natural verticality for the pre-modern paradigm was a pointing *to* (that is, to God in heaven, which – according to Gen. 1.1 – was part of the first creation along with the earth), metaphorical verticality is only a pointing *from* (that is, from the world). It is an image of spiritual thinking which takes God to come from 'outside' or 'beyond' the world, and thus takes the activity of the Holy Spirit within the world to be a path that leads from and out of the world. But the Christian, like anyone else, lives only in the world of space and time. And so by the internalization of such a metaphorical conceptual paradigm which points *out* of the world, the Christian self is drawn to live under alienation *within* the real world, of which there can be no real 'outside'. Thus we Christians who live by this paradigm, may find that we live but poorly in the world, and not at all in any other.[18]

1. Jesus Christ in the World

And so we come to the second half of this chapter and ask the question: how are we to retrieve what has been lost, from within the ancient and fundamental doctrinal inheritance of Christianity? Much of what we have written has been to underline the extent to which many of us will feel that we live today with the awareness that the life of our senses, our sensibility as such, lacks a real relation to the incarnate Christ. His embodiment is recalled historically, and is understood through faith to have been a divine and saving embodiment. The touchstone of faith is likely to be belief in his resurrection, which we celebrate liturgically and sacramentally. But even those of us who inhabit Christian traditions with strong sacramental theologies and practice may wonder how exactly that experience relates to the ordinary life of the senses, to the empirical reality of which we are ordinarily a part. What is thematized within the sacrament, as the liturgical presence of the body and blood of Christ, is unthematized in the world of ordinary sensibility. In short, we have few resources which offer us a sense of connectedness to the living Christ *as embodied*, which is to say a relation with Christ in his continuing or living embodiment as ascended and glorified. The domain of what is for us incontrovertibly *real*, that is the domain of the senses and of sensibility (which is that to which science and publically authoritative knowledge inevitably appeals) appears to stand in some irreducible sense outside the domain of our religious convictions and experience. We struggle to maintain a real relation with the real Christ therefore, but are always invited to fall back into communal memory and traditioned metaphor. Moreover, despite their original dependence upon the real existence of Christ's ascended body, Spirit and Church have surely become for us substitutes for that body, rather than its mediations. The reception of incarnation becomes a matter then principally of the mind, or the imagination, or a certain kind of memory, or a transformational experience in liturgy which – however intense this may be – leaves us with the struggle to transfer it, or to find it again, in the everyday realities of our ordinary, non-liturgical sensibility.

The argument throughout this chapter has been that it is the ascended embodiment which makes possible a real relation between the living Christ and ourselves in the ordinary life of our senses. During the apostolic, patristic, medieval and early Reformation periods, this relation was sustained through a paradigm of height, which meant that our bodies and the ascended body of Christ were at the opposite ends of a continuum which reached from heaven to earth. But it was nevertheless a continuum, and tradition records brief moments when human beings perceived the ascended body in heaven, while still on earth.[19] This is a deeply alien language to us today, for extension, in the modern world, cannot hold heaven and earth together.

The task of repair is likely to be a long one, but the place to begin this reflection is the one depiction of an encounter with the ascended embodiment of Jesus which we have in scripture. In Acts we read how the zealous Pharisee Saul of Tarsus left Jerusalem for Damascus in order to continue his persecution of Christian Jewish communities there. The scriptural record records that he encountered the ascended Jesus, as he approached Damascus. The narrative exists in three versions (Acts 9.3–19; 22.6–16; 26.12–18), though with considerable continuity. Jesus appears to him in a brilliant 'light from heaven'. He fell to the ground[20] and heard a voice, saying: 'Saul, Saul, why do you persecute me?' Paul asked: 'Who are you, Lord?' He received the answer: 'I am Jesus, who you are persecuting. But get up and enter the city, and you will be told what you are to do.' Paul is blinded by this event and is led into Damascus, where he remains unable to see, and cannot eat or drink. Ananias is told by Christ in a vision to go and find Saul in a particular place and to lay his hands upon him so that he may regain his sight and be filled with the Holy Spirit.[21] Saul's sight is restored, he is baptized and begins to eat again. From that time on, Paul will preach Christ crucified, risen and ascended.

At 1 Cor. 15.5–8, Paul tells us that Jesus had appeared after his death to

Cephas and the apostles, and to 'more than five hundred brothers and sisters' and '[l]ast of all, as to someone untimely born, he appeared also to me'. This has frequently been read as suggesting that it was the resurrected Christ who appeared to Paul, but in fact there are some important reasons why we should think of Paul as *not* having seen Christ in his resurrected form, although we may accept that he belongs within the line of those to whom the risen Christ appeared. In his resurrection appearances Christ's body seemed quite ordinary to the extent that he was taken to be someone else, not being recognized for who he was. In the narrative of the encounter on the road to Emmaus, the two apostles failed to identify Jesus and took him quite ordinarily to be someone else (Lk. 24.13–32). Jesus urged Thomas to feel his wounds (Jn 20.24–9), and the disciples saw Jesus standing on the beach in the early morning light but failed to recognize him (Jn 21.4). On the road to Damascus, however, the encounter is accompanied by a brilliance which robs Paul of his physical sight. Paul's physical collapse with the appearance is entirely different in kind from the responses recorded in the Gospels to the resurrection appearances of Jesus: it is of a different order of intensity and becomes itself a primary element in the narrative.

We have to ask the question, therefore, whether it was a vision which Paul experienced, which would place the 'body' entirely within his own subjectivity and close out the possibility that the 'body' might have been seen by anyone else.[22] Or did it in fact display the properties of an ordinary, objective or 'local' body such that others could see it? The evidence on the basis of all three accounts of the appearance is mixed. According to Acts 9, Paul's companions heard the voice of Jesus speaking but did not see the light. If that is the case, then the description of the event as recorded in Acts suggests that the appearance was *both* subjective (to the extent that the light was seen only by Paul) *and* objective (to the extent that Paul's companions heard the voice). What are we to make of such a paradox (which is repeated in inverse form at Acts 22, where his companions 'saw the light' but did not hear the voice)? Is this apparent straddling of objectivity and subjectivity something of which we should take note; or does it point to the constructed character of this narrative? Is it mere inconsistency?

There are reasons for thinking that it may be more than this. In the first place, although the accounts given in Acts 9 and 22 are different, they agree that Paul's perception of the body was both subjective (in the sense that it appeared only to him) and objective (in the sense that it appeared also to others). We can of course attribute this narrative entirely to the spiritual imagination of the early church, and cease to read scripture on its own terms at this point. But there are powerful doctrinal reasons why we should take this feature of the Damascus appearance to Paul at face value (despite the incon-sistency of detail). For these, however, we shall have to return to the funda-mental Christology of the Chalcedonian formula, which states that Jesus Christ has two natures (*physis*) in a single *hypostasis*. Chalcedon affirms the normativity of Christian belief that Jesus Christ is fully human and fully divine and that his humanity and divinity are perfectly united in a single, real, personal existence. The word *hypostasis* here conveys the actuality of his existence, and closes out any attempt to read the Christian faith as allowing only an 'appearance' or temporary manifestation of the divine in the person of Jesus Christ. Jesus Christ is as fully human as he is divine and, as fully human and divine, he is also fully real in this world.

Chalcedon leaves us with the unavoidable conclusion therefore that the body of Jesus is the body both of his humanity and of his divinity (if this is not the case, then his divinity and his humanity are not fully united, and the divinity is not fully incarnate). With our modern forgetfulness about the cosmic nature of the Word, there comes a parallel diminution in our understanding of the nature of the body of Jesus, as body of the incarnate Word.[23] But the Chalcedonian definition affirms what we see in scripture: that this is as much the body of the divinity as it is of the humanity. While the historical body of Jesus manifests all the properties which we associate with our own bodies, it is also the case that it is an extraordinary body. According to Lukan and Matthean tradition, for instance, it is the Holy Spirit who takes the place of a human father in his conception. Jesus' birth is attended by special signs, as is his later mission among the people. His body seems to be the site of a natural and immediate healing power (cf. the woman who is healed at the touch of his hem[24]), and his ability to walk upon water suggests both control of the elements and the capacity to manifest unique physical properties.[25] But it is with the Transfiguration, before he set out on his final journey to Jerusalem, that the divinity which is in Jesus begins to come to the fore: to enter visibility. At this point his body appears to enter a new state, much to the bafflement of the disciples.[26] Shortly afterwards, according to the scriptural narrative, Jesus uses exceptional language about his own body at the Last Supper, when he breaks the bread and says: 'This is my body given for you.'[27] We may forget through familiarity what a very strange thing this is to say. Indeed, it suggests an identification of Jesus' own body with the bread and wine to be consumed at the meal, prefiguring the passion narrative in which we see the body of Jesus suffer and finally die.

If our argument is that the body of Jesus is itself the site of a cosmic drama, which is to say the progression from an embodiment which is primarily human (though within the context of the hypostatic union of the two natures) to an embodiment which is primarily divine (though still within that same union), then we can point to the Easter period as the focal point in that transition. Here the issue is not purely the properties displayed by Jesus' body, but something other comes into view, which now offers a new and unparalleled intensity of meaning. What we see in the Easter narrative is that the transition between the two forms of embodiment (pre- and post-resurrection) entails an act of will on the part of the man Jesus, which is to say an act of total submission to the divine will. Bodies are not just material, they are the living form of the human person, with personality and will. The Easter narrative conveys the comprehensive conforming of the man Jesus to the divine will. Jesus enters an area of profound personal trauma and struggle before God and the divine will, in the face of an imminent and violent death. The divine will is the institution of divine causality in the world; its acceptance by the man Jesus is the inauguration of the kingdom of God on earth. But as the life of the humanity of Jesus and his human will, brought to the limits of its power by the Son–Father relation which subtends it, is worked through, a new life appears. As the Easter narrative unfolds, the divinity of Jesus comes to living expression at the formal level of his own material body. The resurrection body is not a 'new' body: it is the same body of his birth, but now with radically new material properties. It is a wounded body which cannot be contained in any space, but can be touched. It is a body which moves through solid objects and yet can eat.

But if the resurrected body is the same body of Jesus' birth and death (as the empty tomb tradition, and the 'doubting Thomas' passage at Jn 20.24–9, seem to be telling us), though one now of course which lives by divine power beyond the limit of death, then this is still not an 'end-station'. It still retains the dynamically dual and therefore transitional character of Jesus' historical embodiment. This continuing transitional character is given with the *noli me tangere*, when Jesus says to Mary Magdalene in the garden: 'Do not hold on to me, for I have not yet ascended to the Father.'[28] The life of the resurrected body is lived out in the expectation of the Ascension which is a departure that marks a new and definitive state of Jesus' continuing embodied life. If the resurrected embodiment of Jesus, which has a new relation to space and time, still has the authentic characteristics of a wounded human body, then it is also a body, as we shall see, which can remarkably withdraw and yet still remain.

2. Spirit in the World

According to the accounts in John and Luke/Acts, the resurrection of Jesus leads to his Ascension and gives a new role to the Spirit, whose advent as the Spirit of Pentecost – according to Johannine tradition – is dependent upon the 'withdrawal' of the body. Jn 14.26 tells us that the Spirit will come as 'comforter' or 'counsellor' and will teach us 'all things', while Jn 15.26 tells us that the Spirit will 'testify about Jesus' as the 'Spirit of Truth' who comes from the Father. Chalcedon once again can assist us with the Christological and Trinitarian logic in play here.

If the body of Jesus is the body both of his humanity and divinity, and if these two 'natures' interact within history (as they must do if the Word is truly incarnate and thus truly in history), then the progression that we see is the movement from the embodiment of Jesus in which the humanity predominates (birth) to an embodiment in which the divinity predominates (Ascension and heavenly session). The former is an historical and therefore passing event in time, while the second is an irreversible and continuing state, with eschatological meaning.

While we are familiar enough with the human embodiment of Jesus, the divine embodiment often seems alien to modern minds. The scriptural affirmations about the divinity of Christ liken him to Yahweh and identify him with Creator rather than creature. He is the one through whom 'all things were made' (cf. Jn 1.3), in whom 'all things in heaven and on earth were created' (Col. 1.16) and who 'sustains all things' (Heb. 1.3). This is cosmological language which we struggle to combine with what we know about modern scientific accounts of the creation of the universe. But we need not read these scriptural affirmations as proto-scientific in any way. What they point to is Christ's divinity in such a way that we believe in faith that the world itself is 'in' him. The world which we know and of which we are a part is already contained in him since he is the one through whom all things were made and by whom all things are held in being. The reality of new creation of which St Paul speaks is not proto-scientific speculation but the intense language of faith which experiences the making new of all things through Christ's divinity made present to us in the Church through his glorious, embodied life. If we are to acknowledge the fullness of the divinity in Christ, then we have to consider that there is a sense in which the world itself becomes a function of that body, which is the body also of the Creator. In other words, we have to consider that by becoming incarnate, which is to say by entering into our material world, the triune God changed the very nature of the world in which we live, in accordance with his unfathomable and loving creativity. Human redemption then is not something that happens without reference to the world of which we are intrinsically a part. Just as we are part of the world, our redemption, rebirth in the Spirit and new creation are intrinsically part of the world order which is radically transformed by the glorification of Christ's body.

Of course, the cosmic dimensions of this transformation have been eclipsed over a long period of time in favour of its purely human expressions. Part of what we wish to do in this volume is recalibrate the tradition in its modern appropriations by laying out the foundation of the redemption which is *the change in the world itself* that is brought about by Jesus' birth, death, resurrection and Ascension. Human redemption has to be seen as part of that, just as our own lives are themselves only ever constituted within a world. The Word, who – in and with the Father and the Spirit – is Trinity and Creator, has united himself with the man Jesus in such a way as to effect a change in the created order itself, which is now consummated in some real, though for us unfathomable, sense as God's creation. The Pauline language of new creation which attaches to the person of Christ reminds us that the transformed possibilities of faith for us following the death, resurrection and Ascension of Christ, are inseparably part of the transformation of the world itself brought about by the incarnation of the Creator Word made flesh. Since we are truly part of the world, then our new reconciled relation with God has to be seen as part of new creation, which is to say as part of the post-resurrection, post-Ascension world order.

But if we are to think the divinity of the incarnate Christ in such a way, then we have to ask how could we as creatures ever know such a divine body, or embodiment? How can we know representationally that which is the ultimate unity of all things in Christ, in whom God has 'made known to us the mystery of his will [. . .] as a plan for the fullness of time, to gather up all things in him, things in heaven and things on earth' (Eph. 1.9–10)? How can incarnation under such terms be meaningful to us as something real, within our own ordinary embodied human existence? This is the question with which we began this enquiry. We know that we cannot simply turn back to a pre-modern worldview, for that astronomy simply has no meaning for us today. We know also that we must not reify 'world', objectifying it as a totality, which would be to fall into Kant's 'logic of illusion'.[29] World is not a totality to be conceptualized but rather it is a horizon of possibility (of all possible experiences) on the one hand and our actual spatio–temporal reality in the here and now on the other. Our problem then will be to map incarnation as something that is genuinely accessible to us, and real for us, within the tension between what is and what can be.

Let us continue with Chalcedon and its affirmation of a body which is simultaneously divine and human. By virtue of the divinity, we can say that through incarnation the Word has taken to itself the world it created which can now be said to be 'in' the body of Jesus Christ, as new creation. The world rises with him and undergoes glorification by analogy with the 'seed corn' and 'first fruits' of his glorified body.[30] This state of glorification is intimately bound up with the Ascension and the Spirit of Pentecost by which we are inaugurated into new creation: it is by the Spirit that we are reborn, into a world already irreversibly shaped by incarnation, and 'under way' in conformity with the transformation of Christ's body. But – according to the Chalcedonian dialectic – he is present to us also by virtue of his full and continuing humanity. This is to evoke what tradition called the 'local' body of Jesus with its place in heaven; and it is to recall the way in which we can say that in Jesus Christ the Word is also truly 'in' the world as we, who are creatures, are in the world. If we cannot return to the pre-modern cosmology which affirmed the continuing existence of the full humanity of Jesus in heaven above, then we can affirm its basic principle that Christ still lives in his full humanity and that this body must therefore exist in a continuum with our own sensible reality. It is precisely our inability to conceive of this relation in real terms which seems to be at the heart of our failure of reference when we pray the creed.

But what does it mean to affirm that Christ still lives in a continuum with our own sensibility or embodied experience today? In the first place, it means that our relation with Christ must be considered to be something that is not constituted purely as memory or hope. Things remembered and things hoped for are not present to us in that way. People are not present to us in that way. The very essence of a personal relation is that the other is present to us as *given*: we do not have to call them to mind. They stand or sit before us or walk beside us. Of course, after the death of the other, that link, or mode of givenness, is made impossible. But the post-resurrection narratives show that this was not the case with Jesus Christ. He was still present to his disciples in this way after his death. He walked with them, spoke with them and ate with them. This is the givenness of the continuing full relation of one person to another. But the resurrected body, as we have noted, was not a permanent condition or state of that body: for the resurrected Jesus awaited his Ascension to his 'Father in heaven'.

When Ascension came, it was as a removal of the body from view and the advent of the Spirit of Pentecost. It is easy for us today – who struggle to make sense of the notion of heaven as a place in which the transformed though still real body of Christ can be – to think of the ascended body as a complete break with the Christ of history and with the presence of Christ to us within history, which is to say within the world. It is the 'end' of the historical incarnation. From this point on, salvation history becomes figurative and detached from the senses: from our here and now. But paradoxically it is the exact opposite which is the case. While the withdrawal of the body marks the cessation of its visibility (which is to say its objectifiability), it also marks its availability or presence to the senses in an entirely new way. Although Jesus is no longer visibly present, he has told his disciples that he will be with them until 'the end of the age' (Mt. 28.20) and that 'where two or three are gathered in my name, I am there among them' (Mt. 18.20). These are assurances of continuing presence. Rather than taking ascension to be an abrupt disruption through the withdrawal of the body, we need to see the same continuity of the body of Christ which emerged during the post-resurrection appearances, where all the emphasis was upon the identifiability of Christ in terms of his mortal history. If continuity was possible then, after his death, it remains possible still. But the post-resurrection body was a transitional state, to be superseded by his irreversible Ascension into the presence of the Father in heaven and the granting of the Spirit of Pentecost. It is only through the new advent of the Spirit that the presence of Christ in the fullness of his humanity becomes universally possible: to those to whom he is now known in the Spirit through faith. The givenness of present personal relation remains, since the body is now both local, by virtue of his humanity, and, by virtue of his divinity, is glorified as a world-body, which is to say as a body which contains the world, a body which the world itself can now be said to be 'in'; and thus we too, as part of this transformed world, can also be said to be 'in'.

But what does it mean to be 'in' the body in this way: where and how do we follow the ascended and therefore living Christ? Before we can answer this question, we must reflect further upon the role of the Spirit in making real to us the body of Christ. If the body is the body of God, by virtue of the *homoousios*, and thus, by implication, is a body in which the Father is 'visible' or present (cf. Jn 14.9: 'Whoever has seen me has seen the Father'), then it is no less a body 'of the Spirit'. This is a body that we can describe as Trinitarian or triune. If the divinity of the embodied Christ is 'of one being with the Father', then it is the Spirit who 'fathers' that body and so, in one sense, gives it life. But in Johannine tradition, the Spirit takes on another intimate role with respect to the body of Christ. At Jn 20.22, we read that the Spirit is breathed by the risen Jesus upon the apostles when they identified him by the wounds in his hands and side: 'he breathed on them and said to them: "Receive the Holy Spirit [. . .]"'. Johannine tradition also insists that the Spirit of Pentecost is given with the Ascension or 'withdrawal' of the visible body of Jesus. Only when he is no longer visible will the Spirit come as 'Counsellor' and 'Comforter'.[31] Pauline tradition likewise conceives of a profoundly intimate link between the Holy Spirit and the body of Christ. In Romans, for instance, it is 'the Spirit of Christ' who is the 'life' in our bodies, and St Paul tells us that 'the Spirit of him who raised Jesus from the dead [. . .] will give life to your mortal bodies also through his Spirit that dwells in you' (Rom. 8.9–11). For St Paul, baptism is baptism through the Spirit so that we participate in the death of Christ and, as he was 'raised', so also we can 'walk in newness of life' (Rom. 6.4). The Pauline Spirit then appears to link the body of Christ with our own.

The Spirit is central to the life of the body of Jesus; but what exactly is it that the Spirit 'does' with respect to the body? What does it mean to say that the Spirit 'fathers' it? Here we must look back to the characteristic role of the Spirit in the Old Testament, which provides the contexts in which this question can be addressed. The Spirit, of course, has eschatological resonances.[32] But it is the sign also of God's active presence, power or actuality in the world. The Old Testament is full of accounts of the Spirit's power, manifesting through words of persuasion or prophecy, or through mighty actions, shaping history according to the divine will. But the Spirit always manifests in ways that are non-objectifiable. That is to say, it is not known in itself: we do not see or touch it. Rather we know it through its effects, as it transforms people and situations, changing the world. The very term *ruach* (meaning also 'breath' or 'wind') suggests this ubiquitous, pervasive, non-objectifiable presence and power of Spirit in the world.

The relation between the Spirit, who makes the power of God actual in the world, and the body of Jesus Christ, is a vitally important question for Transformation Theology, which is also theology *in* the world. Nothing determines the relation between theology and world as much as the role of the Spirit: does it lead away from our world or into it? I want to suggest the following. In the first place, I think it would be wrong to see the body of Christ as the *objectification* of the Spirit. It is not the case that the non-objectifiable Spirit becomes objectifiably present in the body (which can be seen and touched): that would be to introduce a theme of substitution again. Rather we must think that in the birth of Christ in Bethlehem, who is made incarnate 'by the Holy Spirit of the virgin Mary', the Spirit brings into historical actuality not the body of the Son as such but the eternal birth of the Son from the Father: the Spirit makes real this uncreated and therefore in itself unknowable truth for us within the reality of space and time. It is the making real for us (and not only for us) of the eternal *generation* of the Son by the Father as the *sending* of the Son by the Father, in our world of space and time. And yet the eternal generation of the Son is the act that itself is the ground of the creation ('through whom all things were made'). And so we can say that what the Spirit makes actual or real for us in space and time, by taking on the 'fathering' role of the First Person with respect to the Son, is the movement of love in God which is the genesis or ground of the creation itself. The body of Christ has to be seen first and foremost as the mission or sending of the Son for us by the Father, made present through the Spirit, but it is a sending which also communicates to us in space and time, in ways which we cannot yet discern, the overwhelming and incomprehensible power of the *ex nihilo*, which is to say God's originary creative power.

Something else comes into view here, therefore, which is that the making present by the Spirit of the ascended body of Christ in our own here and now is to bring us into the presence of an incarnational mission or sending which communicates to us what Paul Janz calls 'the command of grace'[33]: it is our commissioning into the ecclesial reality of existence in the new creation. At Jn 20.22 quoted above, where the risen Jesus breathed his Spirit upon the apostles, Jesus also goes on to mandate the apostles: 'As the Father has sent me, so I send you [...] If you forgive the sins of any, they are forgiven them; if you retain the sins of any, they are retained.'[34] The Spirit of the body empowers and commissions, therefore, into a new depth of ecclesial commitment to and for the world.

Earlier we discussed the description of St Paul's encounter with the ascended Jesus on the road to Damascus. This is an event which from one perspective stands outside the realm of our possible experience. In the letter to the Galatians, St Paul writes that he did not receive the gospel from any human source, but 'I received it through a revelation of Jesus Christ'.[35] In other words, Paul did not receive the gospel, as we do, from the proclamation and ministry of the Church, and through or with the Spirit, but rather it came to him directly from Jesus Christ himself. In the post-Ascension body of the Damascus road appearance, St Paul experienced the resurrection with all the immediacy with which the apostles experienced it in the post-resurrection body. The unmediated character of the appearance to St Paul suggests that this appearance should be regarded as integral to the revelation as a whole, no less than the birth, death or resurrection of Jesus, in all of which Christ is present in 'natural' or unmediated form. But from another perspective, the Damascus road appearance and our own ordinary Christian experience of conversion and commissioning cannot be *qualitatively* dissimilar. For unlike the other forms of Christ's embodiment, which were transitional and therefore specific to a particular time frame, the ascended or glorified body is his *current* embodiment. St Paul is brought into relation with the living Christ, in the realization of his promise to be with us 'to the end of the age'.[36] We are unlikely, of course, ever to share either the intensity or the immediacy of this event; we will not be blinded as St Paul was. It will always be communicated to us through the Spirit (rather than before the giving of the Spirit, as in St Paul's case). But for all its uniqueness, the encounter remains paradigmatic of Christian conversion and commissioning, since these things are about coming into relation with Christ as he is for us today, and they require that we should live *from* that relation.

If we take the detail of the account in Acts of St Paul's experience at face value, then the body is both objective and subjective, which means that it breaks the categories of each. This is an entirely new order of existence then if, like world itself, the body of Jesus includes both subjectivity and objectivity, which we ourselves are now in some unfathomable sense 'in', as we are in the world. But being 'in' the body is not like being 'in' something in a physical sense, since it is fundamentally a dynamic relation which occurs in or through the Spirit. It is not known 'representationally' therefore, but rather through 'the command of grace'. The ecclesial mandating and commissioning which it brings is the mode by which it is known. In this respect, St Paul's response is deeply significant for us. Following dominical command, Ananias lays hands upon him and gives him the Spirit, which restores Paul's physical sight. For us, of course, it is the Spirit who brings the spiritual insight of faith. Paul has already encountered Jesus in glory however (for this is primary revelation), but the Spirit still has a role to play. In this case, the Spirit's role is subsequently to recalibrate his physical senses, so that he can function normally in the world which is now for him profoundly changed by incarnation and by the presence of that glorious body. St Paul will later write: 'So if anyone is in Christ, there is a new creation: everything old has passed away; see, everything has become new!'[37] The function of the Spirit, then, following this encounter, is to establish St Paul *in* Christ and in the new creation which Christ brings about. This requires the transformation of his ordinary sensibility; and it is this that is the Spirit's work. Integral to that transformation is his reception of the dominical command, which is his birth into the ecclesial existence by which he belongs to the new creation, brought about in accordance with the originary creative power of the divinity made flesh in Christ's body.

We should note again that this is not the language of transcendence, of the Spirit as a mode of escape from the world, but rather it shows the Spirit as being part of a radical, Christological transformation of the world. The newness of the world in new creation is an effect of 'the generativity of the *ex nihilo*' (in Paul Janz's phrase), and I have argued above that it is precisely this which the Spirit makes present in the incarnation: the generation of the Son from the Father made actual in space and time. We cannot know this truth representationally, however. But we can now say that we 'know' or 'receive' that originary generativity through the transformation of the world of which we ourselves are intrinsically a part. We do not know it directly, but we do receive it in the change that comes upon ourselves as part of that world, as we enter a new sensibility or come to a new condition of sensible existence, through the Spirit. This new sensibility is our ecclesial existence, a new life of mandate and commissioning, which is the mode of our belonging in the world as it is irreversibly changed by incarnation.

But that commissioning is not a general or disembodied one. It has specificity and particularity. In the case of St Paul, it is one which specifically forms part of the particular circumstances of his own life. There is only one hypostatic body of Christ, however, which St Paul also encountered according to its *human* nature: according to its particularity. He knew it 'locally' as tradition puts it. Paul is clear that he has 'seen Jesus our Lord', as he states at 1 Cor. 9.1 (cf. 1 Cor. 15.8). His sense of *physical* sight was profoundly affected by the encounter. In the unity of the one body, St Paul experienced both the divinity and humanity of Christ: he knew both the way that the world is 'in' God through incarnation and how God continues to be 'in' the world. And the act of commissioning which took place during the encounter is the manifestation to him of the unity of the two natures. But this role, like that of the apostles who received the Spirit breathed upon them from the risen Christ, is a particular role with particular meanings. It will not be a general commissioning but a particular one, worked out in the concrete circumstances of an individual life: precisely within and not at an angle to the sensible reality of each and every one who is touched by this commissioning.

Our faith therefore is also of this kind. The Spirit we receive through baptism is the Spirit of the body: it connects us with the body, by setting us in relation to it. The body of the living Christ is present to us, as it was to the disciples during his life on earth, though it is not *objectifiably* so. We cannot touch it or see it. Indeed, St Paul's description seems to describe a manifestation (or what in Galatians he three times calls a 'revelation' of Christ[38]) which takes place as much *within* his sensibility as it does *through* it. At Galatians 1.16, he even says that God was 'pleased to reveal his Son *in* me, so that I might proclaim him among the Gentiles'.[39] This would accord in fact with the Spirit – the Spirit of the body – being present in the senses rather than through the senses. The body, like the Spirit, is non-objectifiable now, but still its signature in faith is the awareness that it is really present to us, in our own here and now. The painter Caravaggio captured this memorably in his masterpiece *The Calling of Matthew* where he shows the apostle, in contemporary clothing, responding open-eyed to the summons of Christ. The painter exactly depicts the startled look of a man addressed. But Christ himself, like St Peter with him, wears clothing of the ancient world.

What are the effects upon us then of being brought, through faith and the Spirit, into relation with the living embodiment of Christ? It calls us, like St Matthew, into a new, real and ecclesial existence: into a discipleship in which we feel summoned in the fullness of our own sensible life to 'follow' him. And there is indeed a directionality at work here, for the body that is made present to us in the Spirit is the body of the one who was 'sent' by the Father, whose incarnational sending was itself a commissioning and the communication to us in turn of the imperative of our own commissioning. This is an encounter then which leads us into an ever-deeper engagement with the world. It marks our entry into the deep bodily practices of the Christian Church: as worship, prayer, mission and penance, as active caring for the needs of others and concern for living things. It is living in the spell of the body of Christ, within its precincts, as it were. It is allowing our own sensibility, which is the primary mode of our being in the world, to be shaped in and through the Spirit of the body, and thus to become conformed to new creation and to learn to live within it. In a world that is irreversibly changed by incarnation, and by the divinity that transformed the human body of Christ, we are made part of new creation. We are ourselves integrated or 'reborn' into it, in the totality of our sensible existence, through the particular commissioning which is always a commissioning through the 'local' body of Christ, which is to say according to the humanity he still shares with us; and so is always particular, to be worked out at *this* time and place, with *these* people.

3. Church in the World

A Chalcedonian theology of the continuing body of Christ as simultaneously expressive both of his true humanity (local or particular) and of his true divinity (cosmic or universal) offers the possibility of understanding the Church as the community of those who share the discovery that the structure of the world is changed through incarnation. The world 'chanced upon' or encountered on the way is itself now new creation. This is, however, not to propose something that must be abstractly understood. It is not presented here as an idea or a concept or an image about how the world is, or about how we should learn to see the world. As noted above, this change cannot be known in this way. It is simply too fundamental. Rather, we need to understand that it is grasped in the moment that we receive and accept a commissioning, which is our own particular commissioning, for the sake of the 'kingdom' or reign of God's will on earth, in terms of the everyday reality of our own ordinary lives. This is thus a re-enactment of the incarnation at the level of each individual: a Trinitarian sending which is made actual to each and every one of us in the humanity of Christ's embodiment which the Spirit makes present to us. And being made part of our sensible reality, it is something which we ourselves enter into and become part of, as we become internal to that sending, for others and for the world. To accept such a commissioning is to live in the world as it has been brought back to its origin in the *ex nihilo*: just as the risen Christ himself lives from the *ex nihilo*. To be in the Church then is also to live within the power of the *ex nihilo* which, as we have seen, underlies the sending or commissioning of the incarnate Christ. We do not experience this directly, but we know it in the transformation of world that is new creation, and in our belonging to that world, through the Spirit, which includes the promise of resurrection into eternal life.

And so we come to the question of what Transformation Theology means for Christian life. We can perhaps say that all human existence is a living in the present which is historically structured by the two cognitive acts of past memory and future intention. We remember the past that has been and look forward to a future that comes. But at times one of the consequences of this structure is that the spontaneity of the present, which is our 'here and now', is fractured or suppressed by the burden or deadness of memory on the one hand or by the weight of future expectation, with all its attendant anxieties, on the other. And it may be that Christian theology itself has, for whatever reason, allowed itself to be shaped by this same structure. It has attenuated the sense of the present reality of Christ, to which we can make present reference in our recital of the creed, in the light of a past to be remembered and retrieved and a future to be hoped for. But neither past nor future have life or real meaning outside the present, for it is there that we encounter the immediacy of a real world through sensibility.

If this is the case, then 'theology in the world' marks a new departure for descriptions of Christian faith. For the intentionality of ecclesial existence, according to this theology, is determined not by human consciousness and will, making sense of things in a rapidly changing environment, looking backward and forward; but rather by the nurturing of a sense of Christ's body as non-objectifiably present to us, communicated to us in the Spirit, in or through sensibility. This is to say that it is determined by the real and personal relation with Christ to us, in the fullness of his humanity, through faith and in the Spirit: a continuing or living humanity for us and for the world which is sustained by the full divinity of his glorious nature. Only in this way do we meet him as truly *alive*.

Life in the Church is always temporal, of course, structured between past and future. But it is also and fundamentally *present*, where presence is the presence to sensibility of the risen body of Christ, made fully particular and universal through its ascended state, in a way that changes our experience of world. To be a Christian then is to live within or from out of this entirely unique relation to world. It is to be called into an intensely personal relation, which is expressed as a 'following', or discipleship of church practice and concern, as we come closer to and grow spiritually in conformity with the living body of Christ. This in turn brings with it a new form of simplicity, as we enter into the givenness of the sensible real: of the 'everyday'. The *telos* or incarnational 'movement' of Christ leads us away from unnecessary complexities and distractions, and from the culture of appetites, into the discovery of present sensible existence as the experience of our own reciprocating movement into a profound simplicity of life. This in turn opens up the possibility of a new kind of detachment, which is the detachment which comes not only with a new purity of the senses but also with the possibility of a new humility of the self: a denial of the self in terms of its overly complex appetites and intentionalities. These two taken together, purity and humility, are both grounded in the simplicity which is a further mark of the Christian community of faith as we receive in our own 'here and now' the Trinitarian sending of the Son by the Father, in the Spirit who makes the dynamic life of the Trinity real for us at the heart of our sensible existence.

But the body comes to us also through its ecclesial mirrorings or mediations, which serve to strengthen us in our relation to him. The Eucharistic body of Mt. 26.26–9 (which Catholic tradition understands to be substantially present in the elements and Zwinglian Reformed tradition takes to be present in the gathered members of the Church) mediates to us Christ's current or ascended embodiment liturgically and cosmically, under the accent of the divinity and new creation. Communion replicates in objective reality the communion we have with him non-objectifiably through the Spirit. The bodies of those in need, in whom Christ is present to us, of Mt. 25.34–46, mediate the ascended body under the accent of its humanity and particularity: that which is shared with us. And there are further mediations which appear in church tradition, in addition to the non-Eucharistic sacraments. There is the presence of Christ among those 'who are gathered in my name' of Mt. 18.20, and Christ's promised presence to his Church to 'the end of the age' of Mt. 28.20. There are the mediations of Christ's presence in the Word as preached, and in the biblical text as received and performed. There are multiple mediations in Christian arts and culture. But however 'mediated', the ascended body always remains directly active. Through the primary ecclesial mediations, the one liturgical and the other caritative, and all their analogues, the ascended body always retains the power to 'disrupt us', as Clemens Sedmak puts it, pushing urgently and disruptively into the 'everyday' of our ordinary lives. And this disruption too is a sign of the Church, perhaps indeed its primary sign. For disruption is the way in which the ascended body claims us for its own. In Church, in its most fundamental dimension, we are conformed to the movement of that body as Trinitarian sending. We are taken up into the urgency of love which is the Father's own presence to the Son, and which defines his bodily existence for us as itself sending and self-giving: made real for us by the Spirit in the actuality of our sensible living. And so we too, as another fundamental sign of Church, become, without ever being able to see it for ourselves, a further mirroring or mediation of that ascended body: and a new realization for others of the unfolding creativity of its divine life.

Notes

1 Klaus Scholder, *The Birth of Modern Critical Theology* (London: SCM Press, 1990, pp. 65–87). See also Scholder, pp. 56–7. Scholder quotes Johannes Kepler's interpretation of this passage: 'God understood Joshua's wish [for an extension of the day] without difficulty from his words and fulfilled it by stopping the movement of the earth, so that to Joshua the sun seemed to stand still' (p. 57).

2 Hans Frei, *The Eclipse of Biblical Narrative* (New Haven and London: Yale University Press, 1974, especially pp. 124–54). See also Scholder, *The Birth of Modern Critical Theology*, pp. 65–87.

3 George A. Lindbeck, *The Nature of Doctrine* (Philadelphia: Westminster, 1984, p. 118).

4 Hans Blumenberg, *Paradigmen zu einer Metaphorologie*, 1960; Paul Ricoeur, *The Rule of Metaphor* (London: Routledge & Kegan Paul, 1978).

5 Thomas F. Torrance, *Space, Time and Incarnation* (Edinburgh: T&T Clark, 1997, pp. 34ff, 48, 76).

6 Torrance argues that Luther is following an Aristotelian account of the universe as finite space (or as *finitum capax infiniti*, following Bonhoeffer's phrase), which provides the ground of his ubiquity theory. It is to Eph. 4.10, with its scriptural cosmology, that Luther appeals, however, in key texts such as those quoted in the previous chapter from *The Sacrament of the Body and Blood of Christ – Against the Fanatics* of 1526 (see Chapter 1, notes 55 and 56). In *That These Words of Christ, 'This is my Body', etc., Still Stand Firm against the Fanatics* of 1527 Luther

explicitly appeals to the doctrine of the creation and to the divine nature of Christ to support his argument from ubiquity (*Luther's Works*, 37, pp. 55–70).

7 *Space, Time and Incarnation*, p. 72.

8 *Space, Time and Incarnation*, p. 75.

9 *Space, Time and Incarnation*, p. 72.

10 *Space, Time and Incarnation*, p. 71.

11 *Space, Time and Incarnation*, p. 70.

12 *Space, Time and Incarnation*, p. 67.

13 *Space, Time and Incarnation*, p. 72.

14 *Space, Time and Incarnation*, p. 72.

15 *Space, Time and Incarnation*, p. 72.

16 *Space, Time and Incarnation*, p. 72.

17 *Space, Time and Incarnation*, p. 67.

18 We can perhaps see further evidence of the effects of this metaphor of height in the kind of theological style which T. F. Torrance applied in *Space, Time and Incarnation*. There seems to be a sense in which the massive inversion of the dimensionality of human embodiment brought about by the 'vertical axis' metaphor drains the actuality of the human body from the content of the piece itself. Nowhere is the incarnation referred to in terms of a body, for instance, any more than human beings are conceived of as bodies or as possessing bodies. Rather, despite the indexicality of the primary metaphor (or perhaps because of it), both Jesus and humankind are only ever referred to as 'place' or as 'a place'. The binary oppositions 'eternal–temporal, spiritual–material' (p. 76) seem to leave no space for the complexity or continuity of the body, either human or divine.

19 See, for instance, Acts 7.55–6, which narrates Stephen's vision of Christ, 'standing at the right hand of God', prior to his martyrdom. We should take this together with the Old Testament accounts of experiencing or seeing heaven from earth. See the previous chapter, pp. 13–14, notes 16–21.

20 Acts 22 states that those accompanying Paul also fell to the ground.

21 This conflates 9.12 and 17.

22 The third account at Acts 26 includes a reference to the event as a 'heavenly vision'.

23 The term *extra calvinisticum* was used polemically by Lutherans to suggest that their Calvinist interlocutors were failing to maintain the full divinity of Jesus Christ, preferring to conceive of the Word in its divine and cosmic functions as being somehow 'outside' or 'beyond' the incarnation. From one perspective this was a function more generally of the Lutheran–Reformed debate concerning the range and nature of the *communicatio idiomatum* within the hypostatic union. But from another perspective (and whatever the purchase of the term as a polemical expression), its emergence coincided with the loss of the rich cosmology and the high, scriptural theology of the Word, and thus pointed to the greater difficulty in conceiving of the full divinity of Christ given the changes in cosmology which had taken place. On the *extra calvinisticum* more generally, see E. David Willis, *Calvin's Catholic Christology: The Function of the So-called Extra Calvinisticum in Calvin's Theology* (Leiden: E. J. Brill, 1966).

24 Mt. 9.20–2.

25 Mt. 14.25–6.

26 Mt. 17.1–13; Mk 9.2–8; Lk. 9.28–36. The use of the Greek term *exodus* for 'departure' can be read as already pointing forward to the Ascension.

27 Lk. 22.19.

28 Jn 20.17.

29 See the previous chapter, note 4.

30 cf. 1 Cor. 15.37–8.

31 Jn 14.26 and Jn 15.26. cf. Acts 1.9.

32 Joel 2.28–9.

33 See Paul Janz's discussion at pp. 107–111 below.

34 Jn 20.21–3.

35 Gal. 1.12. The lines following show that he has the Damascus road experience in mind.
36 Mt. 28.20.
37 2 Cor. 5.17.
38 Gal. 1.12, 16; 2.2.
39 This phrase (*en emoi*) has caused translators some difficulty: in the NRSV, it is given as 'to me'.

PHILOSOPHY

3

Revelation as Divine Causality

Paul D. Janz

The foregoing discussions have brought into focus, in a renewed and sharpened way, the scriptural demand and church confession that it is indeed the same *incarnate* Jesus Christ who, through the transformational power exerted in his resurrection and ascension, is still presently and really alive for human beings in the world today. And the central concern of the following two chapters, in that light, is to show that if we are to take with full seriousness this transformed and transformative present reality of Jesus Christ at the very centre of embodied human life, then this will demand further a fundamental transformation at the very heart of theological questioning, procedure and especially attentiveness today. Or to state this somewhat differently, if the affirmation of the *present reality* of the resurrected and ascended incarnate Jesus is to be taken as seriously by theology as it already is by the Church in the world, then a fundamental refocusing or reorientation will be required in the way that theology must be attentive to 'revelation' today, which is both theology's authenticating ground and its most basic and defining 'subject matter'.

Now the term 'revelation' can of course signify an array of things and can be used in several different ways. But for Christian theology – especially again with a view to questions of its proper procedure and attentiveness – the term has a number of defining characteristics, two of the most basic of which can be expressed as follows. To begin with, the term 'revelation' is meant first and foremost to signify a *divine* disclosure and declaration, a *divine* communication which is the indispensable source, and indeed the very life of Christian belief and practice. This in turn has a vital corollary, one which immediately identifies a basic front on which theology faces challenges that are both uniquely demanding and also uniquely different than those faced by other intellectual disciplines. For as a *divine* disclosure, 'revelation' is meant to denote the communication of a truth or a reality which human beings precisely *cannot* come to by themselves, or cannot attain to from out of themselves, either through any natural empirical discovery, or through anything that the generative spontaneity of human imagination or creative insight could engender from out of itself. Or as Friedrich Schleiermacher has stated this classically, the term revelation in its theological use is 'never applied either to what is discovered in the realm of experience by one person and handed on to others, or to what is excogitated [rationally generated] in thought by one person and so learned by others'.[1] Secondly, revelation at its origin is for the Christian faith also said to be most essentially not merely the disclosure of information or descriptive propositions 'about' God, but is rather declared by the scriptures most fundamentally to be nothing less than the revelation of God himself (e.g., Exod. 5.3; Jn 1.1–14; Jn 14.22; Heb. 1.1–3). Revelation in its Christian sense then is most integrally a divine *self*-communication to the world, which *as* a divine *self*-disclosure comes to its fullest expression in the incarnation of Jesus Christ himself, in whom 'all the fullness of the deity lives in bodily form' (Col. 2.9).

And it is with respect to its attentiveness to the present reality of revelation as such that, as I will be suggesting, a basic transformation is also required in theological orientation and attentiveness *to* that reality. But before coming to the task of explaining what this is intended to mean exactly, let me also insert a note of moderation. For by speaking of a required 'transformation' in theological attentiveness to revelation, I do not mean to make what would be the highly presumptuous suggestion that the discussions over these next two chapters are claiming to introduce anything fundamentally new. The term seeks rather to point to the need for a retrieval or a reinvigoration of a certain vital and indispensable kind of attentiveness to revelation, an attentiveness which throughout much of our past doctrinal heritage has been a virtual commonplace for theological self-understanding, yet which has for several reasons become almost entirely lost to theological questioning over the past two centuries. Indeed, it is a kind of attentiveness which has become so completely submerged today that the very broaching of it here may initially seem mysterious and foreign. It will be helpful therefore, in order to prepare for the reintroduction of the specific kind of attentiveness being suggested, to begin from a more general contextualization. (I might also take this opportunity to add that much of what follows in this initial chapter is a reiteration of aspects of an essay recently published elsewhere, condensed in the current chapter at certain points, and expanded considerably at others.)[2]

1. Theology and the Spirit of Idealism

There is a certain subliminal, but deep-running error that can afflict a great deal of theological questioning today unawares. The error has its roots broadly in the still powerful influence that a particular legacy of classical (German) idealism continues to exert on theology and the human sciences today. The error itself can be stated quite simply. It involves a failure in theological reflection to distinguish properly between *causal* reasons (or explanations) based on *sensible* connections and susceptibilities, and *conceptual* reasons (or explanations) based on *logical* connections and susceptibilities. Or even more directly, it involves a failure to distinguish properly between causal awareness and conceptual awareness, between causal authority and conceptual authority, and thus between causal questioning and conceptual questioning.

Now on many levels – e.g., in the observational sciences, and also in a straightforwardly commonsense way – this distinction between the causal and the conceptual can seem like an obvious and really quite unproblematic one. For example, no one will disagree that the causal-sensible way I am expected to be able to explain or account for the fact of this irregular semicircular scar on my left forearm (an effect caused by a freak gardening accident while pruning a row of enormous holly bushes in a particular suburb of Vancouver, Canada at dusk on 14 November 2002) is fundamentally different than the conceptual-logical way I am expected to be able to explain or account for the mathematical 'fact' that three times five is equal to the half of 30, or for a conclusion deduced via the formal logic of a syllogism. The former kind of explanation has to do with observations of connectedness in the relation of *sensible* processes and events between *extended bodies* in *space and time*; the latter kind of explanation has to do with questions of connectedness in the relation of *logical* processes and computations between *abstract concepts* in *intellection*.

Now as implied above, this distinction has indeed been quite clearly observed and respected throughout most of our theological and philosophical history, and continues to be observed relatively unproblematically today in the natural sciences. I have discussed elsewhere at considerable length the full historical development of this distinction from Aristotle onwards, through Augustine, Aquinas, Ockham, Scotus, Luther and Calvin, and then into the modern period in Hume and Kant.[3] But we must set those discussions aside here in order come directly to the really vital contention as suggested in the opening sentences of this subsection.

The implied point there was that although the causal/logical distinction has indeed been clearly observed throughout most of our theological and philosophical history, nevertheless when we come to developments within the human sciences and theology over the past two centuries, we find that this twofold kind of attentiveness – and especially attentiveness to causal authority – has with a few exceptions almost entirely disappeared from view. Or more exactly, we find that the causal question (that is, the question of sensibility, or sensible awareness) has been entirely absorbed into the conceptual question (that is, the question of intentionality, or intellective awareness). Again, I have elsewhere discussed at length the exact character of this subsumption and the reasons for it, and I restrict myself here simply to expanding briefly on the observation made at the opening.

The current loss of causal attentiveness in theology and the human sciences can be traced back to certain powerful developments within the German idealism, especially that of Fichte and Hegel, which emerged after Kant. And it should be noted as such that while these built indispensably on Kant's 'critical' project, and indeed saw themselves as bringing his 'revolution' in philosophy to a kind of completion, Kant himself saw them as a fundamental abandonment and betrayal of his own critical principles.[4] But let me come directly to the point at hand, and now specifically with respect to the influences of idealism on theology.

What idealism was most crucially able to provide was a set of powerful epistemological mechanisms which opened a path for theology to account for the intelligibility of its own claims about the continuing reality of Jesus Christ today in ways that no longer needed to locate this continuing 'reality' within the world of sensible human embodiment in space and time at all.[5] Or more exactly, at precisely the time when theology was beginning to struggle perhaps most deeply with the intelligible authority and meaning of its own confessions in light of the demands of cosmology and natural science after Newton, Kant, Hume and others: at just this time the spirit of idealism was offering ways of bypassing the new empirical challenges of modern science and cosmology altogether. And it did this most basically through demonstrations of what it claimed was a fundamental supremacy of mind over body and, by extension, a basic supremacy also of the *Geisteswissenschaften* (the human or mental sciences) over the *Naturwissenschaften* (the natural sciences) within the academic disciplines. (This last point is traced with especial lucidity in Hans Georg Gadamer's *Truth and Method*.[6])

The supremacy claim was rooted in the basic argument that sensible experience or sensible reality (and the empirical sciences along with this) was really only capable of offering up what Hegel called the 'the poorest kind of truth'[7] anyway; and even more than this, that the causally dynamic, spatio-temporally extended sentient 'world' may not be spoken of as *properly* 'real' in any case, until only *after* it has come to an appropriately sophisticated 'determination' *as* a 'world' by the *mind*. The extent to which Hegel was willing to push what he called the 'lordship' of the mental over the sensible is made especially evident for example in his unwillingness even to allow that fossil remains were ever living organisms. Contemporary phenomenology avoids such eccentric results altogether by simply bracketing out completely through the 'epoché' any questions that could give rise to them. Or more specifically, in its following of the basic dictum voiced in Husserl's *Ideas*, that nature is to be treated as nothing but a correlate of consciousness, contemporary phenomenology is able simply to set aside certain kinds of objections – for example the objection that the human embryo is generated causally and secretly in the mother's womb before it ever becomes a 'correlate' of consciousness, and therefore with an authority not dependent on consciousness – by relegating such objections to the level of the 'naïve' or the 'brute'. The fundamental affinity with idealism here is clear.[8]

At any rate, it did not take long in the human sciences more broadly for the mind to assert a kind of absolute supremacy over sensible embodiment (indeed, even over that very embodiment within which the enquiring mind finds its origin and source). And as Gadamer so lucidly traces,[9] this 'supremacy' influence of classical idealism would continue to flourish long after the more onerous elements of Hegelian idealism had been abandoned, and that it today remains no less influentially and pervasively embedded within many contemporary versions of phenomenology, textualism, hermeneutics, post-structuralism, aesthetics and so on.

But now for theology, specifically, the single most important consequence of this subsumption of the causal authority governing sensible embodiment into the conceptual authority of the intentional mind has been a shift in the perception of *revelation* itself: a shift away from the more traditional understanding of revelation as a fundamentally *causal* communication to embodied human beings in the real world of space and time, and towards the more contemporary theological treatment of revelation as a fundamentally *conceptual* or mental communication, encounterable more properly in intellective terms directly by the mind. Again, I have worked through more fully elsewhere how this occurs supremely within today's predominantly hermeneutical and especially phenomenological orientations – and indeed, how it comes to expression in even more radicalized ways in the phenomenological appeals to 'phenomenological surplus', 'saturated phenomena', 'economies of superabundance', 'overflow of meaning', 'fecundity', 'excess', 'ontological plus' and so on.

But precisely the same kind of thing also occurs frequently directly within Christian doctrine today as well, and we find what is perhaps the quintessential, and certainly the most influential, expression of this in none other than Karl Barth himself. (Let me before proceeding, however, add an important caveat at this juncture. Even though this chapter will at points take a quite critical stance in relation to Barth, this should quite emphatically not be understood as an attempted vilification or disparagement of the Barthian enterprise per se. Strongly to the contrary, Barthian theology is in my view a theology of massive intellectual power and integrity, with a depth of Christian passion hardly surpassed in recent times, a work of immense value and importance. Any critiques I offer here therefore are to be understood in the spirit of Eberhard Bethge's description of Dietrich Bonhoeffer's often equally intense criticisms of Barth: i.e., that despite the severity of his own objections, Bonhoeffer always 'criticized as an ally'.) But at any rate, it is the undeniable and prominent shift in Barth – reflecting the spirit of idealism – away from an understanding of revelation as a causal communication at the centre of embodied life, to an understanding of it as an essentially mental or conceptual event, which most basically interests me here. And indeed, Barth's own words on this could not be clearer: 'the encounter of God and man takes place primarily, pre-eminently and characteristically in this sphere of *ratio*'; 'it is the divine reason communicating with human reason'; 'revelation in itself and as such ... is talk, speech'.[10] The depth to which this orientation pervades the *Church Dogmatics* is manifested further by Barth's explicit stipulation that revelation cannot for us today be encountered as a 'present reality' at all but always only as a 'concrete concept'.[11] Barth of course does not deny that 'naturally, the reality of revelation stands beyond the concept'.[12] But this is always the reality of a 'specific past' which '*has taken place*' in Jesus Christ, and the reality of a 'specific future' which '*will come*' in the eschaton.[13] He is thus quite explicit in his declaration that in theology today '*we cannot try to deal with the reality*' itself.[14] Theology must rather understand itself today always and only to be 'dealing with the *concept* of revelation, i.e., with the present of God's Word *between the times*'[15] of the past and future *realities* of revelation. One can see the same kinds of commitments prominently at work also in the 'post-liberal' school, as exemplified by George Lindbeck's often-quoted assertion that 'it is the text which absorbs the world rather than the world the text'.[16]

However, if we are unwilling and unable to give up the belief that Jesus Christ is really alive for us today by God's power (2 Cor. 13.4; Gal. 2.20; Col. 3.6); or that the living Christ is really the same today as yesterday and forever (Heb. 12.8); or that the Spirit of God truly dwells in the believer causally with real effects in human life today (1 Cor. 3.16); or that the kingdom of God does not consist *only* in talk or 'grammar', but in real, dynamic, life-changing power in space and time today (2 Cor. 4.20); or again, if it is *really* the parts of our sensible, physical bodies that are to be offered to God as instruments of God's real righteousness in the world today (Rom. 6.13; 12.1): if we are unable to relinquish the commitment to the *present reality* of all of this, then we must return to what throughout the history of Christian thought and practice has been the authoritative and prevailing understanding of God's self-commu-nication. That is, we must return to the view that God works and reveals himself *causally* in the real affairs and to the sensibly embodied lives of human beings today in space and time, with real, life-changing effects. To be sure, and as we shall see, this causality will show itself to be not a mere efficient causality which operates entirely *from within* the causal dynamic order like any natural causality. It is rather a *divine* causality whose origin is not temporal or finite, but infinite; yet whose effects are no less dynamic, no less empirical, no less real for human embodied life today than any natural causality, however 'infinite' these 'effects' may *also* be for the eternal redemption of human beings beyond this life, and for God's reconciliation of the whole world to himself.

Against the prevailing trends, then, the main goal of this chapter is to raise again a certain awareness with regard to the originally *causal* nature of God's self-revelation in the world, as it has been held traditionally in most of doctrinal history, and in the way that Christianity as a genuinely *incarnational* confession of faith demands. And to that end, let me set the basic tone for what follows by laying out a basic postulate or guiding declaration that is fundamentally dif-ferent than the currently predominating phenomenological and idealistic ones. The postulate around which the project presented here will come to develop-ment is as follows. Just as in the empirical sciences we recognize the require-ment to engage in questioning and to give explanations in two fundamentally different ways – *causal* questioning and explanations about connections which are at bottom *sensibly* perceived, and *conceptual* questioning and explanations about connections which are at bottom *logically* perceived: so, too, theology demands both a causal attentiveness and a conceptual or logical attentiveness.

But before getting into the explication and defence of this, let me make four remarks briefly in order to pre-empt certain anticipatable misperceptions about what is being claimed here. First, the distinction I am making will be in no way to posit two different 'realms' – one 'realm' or 'world' of concepts and intellection, and another 'realm' or 'world' of sensibility and corporeal things. Nor will what I am doing be found in any sense to separate the rational from the sensible-causal in actual human life. I will only be drawing attention to specific ways in which the single human organism itself will demand this twofold kind of attentiveness. The human organism itself demands this because, precisely *in its unity*, it recognizes itself as *both* embodied (responsively susceptible to sensible or causal influences) *and* rational (responsively susceptible to conceptual or logical influences).

Secondly, I will in no way be committing myself to a treatment of causality as something 'pre-reflective' in any strict sense of this term. We are, after all, speaking of causal *accounts* or *explanations* or indeed causal *reasons* versus conceptual accounts and reasons; and the whole process of what is going on here as such is already taking place as an *activity* of conscious *reflection*. The point instead is simply that when we reflect on human life and try to explain or account for aspects of it, we will again and again come up against features or forces which we recognize unmistakably as being *not* the *products* of intellection or interpretative consciousness, but rather as being forces which confront the reflecting perceiver with their own originary authority through sensibility.

Thirdly, it will be clear from the prior two points that my treatment of causality here expressly prescinds from any discussion or commitment either way as to the question of its 'metaphysical' character, and thus from any deeper philosophical discussion of the question of causality (for example, as to its status as something 'necessary' when viewed as a principle). I set such metaphysical questions aside here and simply focus on causality as a fundamental and ineluctable aspect of the way human beings experience the world, or the way they understand themselves in the world as thinking bodies, or as rational animals, standing in real sensible proximity to other bodies and events in space and time. I would only add for clarity's sake that if one were to map this on to Aristotle's four kinds of cause (or four factors of causal explanation), much of what follows would fall perhaps most naturally under his 'efficient causality', although even here in a quite straightforwardly empirical way as it is presupposed, for example, in contemporary observational scientific enquiry.

Fourthly, I am most emphatically not arguing for any sort of *favouring* of the sensible and causal over the rational and intellective. I will only mean all of this to work towards the restoration of a proper *balance* between causal and conceptual attentiveness in theology. Or in other words, a 'rediscovery' of the authority of causality for theology will by no means be something which diminishes or compromises the authority of reason (or indeed imagination), but precisely the opposite. It will in fact motivate reason itself to ensure that it operates at the highest levels of its integrity by not overstepping its own proper limits, thus following the best self-critical examples of Aristotelian, Thomist, Kantian, Schleiermacherian or Rahnerian dispositions of thinking.

2. *Causa* and *Ratio* as Authorities for Human Questioning

To engage in questioning reflectively, or to enquire, means most essentially to search for reasons or explanations with regard to some subject of focus. And to search for reasons or explanations means further, by definition, to place some item of interest into some sort of broader contextual relation or connectedness. Now as has already been suggested, there are as such two, and only two, ways in which we can possibly search for reasons or give explanations in this relational way. Reasons will at bottom always be either *conceptual* – that is, having to do with explanations of connectedness in the relation of *logical* processes in *reflective intellection*; or they will be *causal* – that is, having to do with explanations of connectedness in the relation of *sensible* processes and events in *space and time*.[17] Or, for simplicity's sake, we can also speak of two fundamentally different ways in which we can seek to give accounts, or two ways of being *accountable* in questioning: conceptual (or logical) accountability, and causal accountability. Let me make some brief introductory clarifications about each of these before discussing them in greater depth.

First, with regard to ratiocinative or logical questioning, I want for purposes of clarity and precision to follow the common philosophical practice here and call this kind of accountability also by a different name. I want to call it *inferential* accountability in order to identify more precisely the particular function by which, without exception, all intellective or rational connections within discursive consciousness are made. In other words, 'inference' here is not to be understood merely in the colloquial sense of you inferring what I imply, but rather in the full noetic sense as it is used in epistemology and logic, where it denotes the precise internal operation by which all attempted rational justifications and explanations occur. The point is that *all* operations and relations of discursive reason are 'inferential': that is, working towards conclusions which are recognized as 'following' in some way from certain premises or items of evidence. These conclusions can of course have different degrees of reliability or certainty or even veracity, as we shall see. But the initial point is that the basic mechanism by which conclusions are arrived at or accounted for will in each case be 'inferential'.

To make this a bit clearer, it will be helpful to identify and briefly explain three basic different reasoning contexts within which inference is seen today as being able to occur: 'deductive' reasoning, 'inductive' reasoning and 'abductive' reasoning. (a) Reasoning by 'deduction' is inference to *necessity*, i.e., inference to conclusions which follow necessarily from certain premises. For example, if Isobel is taller than Helen, and Helen in taller than Beth, then it follows necessarily through deductive inference that Isobel is taller than Beth. The inference here is said to be one of necessity because if the premises are true the conclusion cannot be false. The indefeasible authority of deductive inference therefore is guaranteed because it is effectively tautological, or a matter of analytical definition. (b) Reasoning by 'induction' is inference to *probability*; and as that definition suggests, the reliability of the conclusions inferred here is not as certain as those yielded by deduction, and in fact can vary quite widely, depending on a broad range of empirical and also methodological factors. For example, predictions in election polling which are made on the basis of a smaller sample group to a larger population are arrived at 'inductively'. Or when the Food and Drug Administration pronounces the safety for general consumption of a new drug, this is done on the basis of conclusions reached inductively through evidence gleaned from trials within a smaller test group. In each case the reliability of the conclusions inferred will depend on an array of factors, including the size of the sample group, methods of sample gathering and analysis, and so on. (c) Reasoning by 'abduction' is inference to the *best explanation*. In biblical scholarship, for example, the way that conclusions are drawn from evidence found in a newly discovered MS (e.g., conclusions as to its authorship, authenticity, etc.) will be derived largely on the basis of a 'best explanation', or abductively, in comparison with other sources of evidence. Now again, it will be clear as such that conclusions reached in the latter two kinds of inference can never come with the same kind of certainty as strict deductive inference. In cases of abductive inference especially, new evidence may come to light (e.g. a new MS) that may raise doubts about the earlier 'best explanation', and which suggests a new 'best explanation' which supersedes the first (whereas proper inference in deductive reasoning yields conclusions which are indefeasible). But the broader unifying point to be made here is that, despite these differences, the basic procedure of inference, that is, *reasoning to* conclusions which can be shown (with varying degrees of reliability) to *follow from* certain given premises or items of empirical evidence, remains the same.

This then is the first – the 'inferential' – side of the broader and more pivotal twofold assertion being made here. That twofold assertion, again, is that there are *two* basic modes or standards for giving reasons – or two basic mechanisms for giving accounts and thus for accountability – one *inferential* (i.e., conceptual) as just discussed, and the other *causal*, and that each carries with it its own *separate* set of obligations and expectations.

So then what can be said about the other, 'causal' explanations more exactly? To begin with, they are *not* inferential. That is, they are not reasons or explanations yielded or produced by mental processes as conclusions which are drawn from premises or from items of evidence. They are discovered rather through attentiveness to sequences and connections which are found to be encountered *originally* in sensible processes. For example, the extreme headache, nausea and muscle stiffness I woke up with this morning is neither a result of, nor a rational conclusion reached by, any mental process involving acquaintance with biochemistry, physiology or medical terminology. It is rather the causal result of a flu-bug I picked up on the airline flight into London Heathrow yesterday. It is of course true that 'inference by abduction' is the way I come to *decide* (on the best explanation) that it must have been the person sitting next to me on yesterday's flight, manifesting exactly the same symptoms as I have today, from whom I picked up the bug. But that *inference* is not itself the *cause* or the explanatory ground of my own headache, stiffness and egestion today. The real causal explanation or ground is rather the physical micro-organism itself that is now working its way through my physical sentient body, yielding these effects.

Or again, the way I understand to account for my late arrival at a theological conference on the theme of the atonement held in Toronto on 11 April 2005 (all flights out of my departure city Denver had been cancelled the evening before due to the massive unseasonal spring snowstorm which brought everything to a standstill) is fundamentally different from the way I understand, in the paper I give at that conference, to account for my arrival at the particular conclusions I have drawn which favour an Irenaean account of atonement over an Augustinian account. The two 'arrivals' are entirely different, and the kinds of accountability expected for each are also entirely different. In the former case what is expected is an explanation which shows my lateness to be the product of a certain causal, empirical and contingent series of events in space and time. But in the latter case, a causal explanation will not satisfy the kind of justification or accountability demanded.

For example, no one will find it *theologically* acceptable if I defend Irenaeus' view of the atonement over Augustine's by appealing causally to a powerful personal religious experience, or to a 'gut feeling' or 'inkling', or to explain that a strange dream I had two weeks ago caused an inexplicable but compelling conviction that I must follow Irenaeus over Augustine. I will rather, for a proper *theological* accounting, be expected to be able to *support* any of my judgements on the basis of reflectively reasoned *inferential* explanations, which show my conclusions (whether my listeners agree with these or not) to be the result of a *conceptually* justificatory connectedness, on the basis of certain commonly understood premises.

From all of this we can see something that will by now perhaps already be patently obvious. The fundamental *internal* mechanisms by which *all* intellectual or scientific disciplines – qua *intellectual* or ratiocinative (and this includes theology as a discipline of the intellect) – must without exception hold themselves to account are *not* causal but conceptual (inferential) or logical. Indeed, in terms of their basic *internal operations*, this will be no less true for the strongly empirically observational science of meteorology than it is for the entirely abstract and non-empirical discipline of elementary formal logic.

But the emphasis on 'internal' here is vitally important. For to say that meteorology and formal logic must be equally attentive to right inference is not of course to say that meteorology doesn't *also* have to be attentive to its sensible-causal subject matter in a way that formal logic does not. It is only to say that when meteorology wants to express and defend itself genuinely as a *science*, it thereby holds its *internal* reasonings to account no less inferentially and logically (albeit primarily by an inductive and abductive logic) than does formal logic, where the inferential movements are purely deductive or analytical, which is to say at bottom tautological.

But we now equally need to say something from the other side. For whereas formal logic, together with any of its analytical compatriots (e.g., various forms of calculus, analytical philosophy of language), must by definition focus their attention intrinsically and exclusively on subject matter which is 'posited' internally to consciousness, the empirical disciplines of meteorology or physics or biochemistry etc. can of course do no such thing. And the basic distinction here has to do with a fundamental difference in *subject matter*. The point is that while the subject matter of analytical or tautological disciplines is limited by definition entirely to what can be posited purely presuppositionally or linguistically or propositionally within consciousness, the empirical disciplines must for their subject matter be attentive through the *bodily senses* to dynamically contingent events in the real world of space and time in a way that logic or philosophy of language need not be.

So let us now look at these two sources of attentiveness or accountability somewhat more closely on their own terms. And I commence from a more careful analysis of attentiveness on the inferential or logical level in order to build from there in a certain way to the particular issue of causal questioning in theology, which is the more fundamental interest of this chapter.

3. Logical or Inferential Accountability in Human Questioning

When we come to ask about this mechanism of 'inference' more exactly, specifically with respect to the basic elements or characteristics by which inferential or logical *integrity* is measured, perhaps certain intellectual 'virtues' may most immediately come to mind: conceptual clarity, critical attentiveness, terminological consistency, argumentative transparency and so on. But as we look more deeply into the precise operation of inference itself in any of its 'modes' (deductive, inductive, abductive or whatever), we will find that almost all such 'virtues' are themselves rooted in two more fundamental underlying axioms. These axioms are so integral to any human discourse or communicative exchange that, without an underlying commitment to them, all possibility of discourse (as communicative exchange) fundamentally breaks down. The axioms themselves are not only fully self-evident and presupposed in the normal flow of everyday life, they are also found explicitly at the very heart of virtually every enterprise of focused enquiry. In fact, they are so obvious that one might perhaps think that they shouldn't even need repeating here. Yet despite what virtually everyone will grant as their obviousness when stated, these two axioms are not infrequently violated in the literature today in subliminal ways and unawares. (And indeed, wherever such a violation occurs, it is usually precisely because logical or inferential attentiveness is not sufficiently distinguished from causal attentiveness, as we shall see.) So we do well to remind ourselves of them here briefly.

The axioms are of course – as they have come to be identified in both the traditional Aristotelian logic and modern propositional logic – the law of identity and the law of non-contradiction. (A third, the law of the excluded middle, is sometimes grouped together with these but its equally axiomatic character is sometimes disputed.) Stated in formal terms, the law of identity says simply that everything is what it is and not something else, or that A=A; or in modern propositional terms, that any proposition *p* implies itself. The law of non-contradiction, which is really another way of affirming the same thing, says simply that I may not simultaneously both affirm something and deny that same thing; or in other words that contradictories cannot both be true together or both be false together. Again, this is clear enough to common sense. No one will disagree with the statement that the Brooklyn Bridge in New York is not the Tower Bridge in London, or that Napoleon's defeat at Waterloo is not the discovery of insulin. Nor will anyone disagree that there is something fundamentally flawed in maintaining that in the year 2005 the Chicago White Sox both won the World Series for the first time in 88 years *and* that they did not do so.

But something further can be added to this. The position I am expressing here as to the 'axiomatic' or self-evident status of these need not be a contentious one. Indeed, when it is understood properly, it can be advanced relatively unproblematically even for the more radically pragmatic, culturally comparative or other self-described 'anti-rationalist' views today, which might normally find themselves inclined to reject any claim to axiomatic status. For the contention here is not that the axioms of identity and non-contradiction are anything like free-standing metaphysical principles 'in themselves', somehow existing 'out there' apart from any context. I am rather simply asserting that they are non-negotiable requirements on which the possibility of any *discourse* at all depends, or on which any genuine communicative exchange or flow of ideas depends. I may not, for example, even from fundamentally anti-rationalist commitments, say something like the following without a complete breakdown of communicative exchange: 'Well, yes, I meant such and such by the term X a moment ago, but I've now changed my mind and I mean something completely different. And yet I want you to take the argumentative impact of what I am saying as if I had intended the same thing in both instances.' Whenever a commitment to identity and non-contradiction of *linguistic intention* is given up in this way, discourse as communicative exchange, even if just in soliloquy (thinking), fundamentally breaks down. And that is what makes identity and non-contradiction axiomatic to discourse or thinking, even for the more openly relativist perspectives.

Now there are some disciplines that operate entirely or exclusively on the basis of inferential or logical attentiveness. That is, the propriety of their operations is measured at bottom entirely against the axioms of identity and non-contradiction and corollaries or derivatives of these. Elementary formal logic, any 'general logic', analytical philosophy of language, and many kinds of calculus are some of the most obvious examples falling under this classification. These are called 'analytical' disciplines because they are most essentially concerned with the conceptual *analysis* of linguistic terms, or with relations of ideas and the logical procedures which define such relations. This can be made most straightforwardly clear in considering simple analytical truth-claims, as follows.

When we say that a statement is 'true analytically' we mean that it is true 'necessarily'; and 'necessity' in this sense can appear in several ways. Some statements can be true just by the definitions of the terms involved. This happens when the predicates or qualities that a sentence affirms about its subject are already contained in the definition of the subject. For example, to say that a triangle is a three-sided figure, or that a bachelor is unmarried, or that all the points on the circumference of a circle are equidistant from its centre, is in each case to make an analytically true and thus necessarily true statement, because what is being affirmed or predicated of the subject is already contained in the very *definition* of the subject. Or in other words, it is again because a careful conceptual *analysis* of the sentence's *subject alone* would yield these predicates that these kinds of truth statement are called 'analytical'.

One begins to see here why it is that all analytical truth-claims are intrinsically entirely about language and logic, and can never be about anything other than this: i.e., never anything about the way things are contingently in embodied sensible reality or empirical history in space and time. Why? Because analytical questioning entirely sets aside all problematical considerations about the truth or reality of the *content* of its premises, and deals with them for entirely *formal* purposes, as sets of linguistic or propositional premises to be brought under logical and grammatical analysis. (It might just be added here that this is the source of Pannenberg's criticism of Barth's theology, i.e., that it constitutes a 'dead end of faith subjectivism', inasmuch as it 'takes the truth of Christian doctrine [to] be established [presuppositionally] in advance of all discussion of its content'.[18] In other words, there is a certain analytical self-enclosedness to Barth's theology under which it suffers in important ways, as we shall see further below.)

Most intellectual disciplines, however, are not 'analytic' but 'synthetic'.[19] That is, they take their subject matter or source of concern from the real world of human experience in space and time, and they must as such be concerned with questions about the truth or reality of their subject matter *in* space and time in a way that analytical disciplines can ignore. The natural sciences, medical sciences, political science, economics etc., are all 'synthetic' in this sense. Again, this is not to say that synthetic disciplines can be any less committed to inferential or conceptual integrity than the analytical ones. It is only to say that because what they seek to make judgements *concerning* are real occurrences observed in space and time – real diseases for medical science, real stock market crashes and housing booms for economics, real problems of immigration and urban ethnic tension for political science – they must, somewhere in their deliberations, be attentive to real particular events in space and time in a way that analytical disciplines need not be. And the deeper point to be emphasized here is that such an attentiveness to the dynamics and contingencies of real life in space and time will always be an attentiveness at bottom to the *causal* dynamism of the world, a causal dynamism which is encountered fundamentally or originally through sensible awareness and through sensible observation.

Indeed, the indispensability of this twofold attentiveness can be shown even in the most abstract or theoretical of the empirical disciplines. In the discussions about black holes in astrophysics, for example, most exchanges are thoroughly abstract or non-empirical, occurring entirely inferentially and conceptually within the domains of pure mathematics and logic. But the point is that even in theoretical physics, if it is truly *physics* that is being undertaken, and not just pure logic or pure mathematics, the *original* subject matter at its core must remain empirical. That is, it must be subject matter having been encountered *causally* through sensible interaction with the real world of space and time. And *this* subject matter will *demand* to be accounted for causally, usually in some quite simple way on the basis of an original sensible observation or experimentation, in the case of black holes involving the observation of behaviours and patterns of light. The point to which all of this is leading is one which has been a commonplace in philosophy from Aristotle to Kant and beyond, and also in modern physics from Newton to the present day, but which has become largely lost to modern theology and the human sciences.

The point is this. Sheer mental intellection, no matter how brilliant or creative, cannot, through its own *abstractive inferential* activity, engender or fully account for the *dynamic causal* processes occurring in the extensive magnitudes of space and time. It must rather *take* this content from what causal, observational interaction with the world of sensible experience *brings to* the intellect. Donald MacKinnon illustrates this aptly in one of his frequent references to Albert Einstein. While Einstein was emphatic in his insistence on 'the extent to which fundamental scientific progress must wait on the development, by spontaneous intellectual activity, of more powerful branches of mathematics', he was just as insistent that 'it would be wrong to attribute to thinking a *Durchdringungskraft*, a penetrative power through which it might reach beyond the supposed veil of sense to an intelligible reality, graspable by pure intellection'.[20] The point is that physics, as a discipline concerned with the real world of sensible experience in space and time, must, even in its most abstract endeavours, nevertheless remain at its *origin* always first attentive *causally* to *sensible reality*. The reason for this is that inferential questioning by definition responds and attends to a fundamentally different set of obligations or requirements than causal or spatio-temporal questioning, which is again why results yielded by the one kind of questioning can never at bottom satisfy the requirements of the other kind of questioning.

4. Revelation as Divine Causality

It may be clear by this time where all of this is meant to be leading. The point is that while theology must indeed, no less than any other intellectual discipline, be able to account for its *internal* operations fundamentally through demonstrations of proper inference on the conceptual level, and not by appeal to causal factors on the sensible level, this may by no means be taken to imply that theological questioning can be *indifferent* to the authority of causality. Far from this, when we come to the *theological* problem of causality we reach the very most dynamic and demanding of all aspects of theological attentiveness. Indeed we reach a kind of gateway through which all considerations about both the *source* and the *subject matter* of theology in its indispensably incarnational (embodied) focus must pass. And this is why in the question of causality we also reach one of the most formidably difficult of all theological challenges, one that remains largely unexplored in any critically ordered way since Schleiermacher's trenchant engagement with it in 1830. Stated most basically, the fundamental problem of causality with which theology is concerned is that of *revelation,* where revelation is understood as the *divine causality* in the world. Or more fully, it is the problem of *the causality of the reality of God in the world.*

Now it will be recognized that in connecting revelation to the question of the divine causality in the world, I am expanding somewhat on what today can be the more usual, narrower application of the term 'divine causality' to treatments within the doctrine of creation *ex nihilo*. But this equal connection of both creation and revelation to the divine causality can be shown to be not only fully legitimate but actually required, in several ways, the most important being the particular character of the *authority* or finality with which both creation *ex nihilo* and revelation declare themselves. Let me explain this, first with regard to creation *ex nihilo*. And in doing so I want to introduce a special kind of term which will become operative in much of what follows.

In the divine causality which is active in the creation of the heavens and the earth out of nothing, theological questioning is confronted with what I want to call an 'authority of non-resolution', or a *finality of non-resolution*. This can be demonstrated in two different ways, but before getting to those, let me first explain a bit more clearly what I mean by this term 'finality of non-resolution'.

Within today's predominantly phenomenological and textually structuralist frameworks of reasoning, any theological study presuming to speak thematic-ally of 'finality', or of authorities making claims to finality, will be likely to be greeted with a certain degree of suspicion. But let me try right away to allay the severest of these suspicions by situating this term 'finality' in a way that I hope will make it seem somewhat less immediately offensive. Finality and authority here will not be used with respect to any specific *positions* to be advocated or put forward, but initially only again with respect to certain basic features of dis-course per se, especially to certain ultimate courts of appeal in relation to which any discourse (as communicative exchange) must inherently locate itself. In this light I want to suggest that there are two fundamentally different ways that authority or finality can meet us in reflective enquiry, whether theological or otherwise.

The distinction put succinctly is this: finalities, or genuinely basic author-ities for discourse, can be encountered in human questioning or enquiry either fundamentally in virtue of their ability to provide mechanisms of *resolution* to human queries, or fundamentally in virtue of their *resistance* to all advances of resolution to human queries. The kind of finality or authority we naturally strive for as such in almost any kind of discourse is an authority of *resolution*. By an authority of resolution I mean one which derives its public persuasiveness or inter-subjective visibility from a certain capacity for settling disputes or problems, specifically by resolving the queries involved, or by bringing into some greater harmony the often conflicting elements in human experience and cognition. As such, the kinds of finality or authority we grant to a mathematical theorem or to a scientific theory or, in theology, to a doctrinal or apologetic strategy or a theodicy: these are always at bottom mechanisms of resolution inasmuch as their authority rests on the way they can be shown either to resolve into proofs, or into 'best explanations', or on some other explanatory capacity they may contain with a view to overall coherence. Indeed, human questioning, by its very nature *as* questioning, strives intrinsically for resolution of some kind, even though in many cases it never reaches it.[21] Reason itself, as Kant showed, is intrinsically a 'faculty of unity', and as such it operates always and everywhere by mechanisms of resolution, even when it cannot reach resolution.

But there a few cases where human questioning comes up against an authority or finality that defies any resolution whatsoever. This kind of authority I want to call a *finality of non-resolution*. By this I do not mean merely intellectual riddles, or undecidabilities, or the quandaries posed by recent developments in quantum physics, or chaos theory etc. For all of these, after all, are still *destinations* of human questioning which have been arrived at inferentially (whether deductively, inductively or 'dialectically', and so on) and thus essentially by resolutional means. Or in other words they are recognized *as* quandaries or *as* undecidabilities by the very *processes* of reason functioning as a faculty of unity on the basis of resolution.

By a genuine finality of non-resolution I mean rather something that confronts human awareness and reflection unmistakably as a *reality*, and yet, precisely in its undeniability as real, utterly *forbids* any ultimate resolution into explanatory mechanisms of any kind. There are in life only a few ways that we encounter this kind of authority, the emergence of our own subjectivity or self-consciousness in embodied life and the passing of this in death being among them. But perhaps the most obvious, and certainly most sobering, encounters during our lives in which human reflection is confronted with a finality of non-resolution, are in cases of unspeakable evil and suffering. What we are confronted with, for example, in Auschwitz, or the killing fields of Cambodia or Rwanda, can only be spoken of as a finality of non-resolution in the sense that any attempt to 'account' for this evil in whatever broader strategy of apologetics, or theodicy, or teleological design, utterly breaks apart and shatters against the actual, tangible particularity of human demise, violation and undoing which comprise these events. Dietrich Ritschl expresses this forcefully in his assertion that 'Anyone who wants to say that Auschwitz – as a paradigm of evil and suffering in our time – is willed by God or good, even if we only realize it later, has to shut up, because such statements mark the end of both theology and humanity.'[22]

There is another way of approaching what is seeking expression here, which is to suggest, along with Donald MacKinnon, that there is something in the authority with which unspeakable evil and suffering announces itself, that has unmistakably the character of the 'tragic'. Or more exactly in MacKinnon's terms, tragedy understood as a form of discourse presents us with a literary mode of representing what he calls the 'sheerly intractable in human life' (as in Auschwitz the 'sheerly intractable' confronts us) in a way that no other form of discourse can. The implied point here is that every other form of discourse will invariably seek to draw the sheerly intractable into some broader resolution or application, however subtly, whether to glean a 'moral' of some sort, or even just to make a further dramatic or poetic 'point'. But tragedy as a form of discourse is *by definition* 'irresolvable'. Whether in Sophocles, Shakespeare or Racine, tragedy as a literary form keeps its integrity, and indeed its identity *as* tragedy, precisely by *disallowing* resolution into a higher *telos* or a higher rationale. If a course of events can be understood as leading to a resolution which somehow 'makes sense' of it, then that course of events is by definition no longer 'tragic'.[23] It is from this perspective that the relation between literary tragedy and the reality of unspeakable evil and suffering can be so aptly illuminated by what I am calling a finality of non-resolution: i.e., because in either case we are dealing with a finality whose utter *resistance* to 'resolution' is taken as the fundamental *basis* of the authority with which it announces itself.

But MacKinnon now goes further and finds the sheer intractability encountered in tragedy to be reflected also in the authority with which Christian transcendence or revelation demands to confront us. In MacKinnon's words, 'tragedy, regarded as a form of discourse, itself provide[s] a way of representing the relation of the familiar to the transcendent' like no other form of discourse.[24] The relation expressed here remains obscure in MacKinnon but my own distinctions between finalities of resolution and non-resolution can help to illuminate it.

The point is that it is precisely this demand of non-resolution that meets us whenever we turn to the content of Christian doctrine itself, in any of its most central and fundamental revelational claims (incarnation, resurrection, Ascension, creation *ex nihilo*, eschaton). Or in other words, what unites all of these as fundamental sources of theological authority is precisely that they derive the *basis* of their authority explicitly from their *inability* or indeed refusal to be 'resolved' into broader systems of explanation. In the Chalcedonian creed, for example, Jesus Christ is precisely *not* the 'resolution' of the divine and human in any way that we could imagine this, but the unfathomable mystery of their *unresolved* union. This indeed so much so that the very authority of orthodox Chalcedonian Christology *issues from* this demand of *non*-resolution, as is proved in the clear observation that any attempts historically to bring the challenge articulated in Chalcedon into some sort of 'resolution' have always ended in either one or the other opposing errors of docetism or Nestorianism. But we need now to explain this further, specifically with regard to our present concern about the divine causality which is active equally in creation and revelation, and the finality of non-resolution that confronts us in it as such. Let me then explain this first with respect to creation *ex nihilo* and then with regard to incarnational revelation.

To begin with, we may of course speak figuratively, as Schleiermacher does, of the divine causality at work in creation out of nothing as that which 'is presupposed as originally setting the whole sphere in motion by a first push'.[25] But we can never really mean this 'first push' in any merely natural sense as simply the first of all causes already *within* the cosmic, spatio-temporal order. That is, we do not mean that the causality spoken of in the doctrine of creation *ex nihilo* is like the cause and effect we perceive between billiard balls when one strikes another, or merely that it is the first of all such material, natural or efficient causes. For any characterization of the created order as the 'product' of an originating cause in this merely *material* or efficient sense would designate a generative activity already originating and occurring from *within* the created material and efficient order (or as such it would already be an element within that order); whereas what we encounter in the demand of creation *ex nihilo* is the origination *of* that whole order itself. In other words, what we encounter in the demand of creation *ex nihilo* is an authoritative declaration which does not offer itself as a causally resolutional *explanation* for anything. For what it announces is not merely the first element within the spatio-temporal or cosmically causal sequence, to which then all subsequent causal events could trace their origin resolutionally. The whole force and function of the '*ex nihilo*' in creation out of nothing is meant to ensure that the authority or finality of the divine causality in the creational event is utterly prohibited from being resolved or subsumed into the cosmic sequence itself, as simply the first cosmic event. It is rather the causally generative *non*-resolutional origin and ground of all cosmic events, *including* the 'first' of these (in whatever way we might try to make even this latter designation meaningful).

But this non-resolutional authority of creation *ex nihilo* which thus becomes evident on the causal level can become even more clearly pronounced on the conceptual level. The point here is that we can have utterly no comprehension even of what we *mean* conceptually when we say 'creation out of nothing'. For although we can *say* it, we can in no way *think* it as a meaningful concept, just as we can *say* the compound term 'square circle' without being able to *think* it (although I am not implying that 'creation out of nothing' is a logical contradiction in the way that this other term is). And the more exact reason that we cannot know what we *mean* when we speak of the 'beginning of time' and the 'beginning of space' is that with any 'beginning' so posited we will always thereby also have to think a 'time' *prior to* and a 'space' *beyond*. (It is impossible for us to escape this.) And this entails in turn that we will have been unable to articulate the genuine beginning or origination we were striving for at all. The point in short is that it is impossible for us to think a beginning of time (indeed, just as it is also impossible for us to think a beginningless time, as Kant showed in his Transcendental Dialectic). And because we cannot *think* it, neither can we therefore have any comprehension whatsoever of what such a locution could possibly *mean*. The really crucial result to be derived from this therefore is that the authority of creation *ex nihilo* does not confront us originally as a *doctrine* within a framework of theological *meaning* at all. It confronts us rather as a *demand* of the dynamically generative *divine causality* which *precedes* all doctrine or theology: precedes it as the very origination of the world in which we find ourselves embodied as sensible and thinking organisms, and thus as the origination of the very possibility even of doctrine itself or of theology itself.

In short, what we are confronted with 'non-resolutionally' in the divine causality which is active in creation *ex nihilo* – or what we are confronted with 'non-resolutionally' in the biblical declaration that 'in the beginning God created the heaven and the earth' – is a limit or a finality at which all thinking simply *stops*. And this means also that in the divine causality we reach a limit or a finality at which all presupposing, all positing, indeed all doctrine or theologizing *stops*. Bonhoeffer is thus exactly right in the opening sentences of his *Creation and Fall*:

> The place where the Bible begins is one where our most impassioned waves of thinking break, are thrown back upon themselves, and lose their strength in spray and foam. The first word of the Bible has hardly for a moment surfaced before us, before the waves frantically rush in upon it again and cover it with wreaths of foam. That the Bible should speak of the beginning provokes the world, provokes us. For we cannot speak of the beginning. Where the beginning begins, there our thinking stops; there it comes to an end.[26]

But we must now bring all of this to bear on our main concern, which is to say along with Schleiermacher and much of the theological tradition preceding him that it is this *same* divine causality, declaring itself with the same finality of non-resolution, which is active also in the authority with which *revelation* declares itself. In light of the above, this can now be stated quite briefly and straightforwardly. For when we look at the demands of revelation carefully – as seen most clearly in the real incarnation of the divine Logos in a physical human body in space and time, and not as an *ideal* 'incarnation' abstractly within 'ratio' – we immediately see as such that revelation too, like creation *ex nihilo*, claims to bring precisely a wholly and utterly 'original' (i.e., non-resolutionally original) element of dynamically *causal* content *ex nihilo* to human apprehension within empirical history.

Or to state this point in the terms discussed above, what we encounter in the incarnational revelation of the eternal Logos in a real physical birth of a human body in Jesus Christ is precisely not merely an intentional-referential communication within 'ratio'. It is not most fundamentally an event of the divine reason communicating directly and purely with human reason, an event which could then guarantee itself analytically or resolutionally in the hiddenness of a faith subjectivism, or within the hidden securities of a miraculous mental event. It is rather, at least in its genuinely incarnational sense, nothing less than the divinely *causal* and *generative* event of a real bodily birth in the real created world, of a real causal coming forth from a mother's womb, of a real human life and a real human death, lived and died in the causal nexus of space and time. And what this chapter will be attempting to say most fundamentally below, along with several others in recent theology, is that revelation must be encountered no less incarnationally *even today* – that is, no less as an activity of the divine causality in the real world of sensible human embodiment in space and time today – than it was exactly and nothing less than this in the days of Jesus' mortal flesh.

But all of this is meant to re-emphasize the basic point being made here. And that is again to say that we must view the divine causality at work in revelation, not as the invitation to a theologically analytical *solution*, but as the same sort of intractably non-resolutional *problem* for theological questioning as the causality at work in the creation of the heavens and the earth out of nothing. Why? Because the problem of the divine causality acting *ex nihilo* as a finality of non-resolution on the real world of space and time, where the effect is empirical and embodied but the cause is infinite or wholly original, is the same for both. This theme will be taken up again on a deeper level in the following chapter.

But there is finally one further and related element that must be addressed in this regard, and it relates directly back to the erroneous subsumption of causal authority into conceptual or mentally 'determining' authority with which this chapter began. The more particular aspect of that error now under the present magnification is this. Because revelation has over the past two centuries come to be misconstrued as an originally mental communication to human intellection rather than an originally causal communication to human beings at the centre of embodied life, this more basic misconstrual has also led further to certain misjudgements or false expectations about what *revelation* as a *causal* communication is able to achieve in the essentially *conceptual* operations internally of *doctrine* or theology. To state the point directly, one of the most pervasive sources of procedural error in theology today – especially with regard to the central Christological doctrines of incarnation, reconciliation, atonement or redemption – is to make a fundamental misjudgement about what the *unity* (between God and the world) announced by these doctrines, and especially the unity engendered *causally* by the *reconciliation* of the world to God in the real body of Jesus Christ on the cross in space and time, is able to yield *conceptually* for *theology*. Or the point in brief is that the 'unity' of *causal reconciliation* between *God and the world* which is accomplished in empirical history on the cross is by no means merely the unity of a *conceptual resolution* within *doctrine*, nor can it in any way guarantee such a resolution. It is rather a unity achieved by the divinely *causal* act of redemption in the real world of human embodiment in space and time.

Karl Barth, as we have seen, makes this kind of conflation openly, and indeed in a doctrinally presupposed way. But the actual lineaments of the error itself become even more obviously visible in certain kinds of contemporary 'kenotic' approaches. Jürgen Moltmann and Eberhart Jüngel, for example, each in his own way, take God's real, causal reconciliation of the world to himself on the cross as an occasion for a radical conceptual or *linguistic redefinition* of the whole theological terrain itself, so as thereby to retain the basic analytical and self-securing character of theology.

Consider the directness and explicitness with which Jüngel, specifically, wants to guarantee and seal the *theological* 'success' of the cross within the definitional linguistic assurances of a doctrinal resolution. It is well known that Jüngel (and Moltmann with him) maintains that there is something fundamentally misconceived and misguided about what he calls the 'classical' or 'traditional' understanding of God as he finds this expressed for example in Aquinas or Anselm or John of Damascus, among others.[27] And Jüngel seeks to offer what he calls a 'significant correction'[28] of the classical doctrine as such. In his own words, the cross of Christ demands that we must come back 'to query again the *linguistic* meaning and function of the word "God"'; or that in light of the cross we must 'learn to *think* God in a new way'.[29] This altered linguistic meaning of God is then given most exactly as follows: 'the *Crucified one* must be the criterion for any possible concept of God'. Indeed, 'for responsible Christian usage of the word "God", the Crucified One is *virtually the real definition* of what is meant with the word "God".'[30]

Now let me be quite clear that my intention here is by no means to undermine Jüngel's theology as a whole. Jüngel is clearly a formidably rigorous and exemplary thinker and his theology is in other ways very powerful. But there is no getting around a certain flimsiness of the merely analytical result achieved on this particular level; and Jüngel along with Barth can act as a good example for a much broader trend I am seeking to identify here. For by linguistically redefining God's nature ahead of time as in its most basic essence radically 'self-emptying', Jüngel makes the cross – or something like it – a virtual analytical (linguistic) corollary *within doctrine* of the very (analytical) *meaning* of the term 'God'.[31] For both Barth and Jüngel therefore, theology is always in the end something like the working through of a kind of supreme tautology – not an onto-theology, to be sure, but still what might be called a tauto-theology. By contrast, Friedrich Schleiermacher, Dietrich Bonhoeffer or Karl Rahner (or likewise, in the recent British tradition, Donald MacKinnon or Rowan Williams) are no less 'kenotic' in their emphases. But for them, in a spirit which in its fundamentals is much closer to the non-resolutional demands of Chalcedon than to the conceptually resolutional opportunities afforded by Hegel, God's self-emptying in the incarnation and on the cross is always set out as the most basic *intractable problem* for theology per se, and not as something which from the outset logically guarantees the *analytical resolution* to its problems.

Indeed, Bonhoeffer's own criticism that Barth's theology engages in a 'positivism of revelation' is precisely a critique of its self-guaranteeing or tautological character as such. For as Bonhoeffer himself states, each element in the Barthian enterprise is 'an equally significant and equally necessary piece of the whole, a whole which must precisely be swallowed as a whole or not at all'.[32] Yet even so, beyond its tautologizing tendencies, there is for Bonhoeffer a much more alarming consequence of such a theology which simply 'posits' revelation analytically or resolutionally already *within* a system of doctrine, a 'positing' against which Schleiermacher had also warned. The more alarming consequence, as Bonhoeffer now says with force, is that such an approach actually *destroys* (*zerreißt*) the inalienably *incarnational* character of revelation, which is to say its inalienably embodied and thus this-worldly character – i.e., 'that Christ has come in the flesh!'.[33] And the 'destruction' of which Bonhoeffer speaks occurs specifically by abstracting the authority of the incarnation from the real world of space and time where it really occurs, and by placing the more primary authority instead within the self-guaranteeing confines of doctrine.

The same violation can occur, as we have seen, in kenotic appeals, whenever these are used as mechanisms which purport to be able to draw the authority or finality of the incarnation and the cross more fundamentally into a doctrinally analytical system of resolution, and to 'validate' it within such an ideality. For such approaches are not merely an illegitimate tautological shortcut; they are also a violation of the finality of non-resolution with which the real incarnation and death of the eternal Logos in human flesh announces itself causally in empirical history. The essential point here is that kenosis, in its causally embodied *reality*, in no way *solves* the theological problem of God's relation to the world on the cross; it rather *defines* this problem in its full and sheer intractability as a finality of non-resolution. And it defines it moreover in the unsurpassable declaration that it is indeed the eternal and immortal one, who is before all things and by whom all things were created, who dies bodily on the cross, and who thereby with real dynamically causal power, and not by a sensibly abstracted mental miracle, achieves the real reconciliation of the world to God.

5. Theology at the Centre of Life

We can sum all of this up now by following Schleiermacher (who as we have seen reflects the predominating traditions historically on this point), and thus by saying the following. It is precisely because of the loss of causal attentiveness to revelation, under the spirit of idealism, that the authority of *revelation itself* has today become effectively absorbed into the authority of *doctrine,* or into some other conceptually resolutional ordering, whether hermeneutical or phenomenological. And the primary motivating concern of the following chapter as such will be to mount a challenge to the currently predominating idea that it is doctrine or theology which must be the guarantor or validator of revelation, and to return instead to the genuinely biblical demand in the other direction: i.e., the demand that it is *revelation* – seen as the causally generative reality of God in the world today – which must be the prior ground and source of doctrine and indeed of any genuinely *theo*logical reflection whatsoever.

What all of this calls for, in other words, is a shift in the way theology must pay attention to its original subject matter, that is, to revelation. And the main point to be emphasized here will by now be clear enough. In order to pay attention to God's self-revelation as a present reality in the world today, theology must relearn what it means to be *attentive causally* or what it is to question causally. But how exactly do we 'question causally'? We do it first and foremost by a reinstatement of human sensible attentiveness to a level of importance equal with that of human interpretative or intellectively 'determining' awareness in theological questioning. But it must be stressed again that this does not mean a favouring of sensibility over intellection, or a favouring of the authority of causation with respect to the body over the authority of inference or logic with respect to the mind. It means only the recovery of a proper balance in attentiveness between the two, in a way that accords appropriately and genuinely with the human experience of the real world of sensible embodiment, which is the very world into which God has come as a real mortal human being in the flesh, and not abstractly as an idea. Or to repeat what was stated at the opening, it accords simply with the human organism itself, which precisely *in its unity* recognizes itself as *both* sensible (responding to bodily or causal influences) *and* rational (responding to conceptual or logical influences).

I am aware that the position I am advancing here runs counter not only to the analytical or self-guaranteeing dispositions in theology today but also to many of the predominating phenomenological, philological or foundationally hermeneutical orientations. But despite the current predominance of these, it is just as important to note again that the incarnational position advanced in this chapter is by no means an entirely isolated one, even within recent theology, and its basic disposition can be found with varying kinds of emphases in several recent thinkers. Perhaps the most obvious among these is the theology of Dietrich Bonhoeffer, where the pervasive and constantly underlying theme is that revelation must *even today* be encountered no less incarnationally, that is, no less in the real world of sensible human embodiment in space and time today, than it was exactly and nothing less than this in the days of Jesus' mortal flesh. It is against this uncompromisingly incarnational or 'this-worldly' backdrop that some of Bonhoeffer's most controversial statements are shown to be not as over-radical or revisionist as they are often taken to be. Consider for example Bonhoeffer's well-known statements that because 'in Jesus Christ the reality of God has entered into the reality of this world', therefore now 'the sacred is to be found *only* in the profane', 'what is Christian is to be found *only* in the worldly', and the 'supernatural' is to be found *only* in the natural;[34] or the summary statement that 'the reality of God is disclosed *only* as it places me completely *into* the reality of the world'.[35] Far from being over-radical or revisionist, any and all such statements are really for Bonhoeffer only an amplification of the consequences of what the incarnation of God in a real human body in Jesus Christ continues to demand even today.

The same basic 'this-worldly' or incarnational disposition can be found elsewhere as well, for example in Karl Rahner, or in recent British theology in Donald MacKinnon or Rowan Williams. Rahner, along exactly these lines, puts forward what he calls an 'axiom for understanding every relationship between God and creatures'. This axiom is that my relational closeness and distance, respectively, to God and to the world, 'do not vary for creatures in inverse [proportion] but in direct proportion'.[36] In other words, it is only as I draw closer to the real world of my own creaturehood, or to the real world of sensible human embodiment in space and time, that I may also draw closer to God. And with every retreat from this world, God also must inevitably become more distant. Or likewise, in the other direction, the closer God draws us to himself, the more deeply we will find ourselves drawn into the real world of sensibly embodied life in space and time. Denys Turner argues for something similar when he cautions that we should not allow ourselves to construe Christian transcendence in 'metaphors of "gaps", even infinitely "big" ones'.[37] In a trenchant discussion of Augustine on a related theme, Turner summarizes perfectly and with succinct clarity the whole thrust of what is seeking expression here: 'Augustine's sense of divine "otherness"', he says, 'is such as to place it, in point of transcendence, *closer* to my creaturehood than it is possible for creatures to be to each other. For creatures are more distinct from each other than God [precisely in his "transcendence" of their creaturehood, and thus also his transcendence of their creaturely "distance"] can possibly be from any of them.'[38]

Let me bring this to a close then by laying out what I want to suggest can offer itself as a new 'threshold question' for fundamental theology today, in light of the discussions in this chapter. That question is as follows. What does it mean for theological questioning that it is not at the limits of cognition on the *margins of intellection* (i.e., 'noumenon', 'saturated phenomenon', the analytical 'gift', or other namesakes), but at the dynamically causal limits of sensibility or sensible embodiment at the *centre of life*, that we must encounter Christian transcendence as a present reality in space and time *today*, or more exactly that we must encounter revelation as the divine causality in the world today? It is this question that the following chapter now takes as its guiding focus.

Notes

1 Friedrich Schleiermacher, *The Christian Faith* (Edinburgh: T&T Clark, 1948, pp. 49–50).

2 Paul D. Janz, 'Divine Causality and the Nature of Theological Questioning', in *Modern Theology* 23:3 (Oxford: Blackwell, 2007).

3 Paul D. Janz, *The Command of Grace: Foundations for a Theology at the Centre of Life* (Edinburgh, New York: T&T Clark, forthcoming 2008).

4 See e.g., Immanuel Kant, 'Open Letter on Fichte's *Wissenschaftslehre*, August 7, 1799' in *Kant: Philosophical Correspondence*, pp. 253–4.

5 See e.g., G. W. F. Hegel, *Hegel's Science of Logic*, trans. A. V. Miller (London: George Allen & Unwin, 1969, pp. 558–69, especially pp. 560–1).

6 See Hans Georg Gadamer, *Truth and Method* (London, New York: Continuum, 1989), particularly in Chapter 1, section 1, 'The Significance of the Humanist Tradition for the Human Sciences', pp. 3–37. See also G. W. F. Hegel, *Phenomenology of Mind* (Oxford: Clarendon, 1977, pp. 114–17, 521, 461).

7 G. W. F. Hegel, *Phenomenology of Mind* (Oxford: Clarendon 1977, p. 55).

8 Again, I have discussed this in considerable detail in Chapter 2 of my forthcoming book, *The Command of Grace*.

9 *Truth and Method*, pp. 3–37.

10 Karl Barth, *Church Dogmatics* I.1 (Edinburgh: T&T Clark, 1975, pp. 132, 135) (hereafter CD).

11 CD I.1, pp. 290, 291.

12 CD I.1, p. 290; see also, e.g., CD IV.1, pp. 7–10 where the same orientation is expressed within Barth's doctrine of reconciliation.

13 CD I.1, p. 290, emphasis added.

14 CD I.1, p. 291, emphasis added.

15 CD I.1, p. 291, emphasis added.

16 George A. Lindbeck, *The Nature of Doctrine* (Philadelphia: Westminster, 1984, p. 118).

17 This twofold way of giving explanations or reasons will be found to apply no less in the practical domains of agency and volition as it does in the discursive domains of representation and cognition.

18 Wolfhart Pannenberg, *Systematic Theology*, Vol. 1 (Grand Rapids: Eerdmans, 1991, pp. 47, 48).

19 I am aware, as some readers may wish to remind me, that W. V. O. Quine's influential essay, 'Two Dogmas of Empiricism', claimed to have done away with the analytical/synthetic distinction in a certain way (in *From a Logical Point of View* (Cambridge, MA: Harvard University Press, 1961, pp. 20–46). But Quine achieves this, in a way not entirely unlike Hegel, by first drawing 'synthetic' claims entirely to within the authority of intentionality, or fully to within a mental jurisdiction, thus once again fully bypassing the real causal issues. At any rate, as influential as that paper was at the time in certain Anglo-American analytical discussions, it has had little noticeable or lasting impact on the way that the designations 'analytic' and 'synthetic' actually continue to be recognized as distinct within both the natural sciences and in broad sectors of contemporary analytical philosophy.

20 Donald MacKinnon, *Explorations in Theology* (London: SCM, 1979, p. 153).

21 Even the self-declared 'anti-rationalist' approaches like post-structuralism or ultra-pragmatism, which resist grand claims to rational resolution (or to meta-narrative), nevertheless must continue to operate resolutionally in more localized ways (as Jacques Derrida freely admitted), even if what they resolve *to* are ersatz resolutional mechanisms like solidarity, social hope, strategic rhythm, undecidability and so on. See Jacques Derrida, 'The Principle of Reason: The University in the Eyes of Its Pupils', *Diacritics Vol. XIX* (spring 1983, pp. 3–20, p. 17).

22 Dietrich Ritschl, *The Logic of Theology* (Philadelphia: Fortress Press, 1987, p. 38).

23 One can of course bring forward examples of literary works that are traditionally included within the genre of tragedy, yet which do not exactly fit this mould (the book of Job is an example) because they resolve into happy ends or even moral lessons of some kind. But that does not diminish the basic point made by MacKinnon here, which is essentially an analytical one about the *meaning* of the term 'tragedy', the stricter denotation of which most literary tragedies do indeed fall into. The book of Job would fit the stricter definition, in the way that *King Lear* or *Phaedra* do, if the epilogue were omitted.

24 Donald MacKinnon, *The Problem of Metaphysics* (Cambridge: Cambridge University Press, 1974, pp. 136, 13).

25 *The Christian Faith*, p. 190.

26 Dietrich Bonhoeffer, *Creation and Fall* (Minneapolis: Fortress, 1997, p. 25).

27 See e.g., Eberhard Jüngel, *God as the Mystery of the World* (Grand Rapids: Eerdmans, 1983, pp. 232ff).

28 *God as the Mystery of the World*, p. 373.

29 *God as the Mystery of the World*, p. 9, original emphasis.

30 *God as the Mystery of the World*, p. 13, emphasis added.

31 *God as the Mystery of the World*, pp. 13, 14, 184, 232–45.

32 Dietrich Bonhoeffer, *Widerstand und Ergebung* (Gütersloh: Christian Kaiser Verlag, 1998, p. 415).
33 *Widerstand und Ergebung*, p. 416.
34 Dietrich Bonhoeffer, *Ethics* (Minneapolis: Fortress, 2005, p. 59), emphasis added.
35 *Ethics*, p. 55, emphasis added.
36 Karl Rahner, *Foundations of Christian Faith* (New York: Crossroad, 1978, p. 226).
37 Denys Turner, *Faith, Reason and the Existence of God* (Cambridge: Cambridge University Press, 2004, p. 214).
38 *Faith, Reason and the Existence of God*, p. 214, original emphasis.

4

The Coming Righteousness

Paul D. Janz

In order to make any constructive headway at all with regard to the question before us, as arrived at in the conclusion of the last chapter, we will have to turn our attention right away to what the scriptural sources themselves have to say about God's self-revelation, specifically now as this demands to meet us causally at the centre of sensibly embodied life in space and time and not 'noumenally' at the margins of intellection. And without question as such, our first concern must be to attend directly to the 'foundational events' themselves of the Christian faith – the incarnation, life, death and resurrection of Jesus Christ. But even here we will need to ask a particular kind of question. We need to ask *what it is* exactly or most fundamentally that according to the scriptures *is* 'revealed' in the man Jesus Christ himself in Palestine some 2,000 years ago; or *what it is* exactly that *is* 'revealed' in the gospel of the eternal Logos having become flesh. Or, if we want to avoid 'what-questions' and to keep to questions of 'Who', we must in Barthian language ask about the basic characteristic by which this revealed Who 'makes himself an authority and a factor' for us.[1] In short, what is the authoritative 'content' by which this revelation declares and identifies itself as the self-revelation of God? Or to put this in language which we shall find below in a discussion with Rowan Williams, what is the 'news' which we encounter in Jesus Christ the 'news *of*'? Several things will be shown to emerge when we look at this carefully.

To begin with, it will be quite obvious that even in the days of his flesh, *what* was revealed of God in Jesus Christ was not just his human 'flesh', but rather the reality of the divine nature as an 'ultimate' or as something final *in* the flesh. Jesus' human body is the real form in which God comes to human beings 'in the likeness of sinful flesh' (Rom. 8.3). But we need to be able to ask further about the essential 'content' by which the God of the Bible, the God of Abraham, Isaac and Jacob, declares himself in the man Jesus Christ: the content and authority by which he makes himself a 'factor' for human beings.

And in fact, when we ask this question with a careful attentiveness not only to the 'form' but also to the 'content' of the gospel, or to what the gospel 'news' is 'news *of*' (which in any case can never be separated), we will find that the scriptures themselves give us an answer that is as unmistakable as it is consistent in its clarity. Put succinctly, in the language of the Epistle to the

Romans, it is this: 'In the gospel *a righteousness from God* is revealed, a righteousness that is by faith from first to last' (Rom. 1.17). Now this demand is
found not only in scattered passages, which one would then have to work
together creatively to yield a less convincing account of the authority being
declared. For this direct identification of God's self-revelation with 'a righteousness which comes from God', or with the divine righteousness, is not only a
dominating theme throughout the Pauline writings, and one of the *most*
dominating of the Epistle to the Romans, but it will also be found to be
expressed indispensably in many other scriptural contexts as well, all of which
point back to the divine righteousness as most fundamentally the authoritative
content of the self-revelation of God. So let us review this briefly.

1. A Righteousness from God

To begin with, after initially identifying the essential character of revelation in
Jesus Christ as 'a righteousness which comes from God' in Rom. 1.17, the same
theme is repeated over and over again, most directly and in this exact locution
in Rom. 3.21, 22; 10.3; and also again in Phil. 3.9. Quoting Romans 3 now:
in the gospel of Jesus Christ *'a righteousness from God*, apart from the law, has
been made known, to which the Law and the Prophets testify. This righteousness from God comes through faith in Jesus Christ to all who believe.'
Further, in Romans 5, 'God's abundant provision of grace' is described precisely
not only in its *content* as 'the gift *of righteousness'*, but also as a gift given
specifically for the *purpose* that 'grace might reign *through righteousness'* (Rom.
5.17, 21). It is in this way too that the assertion of Jesus, 'my kingdom is not
from this world' (Jn 18.36), receives its proper force. For as Romans continues,
this 'kingdom of God [is indeed] *not* food and drink, but *righteousness'* (Rom.
14.17). The same connection is echoed once more in Jesus' own words: 'seek
first the kingdom of God and his *righteousness'* (Mt. 6.33); and this moreover is
again not merely 'a righteousness of my own that comes from the law, but that
which is through faith in Jesus Christ – *the righteousness that comes from God* and
is by faith' (Phil. 3.9). The same clear connection to the divine righteousness is
made also in the passages on the 'new creation' in Christ in 2 Corinthians.
'Therefore, if anyone is in Christ, there is a new creation: everything old has
passed away; see, everything has become new! All this is from God who
reconciled us to himself through Christ and has ... entrust[ed] the message of
reconciliation to us' (2 Cor. 5.17–19). But now what is the content of this
message exactly? As the same passage itself goes on explicitly to answer, it is
that 'for our sake he made him to be sin who knew no sin, so that we might
become the *righteousness of God* in him' (2 Cor. 5.21).

We can carry this even further. Jesus Christ himself, who rules and judges
over the coming kingdom of God (Mt. 25.31–46) is described in Hebrews 7, as
prefigured in Melchizedek, as none other than 'first, by translation of his name,
"*king of righteousness*"' (Heb. 7.2); and again as a king 'the sceptre of [whose]

kingdom' is described as 'the sceptre of righteousness' (Heb. 1.8); and again, as a king whose throne is described as having righteousness as its foundation (Ps. 89.14; 97.2). All of this is echoed further in the prophetic passage in Jeremiah with regard to the 'righteous branch' that will be raised up for David: 'This is the name by which he will be called: *The Lord Our Righteousness*' (Jer. 23.6). Even more directly, Acts 17.52 speaks of the advent of Jesus Christ himself as *'the coming of the Righteous One*' (see also Acts 3.14). And Paul's own account in Acts of his commissioning by Ananias is described as having the specific purpose that Paul might *'see the Righteous One* and to hear the words of his mouth' (Acts 22.14). This is echoed again in the first Johannine Epistle, that 'the one who speaks to the Father in our defence [is] Jesus Christ, *the Righteous One*' (1 Jn 2.1). Indeed the finality of the divine righteousness will be found to be located both in the creation account of Genesis and in the final eschaton. In 2 Peter 'the new heaven and the new earth' itself comes to be identified, with ultimate finality, as nothing less than *'the home of righteousness*' (2 Pet. 3.13). The same emphasis can be found in the creation account, even if less directly. For if it is indeed the eternal Logos, the Righteous One, the Lord of Righteousness by whom all things in heaven and earth were created, who is before all things and in whom all things hold together (Col. 1.15–17), then it is by no other measure than by the *original* righteousness of the Righteous One himself that the creation is also declared again and again to be 'good' (Gen. 1.4–31).

The overall point then is that the understanding of revelation as the disclosure of 'a righteousness which comes from God' carries with it what must be seen as a unique and indispensable fundamental authority for theology. Indeed, as we shall see below, it is an authority which any treatment of fundamental theology in terms of grace, trinity, atonement or even kenotic love, without a proper embeddedness within the demands of the divine righteousness as the fundamental 'content' of these, overlooks.

But we must now ask further about what this righteousness from God *is,* or about the essential character of the divine righteousness which, according to the scriptures, revelation most fundamentally discloses. For the divine righteousness, as a righteousness which comes from God, is precisely *not* like any human righteousness. Indeed as we shall see, it cannot even find an analogue in human righteousness, and there will be a natural tendency to misapprehend it in several ways if this is not kept firmly in mind. Let us then look further at the divine righteousness by focusing on three basic stipulations as demanded by the scriptures, the first in a negative mode, the other two positive.

In the first place, when we look carefully at the scriptures themselves with this question reflectively before us, we will find that the righteousness of God does not announce itself, as we might naturally expect it to do, with an authority or a finality which is most fundamentally directed to anything in or about human *moral consciousness*. Or it is not communicated originally to any naturally moral mode of human apprehension. For it is made quite clear that this is *not* a human righteousness, or a human 'good' at all. And what this means more exactly is that the divine righteousness does not declare itself *originally* with the authority of a righteousness or a 'good' which is defined intrinsically in its *opposition to evil*, as any normal human understanding of righteousness would need to frame it. This is of course not to say that the divine righteousness does not stand in condemnation of the evil that we ourselves engage in and witness in the created order. Nor is it by any means to suggest that the human questions of good and evil can be of no interest to theology. It is only to say that it is not *that* opposition – the opposition between good and evil, even in any radicalized degree – by which the divine righteousness declares its authority and finality as 'a righteousness which comes from God'. The scriptures will provide several reasons for this, but the most immediately obvious one is that human moral consciousness, or any human moral vision, *just is* already a moral vision that has its root in 'the knowledge of good and evil', which is to say in the state of being in sin. Or more fully, this knowledge of good and evil, on which any human righteousness or human moral vision is based, is, according to the creation narrative, in both its evil aspects *and* its good aspects already a falling away from the original righteousness. Or conversely, the falling away from the original righteousness through a corruption of desire, that is, through sin, is described in the creation account as nothing else than the human knowledge of good and evil.[2] This is why throughout our Christian doctrinal heritage sin is almost never simply equated with evil. The question of sin at its root is an essentially different one than simply the question of evil; for the fall into sin is not a fall only into the knowledge of evil; it is a fall into the knowledge of good and evil. It is a fall into the present state of human moral awareness or moral consciousness.

It is for this reason that the scriptures can declare as unequivocally as they do that, when measured against the divine righteousness, 'there is *no one* righteous, not even one'; and again that 'they have *all* fallen away [from the original righteousness], they are all alike perverse; there is *no one* who does good, no, not one' (Rom. 3.10–11; Ps. 14.3; Ps. 53.3). It is for this reason also that Jesus, when addressed as 'good teacher', replies 'Why do you call me good? No one is good but God alone' (Lk. 18.19). The implied point here again is that, according to the measure of human moral consciousness, that is, according to the measure of the human knowledge of good and evil, our good works are just as fallen away from the original righteousness or the divine goodness as our evil works. This, so much so, that Isaiah can declare that even 'all our righteous deeds are like a filthy cloth' (Isa. 64.6).

So what are we then to do? We have been asking how theology can become properly oriented to God's self-revelation as a divinely causal communication at the centre of life, and we have now on two basic fronts found ourselves confronted with a theological impasse. First, in the foregoing chapter we have discovered as false any idea that revelation can for theological reflection be encountered originally as anything like a 'referent' or an intentional-referential 'object' for our thinking consciousness, and that revelation is therefore at its causal origin theologically inaccessible by such a representational consciousness. But we have now also on the moral front already come to a second impasse. For what may have initially, in the recognition of revelation as a declaration of the divine righteousness, looked to be a possible opening for theological orientation to its subject matter as a present reality, has really brought us no further. Or we may indeed have been able to make what appeared to be a certain kind of advance with regard to our question, in the identification of the essential content of all revelation as a righteousness which comes from God. But this was then immediately withdrawn in the further stipulation that the communication of the divine righteousness in Jesus Christ is nothing which can be apprehended within our own moral vision, or our own consciousness of good and evil.

However, it is now precisely at this doubly sharpened impasse that the scriptures themselves will be found to direct us to a new opportunity for a proper theological apprehension of revelation as a righteousness from God at the centre of life. Let me just state this 'new opportunity' in the briefest of terms as follows, before then going on to elucidate it. One of the greatest impediments for theological progress on these matters is the natural tendency for reflective questioning to orient itself to God in terms of 'alterity' or in terms of a reality which is 'Wholly Other'. And I want to suggest that the scriptures themselves can be seen actually as directing us to an orientation to God which is not primarily or fundamentally one of alterity. This is by no means of course to suggest that theology, in finding it necessary to move away from the language of alterity or 'the other', should thereby, using Levinas' term, move back into the language of 'the same'. It is only to say that the language of alterity or 'the other' is, at least for today's intellectual sensitivities, in vital ways inadequate to provide a genuine orientation to what Barth called 'the Godness of God' as he declares himself in his self-revelation. Indeed, I will want to suggest that the reality of God in his self-revelation can for theology today no more be attended to adequately in the human language of the other (even in the language of the 'absolutely other') than the righteousness of God can be attended to adequately through a human understanding of 'good'. Let me then on this basis venture the following preliminary remarks in a different direction.

The way that revelation announces itself causally in the divine righteousness does not in the New Testament scriptures come to expression primarily under the inscription of the 'Wholly Other' but primarily under the inscription of 'The New' – the new creation, the new self, the new mind, the new body, and ultimately a new heaven and a new earth, which is the 'home of righteousness'. We will discuss in full detail in the next section what this distinction between the 'Wholly Other' and 'The New' must mean exactly. But as a way of preparing for that discussion, we can first return preliminarily to an important point made already in the previous chapter with regard to the demands of the divine causality. The preliminary point to be made here in reference to that earlier discussion is as follows. The communication of the divine righteousness in revelation must, *as* 'The New', be seen as no less an *ex nihilo* divine initiative – i.e., as the *wholly* new in the new creation in which '*everything* old has passed away' and '*everything* has become new' (2 Cor. 5.17) – than the 'original' creation of the heavens and the earth out of nothing must be apprehended as an *ex nihilo*

divine initiative. And it is because revelation must indeed – in its announce-
ment of the wholly new – be seen as an *ex nihilo* communication, that even the
language of alterity (which is precisely not an orientation to an 'out of nothing'
but already to 'an other') is insufficient to capture its authority. It is thus the
question of the more precise character of 'The New' which must now concern
us.

2. 'The New'

It is important to remind ourselves to begin with that, although in the scriptures 'the new' or the new creation comes to its final articulation or destination
in 'a new heaven and a new earth', beyond the entropy and decay towards death
of our present bodily existence, it is nevertheless explicitly and unequivocally
presented also as a *present* reality, as we have discussed at length above. What can
this mean? Obviously, it does not mean that when, in the decision of faith, a
person is said to be 'in Christ', and that in virtue of this decision 'everything has
become new' by grace, therefore the constitution of our physical bodies has now
become new, or that the empirical causal-sensible world within which we live as
embodied beings has now constitutively changed. We remain susceptible to the
same ageing of our bodies towards death as before, to disease as before, to the
same changing of the seasons as before and so on. I walk out of the same front
door as I did last Monday morning; the same 8:10 bus meets me at the same bus
stop on my way to work; it is the same porter wearing his usual jacket who
greets me at the college gate. Or as Bonhoeffer says of the new creation,
'*Ausserlich bleibt alles beim alten*'; outwardly, everything remains as it was.

2.1 'The new' and faith-subjectivism

Now as Bonhoeffer's statement already suggests, in its qualification that '*outwardly* everything remains as it was', the most natural or obvious tendency here
will be to interpret the new creation announced in revelation as referring to
something fundamentally or even exclusively 'internal' to the believer's new
self-consciousness in the decision of faith. Or the most natural inclination will
be to pull the authority of the new creation back entirely into the domain of
interiority, and as such to respond to the question of 'the new' or the new
creation with an answer which carries with it the fully secure but still entirely
impoverished authority of a mere faith-subjectivism. Now the reason this
movement to interiority for explaining the new creation has become so prevalent in theology is not only that modern science has made many of the older
more 'externally' oriented 'cosmic' appeals untenable, as Oliver Davies has
discussed at length above. It is just as much for the theological reason, especially in a certain way since Luther and then carried even further after Kant,
that human salvation or *redemption* has for theology become the quintessential

locus, the *sine qua non* of the divine self-disclosure to the world.[3] I will want to suggest instead – and without denying the absolute centrality of redemption in the purposes of revelation – that the more fundamental focus must again be on the divine righteousness which precedes human redemption. And I will also want to suggest that the degree to which this more fundamental orientation to the divine righteousness has faded from view is the degree to which the possibility of interpreting the new creation as something largely interior and faith-subjectivist has been able to occur.

We see the essential human relatedness of the new creation, for example, in the all-surpassing primacy that is accorded by Luther (and indeed by Bonhoeffer who follows him) to the doctrine of the justification of the sinner by faith alone: that is, not *first* to the divine righteousness *itself*, but first to the sinner being *made* righteous or upright through faith.[4] Or again, Schleiermacher's stipulation that *everything* in the Christian faith must be focused through Christ as the *Redeemer* can have the same effect (whether he himself intended this exactly or not), because the new creation is characterized here, accordingly, as a reality always and everywhere relating solely to human redemption and fallenness.[5] The same *essential* relatedness of the new creation *to humans* was seen above in certain kinds of kenotic approaches, such as some contemporary theologies of the cross, which went so far as to redefine the very meaning of the word 'God' as *most essentially* the 'Self-emptying One', in order to contain the 'logic' of the cross within a doctrinal system focused fundamentally on the redemption of human beings. Something similar occurs also in a different way in Kierkegaard's relation of the 'eternal' indispensably to human 'decision', as this is rooted in his own unique development of subjectivity.[6] Even Rahner leans in these directions in his 'Christology from an evolutionary perspective'. After finding human beings to be that in which 'the basic tendency of matter to discover itself in self-conscious mind [*Geist*] reaches its definitive breakthrough',[7] he then goes on to describe the incarnation as that in which this same 'self-transcendence of matter [in human subjectivity, reaches its] ultimate culmination'.[8] Indeed, for Rahner the very 'possibility' of creation itself is only a 'secondary possibility', deriving from the more 'primordial' or primary 'capacity' of God to become incarnate as a human being. The 'capacity' of God to become incarnate in human flesh, in other words, 'precedes' his 'capacity' (Rahner's words) to create the world.[9]

But it is Barth again, as Pannenberg recognizes, who (ironically) radicalizes this human centredness of revelation and the new creation to the highest degree. The irony here of course is that it was precisely the human centredness of nineteenth-century theology, and indeed what Barth perceived as the collapse there of theology into anthropology, which he was trying to overcome. This is by no means to say that Barth's theology itself collapses into anthropology. But it does collapse into a faith-subjectivism so severe that it can on certain basic levels work to a similar kind of effect, and we shall see a particularly startling example of this in a moment. The problem we are faced with on the Barthian view has two elements. The first difficulty proceeds from Barth's doctrinally analytical stipulation that revelation is a self-communication essentially in mental domains – from 'the divine reason [to] human reason'[10] – and not a causal communication to whole sensibly embodied human beings in the real empirical nexus. The problem that arises on this account is that in order for revelation to qualify as a genuine *communication*, it must necessarily involve the *conscious reception* of this in a *human mind* as this is enlivened by the Holy Spirit. For without receptive apprehension of the divine self-disclosure in an enlivened human consciousness, no genuine mental 'communication' – according to the very definition, analytically, of mental communication – will have taken place. And this means further that no *revelation* will have taken place, no new kingdom will have been announced, *except* as this involves also the reception of the communication *in the human mind* as this is enabled by the Holy Spirit.

This then brings us to the second element of the problem on the Barthian view. And in order to illuminate this, consider now the lengths to which Barth is willing to go in preserving at all costs the analyticity or full epistemic security of revelation in a way that doctrine can guarantee. For Barth finds himself willing to say even this: 'As a matter of fact, Jesus did not become revelation to all who met him but only a few ... *Revealing could obviously not be ascribed to his existence as such.*'[11] Now this is a very perplexing statement which, if thought through, yields what must surely be seen as highly unwelcome results. For surely we *must* be able to say that God was indeed really *there*, active and real and self-revealing in the mortal body of Jesus as he stood there before Pilate, even though Pilate did not recognize him as such. The eternal Logos was not 'absent' before Pilate in the body of Jesus Christ merely because Pilate was not able to acknowledge this. To the contrary, if we are to take the incarnational heart of the gospel with the required seriousness, surely we must be able to say that the eternal Logos was no *less* truly *there* in the human body of Jesus Christ before Pilate, who did not confess him as such, than he was truly there in the body of Jesus before Peter in his confession 'You are the Christ, the Son of the Living God' (Mt. 16.16). This, even though the divine efficacy of the exerted authority and power are radically different in the two confrontations. And it is important to recognize that it is only through the proper and genuinely incarnational preservation of the fundamentally causal-sensible (embodied) nature of God's self-disclosure on the real world that we are able to address this difficulty in the appropriate and required way. For on an appropriately causal and dynamic view, God's self-revelation in the world remains a genuine self-disclosure whether it is recognized or not. The considerable extent to which Barth still occupies a basic Hegelian view of 'reality' is especially evident here. But the broader point is to say that it is his tying of revelational disclosure so inextricably to its reception in the human mind (even though it is the Holy Spirit that 'enables' this) which has the effect of yielding in Barth what Pannenberg has called a 'dead end of faith subjectivism'.

However, I do not wish to be misunderstood here. For by moving the focus of the divine activity in the world to something antecedent to human redemption in the divine righteousness, I am by no means suggesting that human beings in the decision of faith do not know and encounter Jesus Christ *first* and fundamentally as their redeemer and saviour. I am only saying that the redemption that we encounter *first* in the decision of faith will under *theological* scrutiny subsequently come to be understood as demanding a different kind of ordering, through what MacKinnon, and Rowan Williams following him, call 'transcription': that is, that 'what we first know is the reality we subsequently come to know as derivative, transposed from what is prior'.[12] What this means in the present context is that it is precisely in encountering Jesus Christ first and supremely as the incarnate redeemer and saviour – and as such, as the bringer of the divine righteousness into human life – that we will also under theological questioning thereby come to see a truth which is 'prior'. What is this 'prior' truth? It is that Jesus Christ, as the 'Righteous One', as 'Lord of righteousness', has *in* that righteousness been filling everything in every way 'all along' from eternity – and this must mean his eternal presence in righteousness in the world even in those times before the earth was populated by humans – and further that 'in keeping with his promise we [can] look forward to a new heaven and a new earth, the home of righteousness' (2 Pet. 3.13).

In summary, all of this has been meant to demonstrate why any essentially 'internalist' or fundamentally faith-subjectivist view is insufficient to capture the 'not merely internal' reality of what is being proclaimed in 'the new' or the new creation. For any such faith-subjectivist view, which ties the new creation most fundamentally to the justification or redemption of the sinner by faith, can have the effect of making the new creation appear as a *product* or a result of the justification of the sinner by faith within the internal life of the believer, rather than the product or the effect of the divine righteousness acting causally in the world, a righteousness which is 'prior' to our justification and salvation, and is indeed the fundamental, not-merely-subjective ground of it.

2.2 'The new' is not 'the Wholly Other'

But how then *are* we to understand the reality of 'the new', if it is not solely or pre-eminently something internal to the believer's subjective consciousness which has somehow become enlivened in the decision of faith? Under normal circumstances, when we speak of something being 'not merely internal' to the perception of a human being, we will find ourselves unavoidably driven to using terms like 'external' or 'exterior' or 'objective' in order to characterize the reality of something which, in the language of a particular kind of philosophical realism, we might want to say 'exists independently of the perception of it'. But beyond the well-known epistemological pitfalls inherent in any such overly *simpliste* accounts of realism, there are also two basic theological reasons why any such objectivist or externalist characterization of the 'not merely internal' authority of the new creation is prohibited from the outset. The first, as Bonhoeffer has already rightly suggested, is that in the new creation 'outwardly, everything remains as it was'. The second is that 'the new' itself, qua *wholly* new, precisely prohibits any objectifying determination or classificatory identification as something merely 'external'. For anything externally 'determinable' or 'classifiable' would by that very operation already be something falling within a comparative ordering. And as something accessibly comparative, it would thereby be something already 'familiar', and hence not wholly new. We thus need to find a different way of attending to the demands of the new creation: a different way which resists apprehension in either internalist (subjectivist) or externalist (objectivist) terms. And in order to press to its full limit what is seeking expression here, let me now return to develop more expansively a theme that was broached preliminarily above.

To come directly to the point, 'the new' is *not* 'the other', whether configured as Barth's 'Wholly Other',[13] or as any phenomenological 'other' (or, for that matter, any of the other-related phenomenological terms such as 'gift' or 'surplus' or 'excess' or 'saturation'). Nor can 'the other' convey, *in any sense*, what 'the new' of the new creation in revelation announces. There are two fundamental reasons for this. The first is that 'the other' qua *alterity* is by its very designation *as* 'other', intrinsically still a *comparative* term, whereas 'the new', as the *wholly* new *ex nihilo* announced in revelation, cannot be apprehended in comparative terms of alterity at all. What this is saying, in short, is that God himself is for Christian theology today misapprehended in an important way when seen as the 'Wholly Other', and that God in his self-revelation must rather be apprehended theologically today as the 'Wholly New'. I will below explain more fully what this means and why it must be demanded of theology. But first let us consider the intrinsically comparative nature of 'the other' more closely, specifically now as Emmanuel Levinas is known to develop this with especial rigour.

Levinas deploys several mechanisms for conveying the 'radical alterity' he has in mind in his project of 'exteriority'. He speaks, for example, of (a) no 'common frontier' being available between 'the same' (the 'I') and 'the other'; or (b) that it is 'the other' itself who 'calls out' of the perceiving subject the proper relation of responsibility towards 'the other'; or again (c) that 'the other' has 'ontological priority' over 'the same', and so on. Levinas seeks to push this to even more radical lengths when he speaks of the '*absolute* remoteness' of *God's* transcendence as 'Other'. In his own words:

> God is not simply the 'first other', the 'other par excellence', or the 'absolutely other', but other than other, other otherwise, other with an alterity prior to the alterity of the other, prior to the ethical bond with another and different from every neighbour, transcendent to the point of absence, to the possible confusion with the stirring of the *there is*.[14]

But now even for all its radicality, the fact remains that by its sheer designation as 'other', the other is unable to sustain its very meaning and intelligibility *as* 'other' except as a *comparative* designation, which in the end always in some way refers back to 'the same'. 'The other' is *intrinsically* comparative, and indeed Levinas himself has no difficulty admitting this point.[15]

But now 'the new' of the new creation, as the *wholly* new of the coming righteousness, or as the *wholly* new of the coming kingdom of God, in which *everything* old has passed away, cannot come to expression in any such language of alterity or 'over-againstness' at all. This, again, for the simple reason that any language of alterity is already inherently comparative and thus unable to express the wholly new. But here we come to a serious problem. For there is of course a sense in which, in our phenomenal or intentional or thinking-consciousness, it will be possible, indeed even *necessary,* to set 'the new' as something comparable *over-against* 'the old'. Or equally, within the present context, it may be objected that by insisting as I am that 'the new' is *not* 'the other', I am thereby treating 'the new' itself comparatively, precisely by contrasting it to 'the other'.

However, such an objection would already be fundamentally to misconstrue the whole nature of what is at issue here. In fact, it would reinforce one of the most central theological points I am trying to make in all of this. It is a point that I have already identified preliminarily in the previous chapter, and which I will be trying to bring to an initial kind of completion below. Stated most basically, it is as follows. 'The new' can *never* be theologically apprehended at its *origin* by our conceptually representational consciousness, which is to say our comparative consciousness *at all*. Or in short, it cannot be apprehended by our 'thinking consciousness' *at all*. Now this may seem a very strange claim to make. For how can 'the new' announced in revelation be – as it must be – a source of *theological* attentiveness at all if it cannot be apprehended at its origin by conceptually representational or noetic (thinking) means? The most basic answer to this can only be given on the briefest terms here, and must await fuller development elsewhere. But the answer in short is that theological orientation to the new in revelation *ex nihilo* will require a reinvigoration of *practical* consciousness. For practical consciousness – as this comes to development for example in Aristotle, Aquinas or Kant – is precisely not at bottom a 'thinking' consciousness or an intentional-representational consciousness at all, in which the use of reason is concerned with the right ordering of concepts. It is rather a willing consciousness, where the use of reason is concerned with the right ordering of desires. Yet our practical consciousness as such will be found to admit no less rigorously of a genuine rational ordering and attentiveness than our thinking or conceptual consciousness. We cannot go into this further at present except to say that attentiveness to practical reason as a genuine discipline of intellectual attentiveness has almost entirely lapsed over the past two centuries, once again under the influence of idealism and also contemporary phenomenology, both of which collapse the practical fully into the conceptual. Indeed, virtually all current discussions in 'ethics' – whether meta-ethics or prescriptive ethics or even applied ethics – remain essentially intentional-referential or discursively rational exercises which deal with ethical concerns as 'themes' on the level of concepts, rather than in genuinely practically rational terms on the level of desire and will. I have addressed all of this at considerable length elsewhere[16] and cannot proceed with it any further here except again simply to emphasize the vital need for a reinvigoration of practical consciousness and practical reason for theological purposes.

For the present, however, let me just try to explain more fully the foregoing statement that 'the new' cannot be theologically apprehended at its origin by our conceptually representational or 'thinking consciousness' *at all*. There are two fundamental reasons for this. The first, as discussed in the previous chapter, is that revelation confronts us originally with the authority precisely of a divine *causality* exerted towards sensibly embodied human beings in the middle of life in space and time, and not originally as a 'miraculous' representational *referent* or 'concrete concept' communicated directly to the mind. The new, at its origin *ex nihilo*, is precisely not a conceptual or representational communication but a causal one. The second is to repeat what has already been stated: namely that discursive or intentional consciousness *just is* 'differentiating' consciousness or 'determining' consciousness, which is to say intrinsically *comparative* consciousness, and any 'newness' encountered here will therefore already always be a 'differentiated new' and as such another 'comparative new', and not the *wholly* new in which everything old has passed away. We can illuminate further what is at stake here by turning analogously again to the demands of the *ex nihilo* in the creational account. For the same basic limitations of conceptual or thinking consciousness for theologically apprehending 'the new' will be encountered in the creational account as well.

Consider then that in the Christian account of creation *ex nihilo* of the present heavens and the earth, one of the most important functions of the '*ex nihilo*' demand, or the 'out of nothing' demand, is to ensure that there is no *conjunctive* connection that could bring Creator and creation into a comparative ordering or a comparative continuum. The reason that any conjunctive connection must be rejected is to ensure that the world is never seen pantheistically to be identified with God, or even panentheistically as a kind of appendage of the Creator. (This, even though we must equally be able to say that God in Christ fills everything in every way, which is precisely the problem before us.) The error of the conjunctive relation between Creator and creation as such will in general be readily acknowledged and granted. For even though we may occasionally speak loosely of the relation between God and the world, or between Creator and creation, as a relation between 'God' and 'all that is not God', we cannot mean this in any strictly conjunctive or quantitatively totalizing terms. For beyond its doctrinal difficulties, this would already commit the logical error of supposing implicitly that something could be 'added' to the non-finite reality of God, as if to yield merely something like an overall increase in 'quantity'. And this of course would already make God not-God for it would implicitly view God from the outset as something essentially quantitative, and thus as something finite, which is to say, as essentially already a component *within* the created order, rather than as the Creator *of* that order. Any 'unity' of God and the world, which we may, for example, speak of as having been achieved through the reconciliation of the world to God in Jesus Christ, can thus never be merely the conjunctive unity of a 'totality'.[17]

But this is only half the matter. For even while the error of the conjunctive connection may as such be readily granted, there is a different kind of mistake that can much more easily befall theological thinking in another direction. For it is exactly in the interests of *avoiding* the error of relating God and the world *con*junctively and pantheistically that there can be a strong natural tendency to want to speak instead of the relation between Creator and creation in the opposing terms of *dis*junction. Now it is precisely this relation of disjunction which is always at bottom involved in any talk of transcendence as 'the other'. But something important is implicitly forgotten as such. What is forgotten is that disjunction is no less a mechanism that brings entities into a comparative relation than is conjunction, even if the disjunctive comparison comes to expression in terms of opposition or over-againstness. And as we have seen, this contrastingly comparative or differentiational character of disjunction is only magnified all the more when it is 'radicalized' through the language of the 'absolutely remote', or the 'otherwise than other', 'the Wholly Other', and so on. For to 'radicalize' is to exponentialize, and thus not to dissolve but indeed to magnify. It is for this reason that in discussing 'the new' I have consistently avoided speaking of it as the 'radically' new, which would still be a comparative or differentiated 'new', and have used instead the language of the *wholly* new. Or to state this in another way, the mechanism of *dis*junction is no less a function of reason as intrinsically a *faculty of unity* or a faculty of coherence than is *con*junction. For reason will still by its very nature look at disjuncts or opposites as essentially connected *by virtue* of their disjunction or opposition. And this is why even the disjunctive language of 'the other' or 'trace of the other' still ultimately collapses inevitably into a totalizing relation.

But now 'the new' as the *wholly* new, in which the old has entirely passed away, is not an 'other' even in any kind of comparatively conceptual *dis*junctive relation to the old. 'The new' is rather that which is alive with the resurrected Christ, just as the old is that which is dead with the dead Christ, and there can be no *conceptual* continuity between the two whatsoever, even as a disjunctive 'continuity'. Bonhoeffer is thus exactly right in his own connection of the new creation with the doctrine of creation *ex nihilo*.

> The dead Jesus Christ of Good Friday and the resurrected kurios of Easter Sunday – *that* is creation out of nothing, creation from the beginning. The fact that Christ was dead did not provide the possibility of his resurrection but its impossibility; it was nothing itself, it was the nihil negativum. There is absolutely no transition, no continuum between the dead Christ and the resurrected Christ but the freedom of God that in the beginning created God's work out of nothing.[18]

2.3 'The new' as *generative*

This now leads to the one statement – and the only statement – that we can and must make in a 'positive' voice about 'the new' of the new creation as announced in revelation: one positive statement from which then several other derivative statements can be shown to follow. It is this. The new of the new creation is not the *radically alterative*, not the radically disjunctive *to* all life and present real (caused) existence. It is rather the *wholly generative ex nihilo* from *within* all life and present real existence, just as the 'original' creation of the heavens and the earth *ex nihilo* is the wholly generative *of* all life and present real existence. Or again, the new creation is no less creation out of nothing than the relation of 'the dead Jesus Christ of Good Friday and the resurrected kurios of Easter Sunday ... is creation out of nothing'.

But how does this help us forward theologically? In a word, it doesn't. In fact it stops theological thinking fully and unequivocally in its tracks. And this means also that it stops even doctrine fully and unequivocally in its tracks. Why? Because the utterly generative character of the divine causality in creation *ex nihilo*, in resurrection, and in the new creation announced in revelation, is the creative generation of the very possibility even of theology or doctrine itself. It is therefore a creative generation which can never be subsumed within theology because it is theology's own generating ground and source. But there is another way of expressing this by looking at the inherent character of theology itself. The point is that as a discursive or thinking discipline, the intrinsic need and nature of theological questioning is to ask fundamentally about questions of *meaning*. Christian doctrine, and theology more broadly, is inherently oriented towards questions of meaning, and it operates on the basis of such questions. And this brings us precisely to the problem from the other direction. For it will quickly become obvious that at the *generative source* or at the divinely *causal origin* of revelation or of the new creation we can ask no such question of 'meaning' at all. Why? Because any question of meaning is already by definition a request for comparative differentiation, for meaning *as* 'signification' is intrinsically both comparative and differentiating. More than this, any question of meaning is already by definition a request for a conceptually *semantic* ordering within a linguistic framework of signifiers and signifieds, of 'intentionalities' and 'referents'. And any such apprehension of the new, in its wholly generative character, has already been entirely excluded through the foregoing discussions.

We can illuminate this further by looking once again at the demand of creation *ex nihilo* and at the utter failure of meaning structures to capture or comprehend what is expressed in this demand. The point here is that it is impossible for us really even to know what we *mean* when we speak of the creation of the spatio-temporal order as a genuine *origination* or 'beginning' of that order. The reason that we cannot know what we 'mean' when we speak of the 'beginning' of time and the 'beginning' of space is that we will always *have to* understand such a 'beginning' as an origination which takes place within a 'time' *prior to* the 'beginning' of time, or a 'space' *beyond* the 'beginning' of space. It is utterly impossible for us to escape this, as the briefest mental exercise in trying to do so will make immediately clear.[19] And we are reminded as such of Bonhoeffer's statement cited earlier: that 'we cannot speak of the beginning. Where the beginning begins, there our thinking stops; there it comes to an end.'[20]

All of this demands something vital. It demands that we must reject unequivocally and absolutely any suggestion that the divinely generative causal authority in either creation *ex nihilo* or revelation *ex nihilo* declares itself as anything like the 'ultimately significant'. For beyond the fact, as Kant has shown, that we ourselves can have utterly no idea what the phrase 'ultimately significant' itself could possibly 'mean', the expression itself on closer scrutiny is revealed to be an outright and self-defeating contradiction. For in its very designation as 'ultimately *significant*', it would still, in Derrida's words, be something which *qua* significant 'refers *beyond* itself', and as such could no longer be 'ultimate'.[21] In the face of the wholly new in revelation, therefore – in the face, that is, of the causally generative source *ex nihilo* of the divine creativity in the new creation – our most impassioned questions of 'meaning' once again utterly disintegrate and vaporize, 'are thrown back upon themselves and lose their strength in spray and foam'.

We can now bring this whole discussion back to its starting point in this subsection and say the following. If there *is* any way that the theological arrival at its own causally generative and conceptually intractable ground and limit in 'the new' can help theological questioning 'forward' at all, it is by pushing it backward–by pushing it backward *from* its intrinsic need to ask about questions of *meaning*, and backward *to* a prior moment, a moment at which such questions must cease entirely; a moment at which it learns to ask instead, more humbly, simply about ways of being *attentive* to the divinely causal generativity in the world. For as we shall see in the final section below, there are different ways of being rationally attentive than merely meaning-oriented forms of attentiveness.

But prior to building towards that destination through a certain engagement with similar themes in Rowan Williams, let me add importantly that nothing in the above is meant to deny that theology can and must be meaningful. It is only to say that its meaning, indeed the very meaningfulness of Christian doctrine itself, is always *derived from* the dynamic and causally generative reality of revelation which comes prior, and that it is not conversely our ability to place revelation into meaning structures that authenticates revelation. And this then brings us back again to a statement which has by now become almost thematic: it is not doctrine which for theology today guarantees the validity of, or gives authority to, the generative reality of the new creation announced in revelation. It is rather conversely the generative reality of revelation in the real world of space and time which grounds and authenticates doctrine.

Now this ordering between revelation and doctrine (or theology) is absolutely vital, and can be illuminated further by attending to similar concerns voiced by Rowan Williams across a pair of essays.[22] Williams is likewise concerned, in a discussion of 'the finality of Christ', to reject any account of this finality fundamentally in terms of 'significance' or 'meaning', especially as this is apt to be interpreted in an ultimate or totalizing sense as 'the meaning of meaning' (or what I have spoken of above as 'ultimate significance'). He wants rather to place the final authority of revelation – exactly as we have been arguing – in its fundamentally *generative* character in the real world of sensible human embodiment today. Indeed, Williams is one of the few current theologians who remain willing to push this with boldness in the directions being

suggested here. Williams ventures to make the courageous claim that the real
authority, even of the 'foundational events' themselves – the incarnation, death
and resurrection of Jesus Christ – cannot be authorized or held secure merely by
doctrine, or dogmatics or apologetics. Or conversely, it is not doctrine or
dogmatics or apologetics which is the most fundamental attestation to the
reality and truth of the foundational events in Jesus Christ as real historical
events. The foundational events themselves are for Williams rather authenti-
cated most fundamentally in the way that, *as* foundational events, they are *still
generative* as a present reality within the embodied life of particular persons and
communities in space and time today.

But it is important to note as such that what will be suggested in this
amplification of Williams is something quite different from, for example, the
attempt by Rudolf Bultmann also to 'authenticate' the gospel by seeking to
bring it into the 'present', even though one should not be too hard on Bultmann himself in this respect. For in a way it was Bultmann who, despite the
unsustainability of his project in more fundamental ways, provided an
important impetus for twentieth-century theology to begin thinking again
along these lines, and he articulated the problem with a kind of critical urgency
largely unparalleled among his contemporaries. It is likewise important, in
fairness to Bultmann, to recognize that he was not advocating his project of
demythologization simply for its own sake. The purpose of demythologization
was rather to explore ways in which the incarnation and the cross can once again
become tangible as present realities, which he saw that they must be. Nevertheless, the 'presence' actually accomplished by Bultmann's theology – in
his identification of revelation so exclusively with proclamation, and in the
unavoidable subjectivism of an 'existential encounter' which followed from this
– was in the end not a *real* incarnational (embodied) presence at all, but again a
merely ideal or mentally internal one, despite its Heideggerian 'existential'
appeals. It thus achieved a merely pseudo-presence – at least by any genuinely
incarnational measure – which could not help but lead directly back again into
what Pannenberg has called a 'dead end of faith-subjectivism'. By contrast,
what is being proposed here, in an amplification of Williams, by no means seeks
either to 'demythologize' the real empirical historicity of the incarnate Logos in
Jesus of Nazareth under the reign of Caesar Augustus, or to put into question
the indispensable authority of these events *as* empirically real. In fact it seeks to
fortify their authority as such in its explicit recognition that the *way* these
events must authenticate themselves *as* the foundational events in empirical
history, which they really were some two millennia ago, is most fundamentally
through their continuing generative power at the centre of life even today – or
in Williams' words, through the way that they are still able to bring about 'the
creative renewal of persons and communities' today[23] – and not most fundamentally through any authentications which can be guaranteed systematically
by doctrine or theology within frameworks of conceptual resolution. Indeed,
Williams will want to bring this presently generative kind of authentication to
bear even more forcefully on human life in the present by locating 'the creative

and generative power' of revelation 'in the form of *grace*' which is always 'creative grace'.[24] So let us look at this a bit more carefully.

We have been asking, along with Williams, about the 'finality of Christ' and, together with this, also about the finality and authority by which revelation declares and authenticates itself originally as a present reality for human beings today. And in attending to this finality, we have found ourselves again and again directed away from questions of 'ultimate meaning' or 'ultimate significance', and rather towards questions of creativity and generativity *ex nihilo*, which is to say towards questions of the divine causality *ex nihilo*, which precedes and grounds any and all questions of meaning. But I want now also to direct all of this further to a certain kind of conclusion, a conclusion which will find its destination inevitably again in the divine righteousness. And in order to pursue this, let me expand somewhat more deeply on the way that these two points (finality as 'ultimate meaning' versus finality as generativity) come to more exact expression within Williams himself. First, Williams agrees (quoting Jacques Pohier) that in Jesus Christ 'we do not have omnipotence of meaning', and that in Jesus Christ 'we do not proclaim to you the totality of meaning'.[25] Or more fully – and now a certain proviso is allowed – insofar as we might persist in asking about the 'universal significance'[26] of Jesus Christ at all, we can only do so within the careful confines of a thoroughly 'kenotic' apprehension. Or in Williams' exact words (now quoting Gerard Loughlin), we can only do so in accordance with the explicit recognition that 'at the heart of the Christian mystery is the full emptiness, the divine absence enacted and disclosed in the life, death and resurrection of Jesus Christ'.[27] Or again, returning to Pohier, insofar as we might persist in speaking of Christ as 'ultimately significant' or as the 'meaning of meaning' at all, we can say only this: that 'we have nothing to proclaim but Jesus dead and risen; we have only this news which has no value as a response to everything or as the totality of meaning, but has value in itself'.[28] In sum, the question of 'the finality of Christ' can never be answered by appeals to 'ultimate significance' or the 'totality of meaning' at all. Or at the very least, if we persist in pursuing the question of Christ's finality with respect to its 'meaning', it will only return an answer which is uncompromisingly 'kenotic' in form, and thus utterly disappointing for any of our normal demands and expectations of meaning. For it points always to a 'meaning' which is 'ultimate' only in virtue of its 'full emptiness' as anything totalizing or resolutional.

But it is here that we come to a certain vital feature of the *way* that Williams' approach is uncompromisingly 'kenotic', in contradistinction to Eberhard Jüngel's kenotic approach within doctrine, as discussed earlier. For kenosis in Williams is precisely not viewed as an opportunity for semantic resolution within structures of meaning, even doctrinal meaning. I have said in the previous chapter that Williams, along with Schleiermacher, Bonhoeffer, Rahner or MacKinnon and others, is no less kenotic in emphasis than thinkers such as Jüngel or Moltmann. But the crucial point, as it was stated there, was that for the former group, the finality and authority of God's self-emptying in the incarnation and on the cross is not a finality which, as a doctrinal end-station, can from the outset logically guarantee the analytical or semantic (meaningful) resolution to its problems within theology per se. It is rather set out as the finality of a fundamentally intractable and defining *problem* for theological questioning, indeed as the very source and ground of theological questioning. Or again, to recall the point exactly as it was stated there: the *reality* of kenosis – that is, kenosis in its real causal embodiment in Jesus Christ on the cross in empirical history – in no way *solves* the theological problem of God's relation to the world on the cross; it rather *defines* this problem in its full and sheer intractability as a finality of non-resolution. And it defines it moreover in the unsurpassable declaration that it is indeed the eternal and immortal one, who is before all things and by whom all things were created, who dies bodily on the cross, and who thereby with real causally dynamic, which is to say with real effective power, achieves the real reconciliation of the world to God. There is therefore no doctrinal resolution being advanced here in Williams' non-semantic appeal to kenosis. And we are in an important way given even further evidence of this basic commitment when, at the end of the essay in question, Williams cautions that we must never allow ourselves to forget what 'the news' of which Pohier speaks is 'news *of*', or what the news revealed and proclaimed in the self-emptying Christ is 'news *of*'. So let us now follow this through a bit more carefully, specifically with regard to what the news *is* 'news of'. For when we do so we will find ourselves directed back squarely again to the foundational observations on the divine righteousness with which this chapter began.

To say as Williams does that 'news' as *news* is always 'news of', or that we cannot possibly be attentive to the former without having already apprehended the latter, immediately implies two things. It implies first that news *qua* news, or gospel *as* gospel, or revelation *as* revelation, cannot be separated from its *content,* and it also implies equally that the gospel news is intrinsically oriented to its *purpose* – i.e., to what it is 'news *of*'. Now with regard to the former, we have above already demonstrated at length that the fundamental 'content' of the gospel news, or what the news revealed in Jesus Christ is 'news of', is 'a righteousness which comes from God': 'In the gospel a righteousness from God is revealed, a righteousness that is by faith from first to last' (Rom. 1.17). And we will now find exactly the same stipulation being made with regard to the 'news of' in terms of its purpose.

We can show this with especial clarity and force by returning specifically again to Williams' two themes – (a) of the finality of Christ as having its 'form' the 'full emptiness' of Christ in kenosis; and (b) of the generative character of revelation as having its 'form' in grace. So then, with regard to the first theme, let us ask: what is the 'purpose', the 'wherefore' or the 'so that', of the news declared kenotically in the message of the self-emptying God? It is this: 'He was [kenotically] made to be sin who knew no sin *so that* we might become *the righteousness of God* in him' (2 Cor. 5.21). Or again 'He himself [kenotically] bore our sins in his body on the cross, *so that*, free from sin, we might *live for righteousness*' (1 Pet. 2.24). And likewise, with respect to the second theme, let us ask: what is the 'purpose', the 'wherefore' or the 'so that' of grace, and thus, according to Williams' discussion, the necessary completion for any discussion of the generative character of revelation? It is, once again, '*so that* ... grace might *reign through righteousness* to bring eternal life through Jesus Christ our Lord' (Rom. 5.21).

3. Pneumatology as Fundamental Theology

All of this now leads to two results which will be indispensable for attending – as this chapter throughout has been aiming to do – to what the fundamentally generative character of the new creation and of revelation demands of theology today. The first is that at every turn we find ourselves directed back to the divine righteousness as both the content and the purpose, the origin and the end, of 'the new' as announced in the revelation of Jesus Christ. For again, to go back to Williams' terms: What is the 'finality of Christ' as it is declared kenotically in the 'full emptiness' which is 'enacted and disclosed in the life, death and resurrection of Jesus Christ'? It is as we have seen the righteousness which comes from God. And what is the 'creative and generative power [of revelation as it] is shown in the form of grace'? It is again the righteousness which comes from God. But this now leads to a second result, which also confronts us in the foregoing discussions. Let me just state this second result straightforwardly before going on to explicate and defend it further.

If there is any way that the divine causality in the world – the present reality of God in the world, the new creation – can at its *generative source ex nihilo* (and not *only* in its 'effects') become a focus of theological attention at all, then it will always and only be through an orientation first to the *will of God* in and for the world, which is to say through an orientation first to the *purposes* of God in and for the world; and this means further through an orientation to the *making real* of the righteousness of God in the world. Or to put this in somewhat different terms, before theology can become oriented to the 'being' of God at all as the 'source' of the divine causality and of the new creation *ex nihilo*, it must first or fundamentally become oriented to the *will* of God. But this needs now to be explained further, and we can press the necessity of it in several ways.

Most importantly, the scriptures themselves clearly demand it. For example, the scriptures do not say that in Jesus Christ God has made known to us the mystery of his 'being', but rather quite explicitly that 'he has made known to us the mystery of his *will*, according to his good pleasure that he set forth in Christ' (Eph. 1.9). Or again, in the Fourth Gospel, Jesus does not say that anyone who resolves to contemplate the 'being' of God will know whether Jesus' own teaching is from God, but rather that 'anyone who resolves to do the *will* of God will *know* whether the teaching is from God or whether I am speaking on my own' (Jn 7. 17). Similarly in Ananias' anointing of Paul, the commissioning declaration is not that Paul has been called to righteousness through the knowledge of the mystery of God's 'being', but rather that 'the God of our ancestors has chosen you to know his *will* [and *thereby*] to *see the*

Righteous One and to hear his own voice; for you will be his witness to all the world of what you have seen and heard' (Acts 22.14, 15). Or again in Romans we are exhorted to be transformed into Christ's image, not so that we may be able to discern something first about the referential 'meaning' of God's 'being', but rather so as to 'be transformed by the renewing of your minds, so that you may discern what is the *will* of God – what is good and acceptable and perfect', as this is measured against the divine righteousness (Rom. 12.2).

The same requirement for theology to become oriented to its subject matter (revelation *ex nihilo*) through attention to the will of God is just as evident in statements concerning the new creation and the coming kingdom of God. The prayer which Christ taught us does not say 'Your kingdom come, your "being" be known', but rather 'Your kingdom come, your *will* be done, on earth as it is in heaven' (Mt. 6.10). Or again, 'not everyone who says to me, "Lord, Lord", will enter the kingdom of heaven, but only one who does the *will* of my Father in heaven' (Mt. 7.21). Moreover, it is precisely this which is the source of 'the boldness that we have in him, that if we ask anything in accordance with his *will* [and not in accordance with an intentional meaning-attentiveness first to his 'being'], he hears us' (1 Jn 5.14). Indeed, it is by the same accordance that we ourselves are declared to be the 'brothers and sisters' of the incarnate one: 'for whoever does the *will* of my Father in heaven is my brother and sister and mother' (Mt. 12.50; see also Heb. 2.11–18). And this is reflected again in what Jesus says even of himself: i.e., that even his own 'nourishment' was found first not in an intentional or meaning-orientedness to God's 'being', but rather that 'my food is to *do the will* of him who sent me and to complete his work' (Jn 4.34).

Now this demand of the scriptures themselves – i.e., that theological orientation to the present reality of God in the world must be first and fundamentally to the will of God and not first to the 'being' of God – means something crucial and decisive. It means that theology must be an *ethics* before it is a *dogmatics* or before it is doctrine. Or somewhat more accurately, it means that Christian dogmatics or Christian doctrine must be grounded foundationally in a 'Christian ethics'. Why exactly? For two reasons. First, because the foundational question of all genuinely Christian ethics must always be nothing other than this: 'What is the will of God?'. And secondly, as we shall see more fully in a moment, because it is Christian ethics which by its very definition *in* this foundational question can have as its only ultimate source of concern precisely the *'making real'* of the *righteousness* of God in the world today.

Or we can put this second point also in somewhat different terms. One of the main underlying concerns in both of these chapters has been to show that it is not doctrine or systematic theology that 'authenticates' revelation within a framework of resolution, but rather conversely that it is *revelation* which as a *generative* present reality must be the ground and source of all doctrine and theology. Now if indeed this is the right ordering, that is, if revelation does indeed precede doctrine and not vice versa, then we are forced also to say the following. Because it is 'Christian ethics' which, in its orientation first to the will of God, has as its fundamental source of concern precisely the *reality today* of the *righteousness* which comes from God, or more exactly the 'becoming real' of God's self-revelation as such: therefore it is 'Christian ethics' which must today take the place of a 'fundamental theology', to which all secondary doctrinal treatments must then always refer back, or within which they must be grounded. I emphasize 'today' because in the past different kinds of cosmologies, as Oliver Davies has explained above, might still have permitted a different kind of grounding. But with the decline of those cosmologies, it is left to Christian ethics, which has as its source of concern the generative character of God's self-revelation as the present reality of the divine righteousness, to take the place of fundamental theology today.

But there is now one further and final element which must be added to this to bring it to a proper completion. And in order to introduce that, let me draw our attention to something strikingly similar that Bonhoeffer is attempting to achieve in his *Ethics*. In the first place, Bonhoeffer takes exactly this position when, after locating 'Christian ethics' most essentially as a response to the question, 'What is the will of God?', he goes on to make a basic distinction between 'Christian ethics' and 'Christian dogmatics' which can be paraphrased as follows. 'Just as the subject matter of *Christian dogmatics* is the *truth* of God's reality revealed in Christ ... so the subject matter of *Christian ethics* is the *becoming real* of God's reality revealed in Christ among God's creatures.'[29] But Bonhoeffer now also expands on this further in an important way by saying that 'the place that in all other ethics is marked out by the antithesis between ought and is, idea and realization, motive and work, is occupied in Christian ethics by the relation between *reality* [the foundational event itself] and *becoming real*', which he then goes on to qualify as most fundamentally 'the relation between Jesus Christ [reality] and the Holy Spirit [becoming real]'.[30]

There is, however, one thing that Bonhoeffer does not do, yet which indeed he must do, or which these very statements implicitly compel him to do. And his *Ethics* as a whole becomes in fact heavily burdened by this omission, as it struggles throughout to address its own initial and formative questions, yet never really succeeds in doing so, as provocative and brilliant as the book is in less basic ways. What Bonhoeffer does not do is to carry all of this through to its necessary completion, and to treat 'Christian ethics' fundamentally within the framework of a *pneumatology*. For it is precisely in the essential 'from below' focus of Christian ethics on the *becoming real* of the reality of God in the world that it will become ineluctably interwoven with pneumatology. Why? Because pneumatology has nothing less than exactly the same concern 'from above'. Christian ethics is thus never properly engaged unless it is engaged pneumatologically, and pneumatology is never addressed correctly unless it is addressed *first* as a Christian ethics.

So where has this new emphasis on the 'making real' of God's self-revelation in the world brought us then with regard to our original operative question as stated at the conclusion of the previous chapter? That question, we will recall, was as follows: 'What does it mean for theological questioning that it is not at the limits of cognition on the margins of intellection, but at the dynamically causal limits of sensibility or sensible embodiment in the *centre of life*, that we must encounter Christian transcendence as a present reality in space and time *today*, or that we must encounter revelation as the divine causality in the world today?'

We can answer this directly now by way of posing a different kind of question. The question is this. What is it – according to the command of grace itself – that is required of us as we orient ourselves to God's self-revelation and 'the new', not first as a *referent* for our intentional or thinking-guiding consciousness with regard to the 'being' of God, but first as a *demand* on our willing and action-guiding consciousness with regard to the *will* of God? Or what is this 'making real' more exactly, which is demanded by grace itself? Stated directly in the Pauline language of Romans, it is expressed once again in nothing less than the command to 'offer the *parts of your body* to God as *instruments of righteousness*' (Rom. 6.13), that is, the righteousness which comes from God. Indeed in even stronger language, the command of unmerited grace itself is 'to offer the parts of your body . . . in *slavery to righteousness*' (Rom. 6.19), that is, to the righteousness which comes from God, so that in *this* way, and at the centre of this *present* life, 'grace might *reign through righteousness*' (Rom. 5.21). Or to state this also in its necessary broader 'cosmic' context we can say the following. It is as we, in our *sensible embodiment* in space and time, become agents of the divine righteousness through the command of grace, that the reality of God is 'made real' *today* in the world of human agency, endeavour and self-understanding at the centre of life. This, just as the divine righteousness is *already* real throughout the infinity of 'the rest' of the cosmic created order, ever since the creation of the world, and just as it will reach its ultimate reality and finality in the new heavens and the new earth which is 'the home of righteousness'. At every point, therefore, the answer to the question of the 'making real' through the command of grace leads us inexorably back again to the righteousness which comes from God.

There is thus a kind of 'participation' which is demanded here. Although we must be very quick to add as such that it is wholly unlike a different kind of 'participation' that is often advocated in theology today, as for example in the work of John Milbank. Milbank advocates a 'participation in the mind of God' through a certain kind of cognitive 'illumination', according to which both revelation and reason are already 'participatory' in the divine intellect itself, and within which 'revelation itself is but a higher measure of such illumination'.[31] Now my objection here is of course not to the idea that revelation and reason are conjoined, as clearly they must be. The objection is rather that the 'participation' which occurs here still does so entirely abstractly and marginally within intellection, and not at the centre of embodied life which is the real and living locus of the Church itself. Indeed not only this, but in this particular instance (in Milbank) it is restricted to a special 'intellectual intuition' of only a few, or more fully, to the intellectual intuition of a certain kind of rare 'prophetically' discriminating mind, which then also opens the way for illumination to others.[32] The whole emphasis on 'participation' in this direction therefore remains fully within a kind of idealized and even gnostic abstraction.[33]

In fundamental contrast to this, the 'participation' of which *we* are speaking, the participation in the *making real* of the reality of God at the centre of life, is nothing less than the demand that the *parts of our physical bodies* are to become *instruments* today of the righteousness which comes from God, in the real history of sensibly embodied life in space and time. The fundamental contrast can therefore be put in the following way. It is not first as discursive or intuitive 'participants' in the mind of God, or even first as discursive or intuitive 'hearers of the word' – necessary and vital as these may be – that we become most fundamentally oriented to God as a present reality. It is rather much more as physically embodied 'instruments of righteousness' that, as Oliver Davies says above, the Spirit sets us today, through a 're-establishment' of the life of our senses, 'into a new relation with the living body of Christ'.

What remains still to be undertaken is to work out what such a 'Christian ethics', based in a pneumatology, must be. What is a 'Christian ethics' which is focused not first through the faculty of conceptual consciousness with attention to 'the deep things of God', but first in attention to the faculty of desire and practical consciousness with regard to the will of God? While this is beyond our present scope, nevertheless as we venture to pursue such an enterprise, we can be assured, through 'the boldness we have in him' (1 Jn 5.14; Eph. 3.12), that Jesus Christ, and the kingdom of God he announces, is truly and real-ly among us in the world as the righteousness which comes from God, especially as we become 'instruments' of that righteousness. Or in other words, we may boldly affirm what Christ himself as the 'King of Righteousness' demands that we affirm, in Mt. 25.34–40:

> Then the king will say to those at his right hand, 'Come, you that are blessed by my Father, inherit the kingdom prepared for you from the foundation of the world; for I was hungry and you gave me food, I was thirsty and you gave me something to drink, I was a stranger and you welcomed me, I was naked and you gave me clothing, I was sick and you took care of me, I was in prison and you visited me.' Then the righteous will answer him, 'Lord, when was it that we saw you hungry and gave you food, or thirsty and gave you something to drink? And when was it that we saw you a stranger and welcomed you, or naked and gave you clothing? And when was it that we saw you sick or in prison and visited you?' And the king will answer them, 'Truly I tell you, just as you did it to one of the least of these … you did it to me.'

The 'boldness' we can affirm in light of this, with regard to the reality of God in the world, the Godness of God at the centre of life is fully consonant with what is affirmed in this passage. For Christ does not say that inasmuch as you have done it unto the least of these, it will be *'as if'* you had done it unto me; but rather that inasmuch as you have done it unto the least of these, you *have* done it *unto me.*

Notes

1 Karl Barth, *Church Dogmatics* I.1 (Edinburgh: T&T Clark, 1975, p. 315) (hereafter CD).
2 See Bonhoeffer's similar extended discussion of this in *Creation and Fall* (Minneapolis: Fortress, 1997, pp. 88–92, 122–5).
3 See Wolfhart Pannenberg's excellent brief account of this in the introduction to his *Anthropology in Theological Perspective* (Philadelphia: Westminster Press, 1985, pp. 11–23).
4 See e.g., Dietrich Bonhoeffer, *Ethics* (Minneapolis: Fortress, 2005, pp. 146ff).
5 See e.g., Friedrich Schleiermacher, *The Christian Faith* (Edinburgh: T&T Clark, 1948, pp. 52ff).
6 See e.g., Søren Kierkegaard, *Philosophical Fragments* (Princeton: Princeton University Press, 1986, pp. 129ff).
7 Karl Rahner, *Foundations of Christian Faith* (New York: Crossroad, 1978, p. 181).
8 *Foundations of Christian Faith*, p. 197.
9 *Foundations of Christian Faith*, pp. 222–3.
10 CD I.1, pp. 132, 135.
11 CD I.1, p. 323.
12 Rowan Williams, *On Christian Theology* (Oxford: Blackwell, 2000, p. 161).
13 See e.g., Karl Barth, *Epistle to the Romans* (Oxford: Oxford University Press, 1965, p. 445).
14 Emmanuel Levinas, *Collected Philosophical Papers* (The Hague: Martinus Nijhoff, 1987, pp. 165–6).
15 See e.g., *In the Time of the Nations* (Bloomington: Indiana University Press, 1994, pp 181–2). I am indebted to Leora Batnitzky's excellent book *Leo Strauss and Emmanuel Levinas* (Cambridge: Cambridge University Press, 2006) for directing me to this reference.
16 Paul D. Janz, *The Command of Grace: Foundations for a Theology at the Centre of Life* (Edinburgh, New York: T&T Clark, forthcoming 2008).
17 I discuss this at considerable length in my forthcoming book *The Command of Grace*.
18 Dietrich Bonhoeffer, *Schöpfung und Fall* (München: Christian Kaiser Verlag, 1989, p. 33).
19 Kant explains exhaustively the human and philosophical reasons for this in the Transcendental Aesthetic and Transcendental Dialectic sections of his first *Critique*.
20 Dietrich Bonhoeffer, *Creation and Fall* (Minneapolis: Fortress Press, 1997, p. 25).
21 Jacques Derrida, 'Differance' in *Speech and Phenomena and Other Essays on Husserl's Theory of Signs* (Evanston, IL: Northwestern University Press, 1973, pp. 129–60; see pp. 154–5).
22 'Trinity and Revelation' and 'The Finality of Christ', in *On Christian Theology*, pp. 131–47 and pp. 93–106.
23 *On Christian Theology*, 37.
24 *On Christian Theology*, 41, original emphasis.
25 *On Christian Theology*, 105.
26 *On Christian Theology*, 37.
27 *On Christian Theology*, 100.
28 *On Christian Theology*, 105.
29 Dietrich Bonhoeffer, *Ethics* (Minneapolis: Fortress, 2005, p. 49); this is a slight paraphrase of the English translation which renders the German with greater clarity.
30 *Ethics*, pp. 49–50.
31 John Milbank, 'The Theological Critique of Philosophy', in *Radical Orthodoxy* (London: Routledge, 1999, pp. 21–37), see p. 24, *emphasis added*.
32 'The Theological Critique of Philosophy', p. 30.
33 See the fuller discussion of Radical Orthodoxy in this regard in my essay 'Radical Orthodoxy and the New Culture of Obscurantism', *Modern Theology* 20:3 (Oxford: Blackwell, 2004, pp. 363–405).

ETHICS

5

The Disruptive Power
of World Hunger

Clemens Sedmak

The call to feed the hungry is not the exhortation to fulfil a rather uncomfortable task. It is the invitation to encounter Christ, the way, the truth and the life. There is little metaphor at work in Mt. 25.31–46. Jesus does not say that feeding the hungry is 'like giving food to Jesus'. It is stronger: recognizing the plight of the hungry is a way of recognizing Christ and reacting to that plight is an encounter with Christ. In the words of Paul Janz: 'Christ does not say that inasmuch as you have done it unto the least of these, it will be "as if" you had done it unto me; but rather that inasmuch as you have done it unto the least of these, you *have* done it *unto me*.' [1] The bold statement in Matthew 25 needs to be taken seriously, and cannot justifiably be rendered harmless and toothless by making the words of Jesus die the death of a thousand qualifications. This passage recognizes the poor and the hungry as well as the prisoners (we might add: also those who are not innocent victims of the system but rightfully incarcerated[2]) as a source of revelation, as a *locus theologicus*. This passage is a strong statement against a theory of protected revelation that would allow for revelation to take place only under very special and rare circumstances. It is not the kind of revelation that can be judged against predefined criteria of orthodoxy. It is not the kind of revelation that can be systematized and squeezed in between two book covers. Using a distinction by Claude Lévi-Strauss, we could say that the encounter with the hungry, the thirsty, the naked or the imprisoned is not a neat, well-ordered, 'processed' revelation, but a dirty and difficult, rogue and 'raw' one. Transformation Theology as a theology in the world is about recognizing 'raw revelation' that has not been appropriated by church traditions or theological interpretations. This 'raw revelation' takes place in the *hic et nunc*, in the midst of the world, and cannot be predicted or controlled by conceptual means. Transformation Theology is called to look into these *loci theologici* one by one, situation by situation, case by case.[3] A *locus theologicus* is an opportunity for transformation. This case-by-case approach reflects a particular interest in and respect for the world and slows down the process of theologizing, it renders the doing of theology more complicated and it does not come to an end since ever-new places of 'raw revelation' open up in the world. It is also a recognition of the need of constant self-transformation since places of revelation say something about our identities, our place in the world. Rowan Williams makes a clear statement in that regard when he says:

> In judging the world, by its confrontation of the world with its own dramatic script, the Church also judges itself: in attempting to show the world a critical truth, it shows itself to itself as Church also. All of which means that we are dealing not with the 'insertion' of definable blocks of material into a well-mapped territory where homes may be found for them, but with *events* of re-telling or re-working traditional narrative patterns in specific human interactions.[4]

The 'messiness' of Transformation Theology, a 'theology in the world', is also a recognition of divine freedom expressed in the works of the Holy Spirit who is sovereign in the where and when of revealing God's presence in the world. This divine freedom is incompatible with predicting and calculating the effects of divine causality in the world. It cannot be contained in conceptual frameworks and theological models, it is a constant disrupter of our conceptual endeavours. To use an image: our conceptual work is being done on the top of a volcano with divine causality as the foundation and source of energy. Transformation Theology is well aware of the provisional nature of its conceptual efforts seeking God's reliability and fidelity on God's terms and not according to human dimensions. It is in this sense that the book of Exodus and the book of Job can be brought into a fruitful dialogue – liberation is not 'cheap liberation': it comes with a price and this price is living in a world exposing aporetic structures and what has been called a finality of non-resolution, situations of tragedy that cannot be remedied in terms of 'restoration'. Transformation Theology is about understanding the revelatory force of worldly phenomena. The statement that the hungry as well as the prisoners do have a revelatory force implies that they teach us something about God's presence in the world. Hence, the philosophical challenge of encountering large-scale social problems such as world hunger and famines, refugees and migration, wars and violence is theologically deepened.

1. World Hunger and the Structure of the World

Christ invites us to touch him in the encounter with the hungry. There is little room to metaphorize on 'the hungry'. People go hungry and people starve. Twenty-four thousand people die from hunger each and every day. Millions of people are suffering from the ravages of undernourishment, malnutrition, lack of food security, hunger and famines. Millions of children are affected whose precarious nutritional state weakens them in their efforts to cope with life and forces them into conditions of chronic disease. People suffering from hunger are in many cases deprived of the right to act morally. Hunger makes people fall into apathy, it renders them indifferent to their surroundings, it destroys their sense of belonging and shatters their commitments. Because of its causal strength we cannot do justice to world hunger by using lukewarm and shallow concepts or metaphors. In order to see the extent of the tragedy of world hunger, we are in need of thick, deep and fresh concepts. A thick concept is associated with personal experiences and local examples.[5] A deep concept is laden with emotions and shows not only a cognitive but also an affective content. A fresh concept is a concept that has a provocative 'sting' to it that calls for an ongoing *relecture* and reappraisal, a concept that opens up new avenues of investigation and invites us to take a fresh look at causal realities and conceptual frameworks. We need thickness, depth and freshness of our concepts if we want to do ethics in the midst of world hunger. It will not do to say that world hunger is a tragic reality and as a tragedy it bears the sign of inevitability. It will not do to say that the fact that the world is not just is one of the reasons why we have to do ethics under non-ideal conditions. It will not do to treat world hunger on a conceptual level. Swiss sociologist Jean Ziegler was convinced for many years that dying from hunger is a sad thing to happen, but not a painful reality. He was convinced that people dying from hunger would continuously lose strength and would finally go out like a candle. But then he witnessed dying from hunger in Ethiopia and saw how a child painfully died with cramps and convulsions, the experience dramatically changing his outlook on the concepts of 'hunger', 'starving' and 'dying from hunger'.[6] What does that mean? It seems that our concepts have to be immersed in the realities of life in order to become thick, deep and fresh. Our concepts have to gain affective weight.

If we are ready to develop thick, deep and fresh concepts in the fields of poverty and world hunger, we have to accept poor people as our teachers.[7] This is an application of the above-mentioned verses of Matthew 25 to the field of ethics. We have to discover poor people as sources of ethically relevant knowledge. No doubt, a person who knows what it is like to be hungry, knows more than a person who knows everything one can know about hunger from their reading.[8] We can imagine a person who knows everything there is to know about hunger, starvation, famines, food, fasting and starving. But she has never experienced hunger and is well fed and lives in 'food security'. And we would admit that should this person ever find herself in a situation where food security is threatened, she would learn something new. She would learn what it means to be hungry. Later on, I will argue that one way to gain this kind of knowledge under our ordinary life circumstances is through fasting. Accepting poor people as teachers calls us to enter relationships with people affected by poverty. Pedro Arrupe, the former Superior General of the Jesuits, mentioned in a letter to the Society of Jesus that material poverty can teach us about all other kinds of poverty and that the way material poverty teaches us is the ruthless and brutal way of direct experience.[9] In a way, material poverty tells us about non-metaphorical ways of understanding poverty and it does that in a non-metaphorical way. But by doing so, it also teaches us metaphorically about other types of poverty such as spiritual poverty or social exclusion or intellectual poverty. Arrupe was well aware of the fact that most Jesuits cannot fulfil their duties as college professors or doctors under conditions of serious material poverty but he insists that they should have personal experience of material poverty during their formation period and that they should foster relationships (friendships!) with people affected by material poverty. In other words: it is one thing to conceptualize about material poverty and it is another thing to have an insider's perspective on what it means to be materially poor. Arrupe described the transformative effect an experience of material poverty has on the Jesuits who immerse themselves in that experience. It is a kind of transformation that could not happen without such direct experience. This way of learning cannot be replaced with 'knowledge by description'. It is personal knowledge of acquaintance, insider's knowledge that allows one to make first-person statements understanding a literal sense of what it means to 'go hungry'. Understanding the tragedy of world hunger is about retrieving a literal sense of the concepts we use by establishing a connection with causal mechanisms at work in the world of the hungry.

Understanding world hunger is also about understanding the moral tragedy we have to accept. Hunger makes people commit deeds of despair: parents murdering their children since they cannot listen to their cries any longer,[10] people committing suicide, people exercising violence trying to obtain food, people plundering natural resources in order to alleviate food shortage. It seems quite plausible that our ethical ideas experience disruption in the face of hunger. It is one thing to talk about respecting children's rights and it is another thing to ask the helpless father of a starving child to respects his child's rights. Who is in a position to throw a stone at a mother who beats her child because she cannot feed it and cannot cope with the cries and sighs, pains and cramps any more?

There is a simple lesson to be learnt, the lesson that there must be such a right to act morally. People affected from hunger and famines are threatened in their right to act morally. Acting morally requires the possibility to choose among alternative routes of action, it requires the capability to make judgements facing these alternatives, it requires the possibility to build up moral resources such as basic convictions, and it requires the freedom to develop, protect and express one's identity, one's 'place in the world'. World hunger challenges the very way we do ethics since the way we think ethically is built upon the idea that people are in a position to act morally. But this is not necessarily the case. Maximilian Kolbe who chose death from starvation voluntarily was in a position to act morally since he had built up moral resources including a strong sense of purpose and a sense of belonging. A child who is trained to see life as a ruthless battle fighting for survival does not find herself in the same situation. In other words: ethics cannot stop at the development and the application of principles, or let us also say, it cannot start there. It has to start 'in the midst' of the human condition that is not only about unfair distribution of material resources but also about unequal distribution of moral resources. Moral resources are about commitments and identifications, about the constitution of a 'Self'. The Self as one's personal identity is developed on the basis of commitments and identifications[11] whereby commitment involves both an active process of committing oneself to someone or something and a passive moment of allowing oneself to be shaped and moulded by commitments.[12] Moral resources are to be found in commitments and identifications. We know that people with high ideals and strong commitments break least easily under torture – people with moral resources – and these moral resources have been built up within dialogical and communal structures. It is in this sense that moral autonomy is founded on commitments and relationships.

World hunger reminds us that ethics is being done in the world under non-ideal conditions. If we want to do ethics as if people mattered we have to acknowledge the fact that we do ethics not in a laboratory of artificial situations but in the mess of the world. Doing ethics under non-ideal conditions means that we do not start from a *tabula rasa*. It is not the case that we have a plain sheet of paper which we are about to fill. It is not the case that we are confronted with the task of designing a justifiable life. Whoever does ethics and whoever is addressed by ethical reflections has already written a number of pages in the book of his or her life and is part of a complicated situation with commitments and connections and consequences from previous decisions. Thinking about world hunger as if people mattered cannot afford the luxury of a green table distanced from the realities of hunger and starvation as if nothing had happened so far. Doing ethics in the midst of world hunger has to justify the interests it pursues, the concepts it applies, the categories it introduces and the consequences it requires *vis-à-vis* those who have no food security. We have to do ethics in the face of those who do not have sufficient moral resources, who are being denied the right to act morally. This does not turn ethics into social work, but it will have an impact on the claims made, the concepts employed and the categories used. World hunger points to the limits of ethics – the limits of moral resources available for people and the limits of the impact of ethical reasoning. It has to be recognized that conceptual clarity and purity is not enough. Doing ethics is a way of acting and as such is embedded in causal structures – there are chapters already written in the book and pages to be filled after and besides our ethical reflections. Ethics as if people mattered cannot be done in a closed setting. It has to be open to disruptions. A disruption is a process by which established points of reference for identity are being called into question. Disruptions stop the status quo. Disruptive processes change the coordinates of the unquestionable, of what is simply accepted. In this sense, a disruption is different from 'challenges' or 'problems'. Disruptions change the 'structures of relevance' (Alfred Schuetz) so much so that the relevance of relevance becomes an issue. Disruptions change the 'systems of acceptance' (Keith Lehrer) so much so that the very idea of acceptability becomes questionable. We could distinguish between challenges and disruptions. A challenge is an obstacle in the way that can be removed. We can continue our journey down that very road. We may have to slow down, we may even come to a stop for a while, but we do not have to change our fundamental plans. Life is full of challenges, impediments to be overcome. As long as there is a sound foundation, we do have the means to cope with such challenges. Disruptions, on the other hand, are a more serious matter. Disruptions shatter the foundations of our life plans and life forms. Disruptions call for a new reading of our life, a new life plan, a new quest for identity, a new way of being on the world. That is why the term 'disruption' should be used with caution and care. Disruptions are fundamental invitations to begin yet again, to make a fresh start. The disturbing nature of world hunger is an ongoing challenge to all closed systems and refined theories. Ethics sensitive to disruptions cannot neglect the causal structures of which the doing of ethics is being part. Facing world hunger will ask the ethicist to reflect upon the nature of ethics itself.

2. Doing Ethics and the Challenge of Dikedicy

We could illuminate the urgency of this challenge by thinking about reflecting on world hunger facing the victims. It makes a difference whether one reflects on human misery in general terms or whether one has encountered victims. Jean Ziegler's painful experience changed his conceptual grasp on world hunger. Japanese author Haruki Murakami interviewed victims of the 1995 nerve gas attack on the Tokyo underground and he was confronted with personal depths of the incident that make us conceive of this event as a tragedy. A mother of one of the victims whose brain was severely damaged in the attack said that it would have been better for her daughter to die in the attack. Murakami described his speechlessness – he, the gifted author, did not know what to say. What do you answer a mother who is convinced that her daughter would have been better off dead?[13] Similarly in the case of hunger. It is quite comfortable to reflect on the problem of world hunger in abstract terms with starving people turned into 'epistemic objects'[14] that can be fitted into theories. We are not confronted with bodies and their resistance but with concepts and categories. And the bodies are fitted into our categories – we do not think of individual persons but of categories ('undernourished', 'starving') and the starving person is not so much a person but a case of starvation. The frog that is described in a scientific journal has been transformed into an epistemic object. In most cases the object dies on that journey. Similarly, the category 'starving people' transforms people with their history into epistemic objects. This dynamics is unavoidable given the context of scholarship with its tendency towards the general and the abstract.[15] But it makes a difference whether the epistemic objects are the only sources of knowledge used. If a person did a PhD thesis on world hunger based on books and articles the thesis would be built on epistemic objects that have been built, in many cases, on the basis of other epistemic objects. If Jenny Edkins criticizes Amartya Sen's account of famines and the alleviation of world hunger by mentioning that he overestimated the reliability of legal systems she is engaging in a meta-debate on epistemic objects where the particular starving person is conceptually transformed beyond recognition.[16] Amartya Sen himself will mention the fact that he has experienced famine as a boy and this point will be very important for the way we judge the architecture of his theory, since we can locate and identify a point where 'the spade is turned', to use a memorable phrase by Ludwig Wittgenstein.[17] Thinking about world hunger without these points of reference where concepts deal with the particularities and messiness of reality can hardly stand the test of being able to face the victims. How would a reflection on world hunger look in the eyes of the victims?

There is a moment of irritation here that forces us to reflect upon the way we do ethics. We could conceive of a universal gathering of victims of world hunger – without the veil of cheap consolation, generalization or ignorance. The victims would come bearing their wounds and scars, carrying the weight of their stories and history. Such a conference would confront us with the very question of justifying ethics in a broken world. Victims of world hunger – as well as victims of war, torture, rape, land mines, exploitation – would not only witness to what humans can do to one another, they would also challenge the very possibility of ethics. Judith Shklar, Jonathan Glover or Susan Neiman identify the world as a place of atrocities, an inhospitable place where human beings experience faces of injustice, a place in need of healing.[18] We could conceive of a gathering of victims of famines who have seen their family members die, who have, perhaps, committed crimes in the desperate attempt to fight death. We could conceive of an ethicist who is invited to attend such a meeting and give a paper on the ethical challenge of world hunger. We could imagine that our ethicist would feel uneasy, and would try to find a way of balancing an attitude of scholarly distance with human empathy, of balancing politeness with clarity, of balancing individual stories with a broader picture. We can assume that this ethicist's presentation will be different from an academic conference where we can discuss the advantages or disadvantages of the Neo-Malthusian model telling us that there are too many people in this world and that this surplus of people would account for a shortage of food and the destruction of the environment. Surely, one would not dare to make a statement about 'surplus people' facing candidates for this category?[19]

But if we cannot say what we think in the eyes of the victim there seems to be something wrong with the way we do ethics. It cannot be that we have to do ethics 'behind the backs of the victims' or only 'ethics with epistemic objects'. It cannot be that we have to do ethics following standards of generalizations and abstraction that would not be compatible with thinking of particular people and their stories. In any case, we are confronted with the question of what to expect from doing ethics. Or to put it more bluntly: why ethics? The problem of justifying ethics in the dark night of suffering shall be called '*dikedicy*'. It poses the question of the meaning of ethics. The term is coined in analogy to the well-known term of theodicy, coming from the Greek words e (theós, 'God') and d (díke, 'justice'), meaning literally 'the justice of God'. It is a term introduced by Gottfried Leibniz in his *Essais de Théodicée sur la bonté de Dieu, la liberté de l'homme et l'origine du mal* (1710) and thematizes the question of reconciling the existence of evil in the world with God's moral perfection and omnipotence. Without trying to be 'original' at all costs, the term *dikedicy* seems to be adequate to make sense of the ethicist's situation confronted with causes for disruption. The term literally means 'the justice of justice' and points to the question of justifying ethics with its conceptual efforts around justice against the background of disruptions such as world hunger. It has been said that a disruption turns the relevance of relevance into an issue and the very idea of acceptability. A disruption of ethical reasoning calls the very idea of ethics into question. We have to reconcile our conceptual efforts in ethics with the causal realities that we encounter. World hunger urges us to ask the question: why ethics? Ethical concepts and ethical theories may have been useful and are probably still useful on the level of conceptual clarification, but on the causal level of transforming people's lives ethics seems to be a failure. People cannot eat the books written on or even against world hunger. In fact, the resources needed to produce these books may cost people's lives and contribute to the structural injustice that is expressed by world hunger. A gathering of victims would ask ethicists to account for their discipline not only in a conceptual, but also in a causal way. According to Harry Frankfurt ethics is mostly over-estimated in what it can offer.[20] Any ethical approach that is committed to taking the world as a place of human experience seriously has to struggle with the question of dikedicy: is ethics a meaningful project?

The problem of dikedicy gains weight and plausibility within the context of a gathering of victims. Such a gathering would also remind us that thinking about world hunger is sad. To think about world hunger is not a carefree task which may be finished like a crossword puzzle. First, it is not carefree, because it (a) requires care in order to be recognized as a challenge and problem, and (b) any outcome of thinking about world hunger will have an impact on our structures of care. Secondly, it is not a question that can be answered like a crossword puzzle, since it is not a problem that can be solved. Why? The issue of world hunger is about people and their bodies and not about a mechanical problem, such as that of a steering wheel. The issue of world hunger is not so much about sciences and chemistry,[21] but about policy and ethics, media and distribution of goods and services. This mixture of helplessness and knowing that something can be done makes us sad. This sadness is connected with the problem of dikedicy. The more we expose ourselves to the world in trying to make sense of it the more we develop a sense of sadness and guilt. In George Steiner's words: 'A veil of sadness (tristitia) is cast over the passage, however positive, from homo to homo sapiens. Thought carries within itself a legacy of guilt.'[22] It is also the guilt of not being able to give adequate answers, of not being able to transform ourselves and the world as deeply as an issue would invite us to. Facing world hunger we can understand George Steiner's frustration:

> On absolutely decisive fronts we arrive at no satisfactory, let alone conclusive answers however inspired, however consequent the process of thought, either individual or collective, either philosophical or scientific. This internal contradiction (aporia), this destined ambiguity is inherent in all acts of thought, in all

conceptualizations and intuitions. Listen closely to the rush of thought and you will hear, at its inviolate centre, doubt and frustration.[23]

For Steiner, this is a motive for *Schwermut*, for heaviness of heart. World hunger, we can take it from Paul Janz, is 'something that confronts human experience and reflection unmistakably as a reality, and yet, precisely in its undeniability as real, unmistakably forbids any ultimate resolution into explanatory mechanisms of any kind'. It is especially in the face of unspeakable evil and suffering that we find ourselves exposed to encounters with the authority of non-resolution. And again we are confronted with the nagging question: why ethics? How can we justify ethics in the midst of suffering?

I would like to suggest two meaningful reactions to this challenge of dikedicy. A first response I would support is the attention we pay to the bread value of our ethics. I would suggest that ethics is to be measured by its bread value. The bread value of ethics can be taken to be its contribution to a better world in the light of the ethical principles brought forward. It was William James who introduced the idea of the cash value of theories and meanings into pragmatism by telling us that truth lives on a credit system.[24] The cash value that is needed is the pragmatic difference it makes.[25] Similarly, the bread value of ethical reflections lies in the moral difference these reflections can make 'in the real world', the world of causes and effects, the world ordered by schemes of causality. Any justification of ethical models will respect two levels: the level of conceptual integrity and the level of causal accountability. The bread value of ethical reflection lies in its force to disrupt causal chains and to transform causal dynamics of the world by breaking cause–effect cycles and by initiating new causal chains. A gathering of victims will remind the ethicist of her double responsibility. The bread value of ethical judgements lies in the difference it can make to the moral landscape, to the way people act and interact. The bread value of ethical reasoning can be found in its disruptive power. Bernhard Bolzano has introduced the concept of 'the important sentence'.[26] The important sentence is one that has a general influence on our virtues and our eternal well-being. In other words, the acceptance or non-acceptance of this proposition makes a difference to one's attitude towards life as such and towards the world as a whole. Similarly, we could introduce the idea that propositions that we accept do have an impact: it could be a merely conceptual impact on the beliefs we hold and the set of propositions that we accept; it could also go beyond that and present itself as a causal impact that changes our ways of acting. Accepting an important sentence in Bolzano's understanding will have a sustainable and far-reaching causal impact. We will enter practical commitments with the acceptance of such propositions, commitments that direct our actions. The bread value of our ethics is the causal impact of our ethics: the set of practical commitments that we enter and the practical transformations connected with these commitments. Reflecting on the bread value of ethical thinking will be one plausible reaction to the challenge of dikedicy. The bread value of the initiative of 'Mary's meals' may be much higher than the bread value of a scholarly book, 'Introduction to the Ethical Problem of World Hunger'. Obviously, the bread value of ethics would not be a standard introduced by ethicists, but I cannot help but think that victims of world hunger are more interested in the bread value of ethical thinking about world hunger than in conceptual disputes concerning, for example, defining 'famine'. Hence, a first response to the challenge is the focus on the bread value of ethical reflection. It is also a way of taking the fact that ethics is being done 'in the world' seriously. A special variation of this answer to the challenge of dikedicy is the commitment to self-transformation. If the way one does ethics leads to self-transformation and self-renewal, ethics can cultivate the bread value of ethics. The doing of ethics, the reading, writing, thinking and encountering of reality, has to touch us on the level of our identities.[27] Ethics using 'important sentences' will inevitably lead to transformation and self-transformation.

A second response to the challenge of justifying ethics in the midst of a morally defective environment is the hint that there is no viable alternative. The price for the possibility of ethics is the imperfection of the world. We do ethics because we live under conditions of freedom and deprivation of guidance. There seems to be consensus that ethics ceases to be a very promising job in heaven. Theologically speaking, ethical reflection as theory-building will lose its point under the condition of the *visio beatifica*. But we are not there yet. World hunger is a brutal reminder that we are living in a world where ethics is necessary since we have created a morally defective context that makes people starve. The basic condition for the possibility of ethics is the 'openness' of the world: there is no *one* way of reading the world and there is no *one* way of acting in the world. Both Aristotle and Kant reminded us of the unity of *percepta* and *concepta*. Aristotle has defined matter as 'that which in itself is neither a particular thing nor of a certain quantity nor assigned to any other of the categories by which being is determined'.[28] Matter is open to many predications, to alternative categorizations. This openness of the world can also be shown in the contingency of language and the fact that our linguistic devices could be construed differently. The openness of the world can thirdly be demonstrated on the epistemic level, showing that human judgements on existential questions (the problems of life, as Wittgenstein had called them) do not reach universal consensus – these questions are of an adjudicative nature where each judgement brought forward has to accept the possibility and existence of alternative judgements.[29] Finally, the openness of the world is expressed in the alternative ways of living human praxis in its contextuality of many cultural frameworks. This fourfold openness of the world – ontological, epistemic, linguistic and practical – is the condition for the possibility of ethics. Because this openness implies (a) that it makes a difference to how we act, and (b) that there is an alternative to the way we are in the world. Ethics ceases to be necessary (and possible) in a closed world where we are deprived of alternatives to our way of acting and to our way of thinking. Take Huxley's scenario in his *Brave New World* as an example. Ethics has lost its point for the vast majority of inhabitants of this world. Only the world counsellors and a few chosen members of the elite would feel the need for ethical reflection. The Huxley world is without pain, but also without growth and compassion, love and hope. If the challenge of dikedicy ceases to exist, then ethics has been rendered superfluous. In other words: the justification for ethics is the argument that there is no alternative given the world we live in. It is the price we have to pay for contingency. If world hunger ceases to be a source of irritation, pain and anger, then the burden of justifying ethics has been lifted or at least lost a lot of its weight. But this is a bad sign. If we consider poverty and hunger part of the human condition in the sense that most members of the Huxley world accept rigid social stratification and unequal distribution of privileges, then we have made a huge step towards a closed world. If the community of ethicists restricts itself to reasoning on a conceptual level, the disruptive power of causal realities is abolished and the community of ethicists has turned into enemies of Popper's open society to be characterized by the ability to make new starts on the basis of experiences of disruption. Ethics is about maintaining the consciousness that there are alternatives. Ethics is about disrupting established ways of silent acquiescence, of resignation or tacit affirmation.

These answers have to be taken as a cluster. The challenge of world hunger as intensified by the gathering of victims urges us to consider the bread value of the kind of ethical reflection we are undertaking; it reminds us of the price we have to pay to live in a world.[30] And the world is full of ethical challenges. This is part of the pain, but also part of the dignity of living in the world. Ethics in the world accepts the world as a place of learning and accepts experience and even suffering as an important source of knowledge. Ethics in the world emphasizes the value of incarnational knowledge, the kind of knowledge that is 'suffered' and that is applied to oneself. Insights into the human condition are always also insights into oneself. World hunger, starvation and famines are points of resistance where our conceptual strategies seem to fail: can we claim that we understand the phenomenon of world hunger? World hunger is also a tragedy where our agent causality (the ability to initiate causal chains) comes to a point of frustration: can we claim that we can overcome world hunger? But, as this point of resistance, world hunger provides insights into the structure of the world.

3. World Hunger, Sapiential Skills and the Structure of the World

World hunger teaches us a lot about the world, about ourselves. 'Famine acts as a revealing commentary upon a society's deeper and more enduring difficulties.'[31] World hunger is a 'window into the world'.[32] It teaches us in a deep and honest way about the structure of the world. It confronts us with hard facts; facts that are hard to accept and facts that are hard to deny. 'One of the hardest facts of life is that living itself is so painful to large numbers of people.'[33] Hard facts provide the friction we need in order to have concepts that work.[34] If ethical concepts want to be fresh in the above-mentioned sense, they have to be open to disruption, the kind of disruption made possible through contact with the resistance of the real world. World hunger teaches us about the structure of the global food system.[35] It forces us to look at our planet as a whole to realize that we are throwing away food on the one hand and that we allow people to starve on the other. World hunger teaches us about our human conditions, about our bodies. The body is the prime place of resistance to the real world and of resistance by the world. People who starve touch the world with their bodies in a tragic manner – tragic because of the non-necessity of this destiny, and tragic because a starving person can do nothing about his or her own death. The tragedy of world hunger tells us in no uncertain terms in what ways our thinking about the world has to be disrupted, as it tells us too about the point of contact between our bodies and the world. Again, there is little that is metaphorical about the experience of starving. People who starve are embodied human beings in the real world of sensible experience in space and time. We have to face the ethical challenge of not retreating from this real world of space and time as the proper focus of our attention, of not fleeing into abstract domains of conceptual constructions. The memory of the body cannot be substituted by conceptual memories. People who have experienced hunger have access to a particular memory that serves as a reference point for understanding key concepts of our faith more deeply, such as the concepts 'hunger for justice', 'fasting', 'feeding the hungry', 'sharing bread at the Eucharist' etc. Hunger is an experience that tells us something about how and where we touch reality. World hunger also teaches us a great deal about the human body since we can understand that food is more than 'fuel for the human machine'. 'Levels of food consumption are not dictated by some absolute biological need, but by requirements of labour and its reproduction.'[36] World hunger is a window into the world and a window into our Selves.

Because of the deep insights it offers, insights dealing with our identities, world hunger cannot be solved in the sense that there is a question and once an answer is found the question ceases to be a question. There are questions of that kind that can be answered by turning to an encyclopaedia. Let us call these questions 'encyclopaedic questions'. If I do not know when Mozart was born I can answer the question by consulting an encyclopaedia and with the knowledge that Mozart was born on 27 January 1756 the question is closed and the problem is solved. Similarly, if I have a problem in solving a crossword puzzle or a problem in an intelligence test there are solutions that make the problems lose their problematic character. Ethical problems are not of that kind. It would be nice to be able to consider 'world hunger' a problem to be solved rather than a disruption. It would be even nicer to be in a position to say that world hunger is no problem at all: it is a sad thing to happen, but a necessary evil. Aren't we tempted to say: unemployment is an important ingredient for a functioning economy; similarly, poverty is an important ingredient for a functioning economy and in this sense we also need world hunger? Then, world hunger is not even a problem, we only face the challenge of minimizing the ugliness of it. Would we dare to say that during a gathering of victims? Even without this litmus test of integrity (can you cope with encountering the victims?) it seems to me out of the question to argue like that. There are too many decisions involved in the causation and preservation of the conditions of world hunger to consider world hunger a necessity, there is too much of human freedom shown in the causal dynamics of world hunger. The temptation, it seems, is not so much about denying that there is something to be said about world hunger, as to treat world hunger as a problem.

The temptation to see world hunger as a problem is understandable. To yield to it is actually fair and just. There are 'encyclopaedic' elements of world hunger. There is a predictable distribution of the risk of starvation and the ways people are affected by droughts or famines reflect the social structure of this region. 'Indeed, it is by no means clear that there has ever occurred a famine in which all groups in a country have suffered from starvation, since different groups typically do have very different commanding powers over food, and an overall shortage brings out the contrasting powers in stark clarity.'[37] There are different levels of vulnerability.[38] There is the temptation to see world hunger in terms of shortage of food and/or surplus of people that can be solved by soil fertilization and birth control. There is the question of food taboos, of the role of women (e.g. as 'gatekeepers' for food entering a household[39]) and of the status of children (as those who eat last and least allowing the male adult breadwinner to keep going), of the role of violence and war and generally of the political dimension of food. The temptation to treat world hunger as a problem that can be solved is well grounded in the possibility to construct well-justified and important theories. Amartya Sen has developed an influential and differentiated account of world hunger. He has shown that famines occur significantly less often in democratic regimes than in non-democratic regimes, linking that phenomenon with questions of distribution of food as well as of information.[40] Sen analyses world hunger as a matter of unfair distribution of access to entitlements. He has argued for the view that famines are political phenomena and that world hunger has to be seen in terms of political economy. Sen's entitlement approach concentrates on the ability of people to command food through the legal means available in the society. A person starves because she does not use or does not have the ability to command enough food. Starvation statements are about the relationship of persons to food as a commodity; hunger is mainly about questions of ownership of food and entitlements. A focus on entitlements presents an alternative to a food-centred view that does not tell us why people in the same area are affected differently from droughts and how starvation can develop – demonstrated by Sen – even without a decline in food availability. World hunger is a much more complicated story than a story about food.

Effective famine prevention calls for much more than simply rushing food to the victims when they have started dying of starvation. It involves a network of decisions relating to diverse policy areas such as the generation of incomes, the delivery of health care, the stabilization of food prices, the provision of drinking water, and the rehabilitation of the rural economy.[41]

Strategies to fight world hunger according to the entitlement approach are systems of public welfare as well as legal frameworks and information freedom. Sen's approach concentrates on the ability of people to command food through the legal means available in the society. It is a problem-solving strategy. This strategy, however, can only work if there is ethical consciousness on the level of individual ethics and a reform of people's hearts. It does not work under conditions of greed and corruption. The non-moral sphere plays only a limited part in the tragedy of world hunger. The temptation to see world hunger as a problem, even a complex problem that cannot be isolated,[42] is plausible. This temptation is also at work when we find ourselves tempted to see world hunger as a *moral problem*.

As a moral problem, world hunger is about negotiating conditions and questioning decisions. A moral analysis could critically analyse the discourse on world hunger and identify interests and advantages. There are not only conditions to bring about world hunger but also conditions that preserve and maintain world hunger. To put it bluntly: somebody must have an interest and take a profit from the structures that produce and preserve world hunger. There must be positive functions of world hunger.[43] There is an undeniable connection with greed bridging the gap between individual ethics and social ethics: in the case of hunger:

> the craving for money, power and a public image, as ends in themselves, is evidenced by a diminished sense of public service for the sole benefit of individuals or worthy groups; this is accompanied by a high level of corruption in a variety of different forms, from which no country may fairly claim to be exempt. [44]

As a moral problem world hunger calls for strategies, solutions – and it calls for basic decisions. World hunger irritates our way of looking at the world and forces us to step back and make five basic conceptual decisions: there is the basic decision as to whether world hunger is to be reconstructed as a technical/scientific problem or rather as a political/economic challenge.[45] There is the second decision as to whether world hunger indicates failure of a generally well-functioning system or whether world hunger is the price to be paid for the system that regulates our economy. The third decision concerns our image of human beings. Is a human being an autonomous individual who needs food in a way similar to an engine needing fuel or are we part of a community where food is a cultural and social good? The fourth decision concerns the ethical status of the problem: 'Is hunger a misfortune which calls for beneficence and help? The pervasive use of the term "aid" to describe responses to hunger suggests as much. Or is ending distant hunger a matter of justice?'[46] A fifth decision concerns the concept of the victims of world hunger: are we to see people affected by famines or by world hunger as mere victims, as passive 'patients' or as active subjects as well? Should we acknowledge the fact that victims of world hunger in most cases design coping strategies and pursue interests?[47]

These five decisions are important ingredients towards a moral theory of world hunger. Such a moral theory of world hunger is precious and valuable: treating world hunger as a moral problem is an important step in transforming inhumane conditions. But it will not do. As a moral problem it can be pressing and painful, but it can still be separated from my Self, from my identity. Even as a moral problem I can turn world hunger into a challenge that does not involve life-shaping commitments and identifications. I can treat world hunger just like the moral problem of, let us say, genetic testing at the workplace, where I may even develop a position and where I may even know of people involved and concerned. But the challenge of genetic testing at the workplace would still be a clearly defined and conceptually controllable problem that does not call my identity into question. Again, it is an honourable and important enterprise to construct a theory about world hunger, but it will not do. It will not do since taking away the right to act morally from masses of people will also take away our right to act morally. It will affect our 'illusion of innocence'[48], our self-understanding, the constitution of our Selves, the negotiation of our place in the world. How can we claim that we are in a position to act morally facing the ugliness of world hunger? A gathering of victims of world hunger as sketched out above would remind us that there is something wrong with the world, something wrong with us. It would remind us that we are doing ethics under non-ideal conditions. World hunger teaches us a lot about the structures of sin and the usefulness of the concept of 'sin'.[49] We are faced in the tragedy of world hunger with a dynamics which means that we cannot escape the conceptual as well as the causal kind of accountability.

Let us be honest about the topic: it is not about redistribution of food or access to calories; it is basically about the redistribution of moral resources, resources for identity building. The issue of world hunger is not primarily about food and it is not primarily about money. It is about Selves. Wouldn't we say that both our ignorance and our inertia say something about who we are? 'Our capacity to feel justified in ignoring illness and starvation already provokes a widespread sense of uneasiness which is well expressed by Philippa Foot when she muses that "there is surely something wrong with us" in allowing this state of affairs to continue.'[50] World hunger takes away our illusion of innocence. There are several roles to be distributed facing world hunger: the roles of perpetrators and gainers, the roles of victims and losers, the roles of bystanders and silent supporters, the roles of resisters and disrupters. There is no role for a neutral observer or the innocent analyst. There is no role for ethics without justification. World hunger is not a problem, it is a disruption.

4. World Hunger and Disruptive Transformations

Accepting world hunger as a disruption is a difficult task with far-reaching consequences. 'Our capacity to help end world hunger is infinite, for the roots of hunger touch every aspect of our lives.'[51] Accepting world hunger as a disruption is much more than simply stating that the fact that 24,000 people die from hunger each day is disturbing. It is more than that. It claims a bread value in the transformation of our lives. And it claims transformations in our ways of being in the world.

The world is the place where we are supposed to live a fruitful life and where we encounter world hunger. The world as the context and foundation of human experience is a 'locus ethicus' where resistance and disruption are experienced. World hunger is an expression of this disruption. Our concepts, theories and positions are being disrupted by brokenness and fragmentation, destruction and loss. Doing ethics in the world will have to acknowledge the brokenness of the world, and will have to face reality beyond a veil of conceptual disguises. The persistent scourge of world hunger has to be brought into ethical discourse by honouring the disruptive power of death from hunger, famine and starvation. The very first thing we have to acknowledge is the conviction that world hunger is a disruption. What does that mean?

The role of disrupters for ethics can hardly be underestimated. The importance of disruption is linked with the inapplicability of falsification. Karl Popper introduced the criterion of falsifiability as a criterion to distinguish scientific theories from other types of theories. A theory is falsifiable if we can identify circumstances that would render the theory false. A good theory 'forbids' the occurrence of particular events. The more events a theory forbids the better it is. Any scientific system must be able to fail empirically. A serious examination of a theory consists in systematic attempts to falsify it.[52] The criterion of falsifiability cannot be applied to ethics. This is a blessing and a curse. The blessing lies in the openness we face which has been outlined above. The curse is connected with the lack of consensus we are forced to acknowledge, in basic ethical matters such as 'rights of the unborn', 'duty to relieve suffering', 'justifiability of the death penalty', 'justification of active euthanasia'. If a person holds the position that abortion is murder what scenario could we present that would 'falsify' such a position? Similarly, if a person claims that abortion is a procedure like removing a scar, what situations would falsify this position? We could think of situations that bring about a change of mind and heart of the person holding these beliefs. I may be a proponent of the death penalty but then I find a dear friend of mine in death row. This may change my point of view. I may be a proponent of abortion but then I have an encounter with a woman whom I fall in love with and who suffers from the effects of an abortion she had many years ago, and I share her sufferings. This may change my point of view. But these 'positional conversions' cannot be called 'falsifications'. If a Catholic believes that Mary is the Mother of God and that she can rightly be called 'theotokos', then no fact in the world can falsify this belief. Not even an apparition of Mary contradicting this to the recipient of the vision – since the apparition would then, for principal reasons, never be accepted as genuine. The nature of ethical questions as adjudicative problems makes it impossible to apply the concept of 'falsification' to ethical discourse. This is painful in the sense that a person considering world hunger in terms of a lifeboat ethics[53] cannot be won over with knockdown procedures.

If we accept that we cannot falsify ethical positions, then we have to do something to limit the potential epistemic damage. There have to be criteria by which to judge ethical models. I would suggest that we take the courage to face the gathering of victims of world hunger (or even victims of other types of atrocities) to discuss this question. We have raised the issue of dikedicy and we have offered two answers to that challenge. Both replies deal with the double accountability of ethics, both on a conceptual and on a causal level. This is especially obvious in the case of world hunger: 'Paradoxically, a *theoretical* turn is needed if famine and hunger are to be seen as *practical* problems, also if we are to determine what sorts of practical problems they raise.'[54] The conceptual and the causal are intertwined. If we cannot 'reach' the world by means of falsification procedures, we have to introduce other 'points of friction' between ethical reflection and the world. I would like to call these points of friction 'disrupters'. Ethical theories cannot be falsified, but they can be disrupted, they can be irritated and they can be challenged. Ethical problems involve the ethicist. Disruptions are 'epistemological crises'[55] applied to the constitution of the self. The fact that a theory can be disrupted places that theory on the level of causal tangibility, on the level where this theory can be touched and influenced by experiences. Only theories that touch the world, that reach these points of friction, can be called functioning theories. A disrupter is an event that questions the foundations of my theories and the basis for my identity. A theory that cannot be disrupted is a theory that is not placed on a causally relevant level, within the world. Transformation Theology is about constructing disruptable theories. This is a statement about the theories produced and the theologian at work.

During a gathering of victims of world hunger probably no ethicist would dare to come forward with the theory that world hunger is a mere problem to be solved. The victims facing the ongoing tragedy of world hunger and the extent of this tragedy would call for the disruptive power of world hunger in a way similar to the 'ethics of memory' after the Second World War, reminding us that Auschwitz has been a disruption that has always to be acknowledged as disruption with its disruptive force.[56] World hunger, victims will remind us, has to be recognized as a disrupter. The fact that theories can be disrupted turns ethics into an ongoing enterprise, a continuous reflection. In this sense world hunger is a 'thorn in the flesh' of our ethical theories. From the point of view of a dikedicy and reflective conscious ethics, world hunger disrupts our ideas about the world continuously.

How can we conceive of continuous disruption? How can we conceive of disruption as a continuous phenomenon, as a condition so to speak – as a condition that transforms our ethical thinking into 'thinking at the margins'? The answer to this question could be the hint in the story of Job. This story disrupts our ideas about reconciling God with the world since (a) it does not give an answer, and (b) it describes the relationship between God and the world as disruptive. In this sense, the story of Job is inexhaustible, a constant source of newness and freshness, deep insights. It has been said, by the way, that classical texts ('primary sources') provide this kind of inexhaustibility that is always

open to new interpretations. The book of Job teaches many lessons on disruption.[57] Job is wrestling with his identity, with the pillars of his outlook on
life and his worldview. He is disrupted by the messages he receives through the
law. He calls his whole system of orientation into question. He is disturbed by
the messages he receives. He has to learn the lesson that a 'prophetic language'
which operates out of a certain system of judgements is limited; he has to learn
yet another language, a mystical language that teaches him that God's justice
cannot be measured and reconstructed in terms of human justice.[58] Job has to
learn a disturbing lesson that calls for trust in God. The lessons that are taught
by the book of Job about our being in the world cannot be exhausted by one
course of interpretation. The same applies to world hunger. In this sense world
hunger is a constant disruption. The faces of hunger are changing.[59] Hunger
provides us with the epistemic challenges of understanding the relevant concepts: 'One of the problems with famine – as a concept and as an historical
phenomenon – is that it presents us with a fundamental paradox. It is both
event and structure.'[60] Revelation for Job is both event and structure, both
conceptual reflection and causal reality – and Job is disrupted on both levels.
World hunger displays its disruptive force on the conceptual and the causal
level as well. As a constant disruption world hunger makes statements about
the human condition just like the creation story with its account of the fall.
One disruptive lesson of world hunger is that we are not innocent. In this sense,
the challenge of world hunger could bring us to a new understanding of the
story of Job and the questions concerning Job's life. Let us imagine that Job was
a pious man and a diligent worker. One summer there was a drought and Job's
family was close to starvation. Job tried hard to provide for his family but he
made some wrong business decisions, entered commitments he could not
honour and lost the basis of his livelihood. His children were fighting over the
scarce food and Job could not give them their share. His wife forced him to eat
in order to be able to take care of the family. Since he was supposed to be the
breadwinner he ate, in a hidden place, filled with guilt and shame. The children
got sicker and weaker and the parents had to watch their children die. Finally,
Job's wife got sick and he did not know what to do. He could not help her. This
is the essential structure of the new version of the story. We could add elements
to make it more complicated, but the basic message is the same. Possible
additional elements could be his wife asking him to kill her since she could not
bear the pain of starving any longer. We could also think of Job and his wife
being exposed to the challenge of cannibalism. We could also add the element
of Job's visit to a rich man, a detail that could be told in the following way. At
the same time Job knew about a rich man in the neighbourhood who was living
from the ample stock he had accumulated. When he approached the rich man
for help, Job was turned down, not even with violence but with politeness, the
politeness of Job's friends: 'See, I have to provide for my family and we do not
know how long this miserable situation will last. It is out of this sense of
responsibility that I have to decline to give food to you. I am very sorry about
that. I will pray for you and I am sure that God will provide.'

Again, the story is essentially about mistakes Job made and a situation where he was denied the right to act morally. This version of the story of Job is even more painful than the version we find in the Old Testament. The difference can be identified by exploring the concept of 'innocence'. In the Old Testament version, Job is the incarnation of innocence. The evil that befalls him is not of his doing. There is no direct causal connection between decisions he has made and his tragedy. This causal connection has been established by God. Job has not done anything for which he has himself to blame. This lack of culpability accounts for the dynamics of the book. The innocent human creature is wrestling with God. It is, without any doubt, a very challenging and engaged way of seeking the face of God in the midst of undeserved suffering. It is what we can call 'theodicy on the third level' – the first level being a theoretical reflection on the potential compatibility between God's omniscience, omnipotence and goodness, and evil in the world; the second level being the reflection of a believer in secure circumstances. The third level of theodicy is the level of a devout believer whose life is hit by misery and whose belief is existentially challenged by the circumstances. It is on this level that C. S. Lewis could say: 'Not that I am (I think) in much danger of ceasing to believe in God. The real danger is of coming to believe such dreadful things about Him.'[61] It is also on this level that we find Job – the option to deny God's existence is never an option. There is only the range of beliefs we may or may not hold about God. In a hunger-shaped version of the Job story outlined above, the dynamics change significantly. It is not only *vis-à-vis* God that a person has to justify herself. It is also *vis-à-vis* one's family. And it is not in the light of supposed innocence but in the darkness of recognized wrongdoing with severe consequences. The cry to God is the cry of a person who has been denied the right to act morally, who has been thrown into conditions that make it impossible to act without causing harm. The right to act morally is denied if I am only to choose between two or more bad alternatives. We can think of a scenario of 'Sophie's choice' where a mother has the freedom to choose which of her two children shall enter the concentration camp and which one shall be killed immediately. Whatever Sophie, the mother, does, she will find herself woven into a story of guilt and darkness, of wrongdoing and irreversible harm. We will come back to that situation in the next chapter.

People afflicted by world hunger can find themselves in these situations without the possibility to act morally. Frithjof Bergmann has rightly observed that freedom cannot primarily be about making choices since a choice between bad alternatives (do you want to starve or do you want to die from Aids?) cannot be called freedom.[62] World hunger brings about situations without the possibility of acting morally. A Job in such a situation may struggle with his family, with his community and the structures of his society, with his God – but he does all this in the consciousness of being guilty, of having caused irreversible harm. Job will hardly be convinced that ethics can make a difference in a world where his hands get dirty simply by touching the world. Doing ethics in a world where simply being in the world dirties your hands raises ethical issues. The problem of dikedicy becomes urgent in the darkness of a hunger-shaped situation such as that which faces Job. Why ethics? Is ethics the luxury of those who have bread? Is moral capital just one more kind of capital next to financial, intellectual and social capital? Is ethical wisdom just one more kind of intelligence besides social and emotional intelligence?

World hunger invites us to tell Job's story in a new version. A variant of this version can actually be found in Liam O'Flaherty's novel *Famine* (FF),[63] a novel that depicts the Irish potato famine in the 1840s. In this story we find strong versions of Job's challenge: 'Mary suddenly wanted to scream and to cry out to God in revolt against the tortures of this poverty. Immediately she was taken by a great fear of having sinned. Meekly, she crossed herself and begged God to forgive her. Then peace descended on her' (FF 40). '"God helps them that help themselves," said Mary' (FF 63). In situations of moral strain the relationship with God is challenged as well. A phenomenon such as hunger makes it very difficult to act morally. Scarcity generates conflicts. In O'Flaherty's story Michael is a young man who falls sick in the middle of the hunger period and is given the best available food until he dies. His sister-in-law who is pregnant at the time cannot accept his unequal distribution of food. She is tormented with feelings of jealousy and after Michael's death feels a sense of relief. 'I am glad Michael is gone, God forgive me. He was like a worm eating us out of house and home. Now there isn't a pig, or a hen, or a duck left. And my baby coming' (FF 200). 'God forgive me, I'm so glad poor Michael is dead. He was like a worm devouring everything and him wasting away' (FF 204). The right to act morally is something which ethics in the world cannot take for granted. This is not to underline the truth of the statement 'Erst kommt das Fressen und dann die Moral' (Bertolt Brecht) but to see that there is indeed a material basis for our concepts, a bread value as we have called it. From a theological point of view we must also accept that poverty means new forms of temptation, such as the temptation of the poor man to send a curse of God on a rich man (FF 263). The poor person is not in a morally better position than anyone else. This makes any excuse of the second-order kind ('The poor will get their reward in heaven') even more difficult – not only are the well-to-do better off materially, they also have better access to moral resources. They do not find themselves as easily in a situation where there is no possibility to act morally; they generally live lives where their right to act morally is respected.

Let us then read the story of Job in its new version not as a parable about situations with limited moral opportunities but as a parable about the challenge of life after the loss of innocence. If we were to imagine Job as a happy person after all he went through and did, we would surely think that there was something wrong with him. Accepting a loss of innocence is not only a challenge for obvious perpetrators. In the light of world hunger, we have all lost our innocence. It is not only through acting but also through omissions that we lose our innocence in the face of world hunger. Being in a position to prevent the death of a starving person, and failing to act on that possibility, can be translated into 'having killed a person'.[64] We all benefit from famine, as Amrita

Rangasami has pointed out: 'Through our acceptance of a system of law that regulates ownership through violence, forgetting the violence at the root of the law, we are all complicit in starvations and famine.'[65] Nobody can claim to be innocent in an Old Testament kind of Job situation any longer. We are doing ethics in a world that makes us guilty. In fact, it is part of the responsibility of ethics to increase the consciousness of the level of the loss of innocence. In analogy to the above-mentioned three levels of theodicy, the challenge of dikedicy can also be developed on three levels: on the level of a neutral scholar, on the level of a personally engaged scholar who believes in ethics and its merits but does not live in conditions of self-ascribed guilt, and on the level of an engaged ethicist who knows that she is not innocent. It is on this third level of dikedicy that the problem presents itself in the reality of world hunger. And because of the loss of our innocence and because of the fact that 'being in the world' is a guilty condition, world hunger is not a moral problem, but a disruption. And this disruption does not call for a solution, but for redemption, hence for conversion and self-transformation.

How can we do ethics in the midst of misery and as people who have lost their innocence? Let us be very clear about the challenge posed by world hunger. It is the challenge of compatibility. Can we know about world hunger and be at peace at the same time? This question is a variation of Schleiermacher's incompatibility argument. Schleiermacher argues that the eternal damnation of even one single person is incompatible with the eternal blessedness of anyone.[66] This argument has been further developed by Thomas Talbott[67] and reminds us of the fact that blessedness has to be compatible with knowledge of the state of the world. Knowledge of the suffering of even one single person would have an effect on my happiness that would thus be undermined. In other words: if there is still someone suffering in hell, how could anyone be totally happy? If we take the condition of the saved to be a condition of knowing and understanding as well as a condition of loving and forgiving – then the problem cannot be denied. How could anyone be happy if her child is in hell? Or how can anyone be happy if he does not know what happened to his child after death? And what would it say about the love of this person if he did not care about the eternal destiny of his child?

What does this argument mean for world hunger? It challenges the right to happiness. Can we know about world hunger and be at peace at the same time? We can hardly assume that peace of mind has to be bought at the expense of knowledge, at the price of accepting ignorance. World hunger challenges our being in the world in the sense that we cannot be 'at home' in the world. World hunger does not allow us to see the world as the ultimate horizon. World hunger challenges us to see ourselves as strangers, strangers in a world that seems so deaf to human cries.[68] In this sense, world hunger is an ongoing disruption that would not permit a coming to rest either in the bed of cosy concepts or in the bed of controlled causality. What we do is never enough. And what we think is never adequate. The two answers I suggested to the challenge of dikedicy do not make the challenge disappear. In a way, this challenge becomes more urgent, so much so that our ethical thinking depends on the way we deal with this challenge. We can be at peace in the sense that we accept our limits, but we cannot be at peace in the sense that we accept the way we deal with our limits. In this sense, world hunger is a source of disruptions that does not go dry – as much as the book of Job is an ongoing disruption to our images of God and to our models about human suffering.

In a nutshell: ethical positions and concepts can be constantly challenged and disrupted by the resistance given by human experience of the world and human experiences in the world. The price to be paid for this disruptability is an ongoing struggle with the question of dikedicy. In other words, the fact that dikedicy can be posed as a problem points to the meaning of ethics in a broken world, a world that can challenge, break and disrupt ethics. Ethics in the world is not 'falsifiable' but 'disruptable' – and the 'disrupters' are to be found 'in the world'. Ethics is a project of transformation, a project of disrupting our concepts and theories and the ways we act. And ethics itself is being constantly disrupted by the way the world is, and by the ways we shape the world and ourselves in the world. World hunger disrupts the way we do ethics and calls our identities into question.

Notes

1 Let me express at this point my sincere gratitude to Oliver Davies and Paul Janz both for critical comments on previous versions of these chapters as well as for their efforts in anglicizing the language used. Working on this project has transformed our relationships, deepening our friendships. And this self-transformation that I experience as a sense of gratefulness is a good sign for the theology at work in this book.

2 The way we treat rightfully and lawfully convicted criminals can be seen as the litmus test for the decency of a society – cf. Avishai Margalit, *The Decent Society* (Cambridge, MA: Harvard University Press, 1996). It can also, it seems, serve as a litmus test for the integrity of our concept of revelation.

3 Cf. Clemens Sedmak, *Doing Local Theology* (Marknoll, NY: Orbis, 2002).

4 Rowan Williams, 'The Judgement of the World', in Rowan Williams, *On Christian Theology* (Oxford: Blackwell, 2001, pp. 29–43, 31).

5 Concerning the understanding of the thickness of descriptions cf. Gilbert Ryle, *The Thinking of Thoughts: Collected Papers II* (London: Hutchinson, 1971, pp. 480–96); Clifford Geertz, *The Interpretation of Cultures* (New York: Basic Books, 1993, p. 6ff); concerning 'thick concepts'; Bernard Williams, *Ethics and the Limits of Philosophy* (London: Routledge 2006, pp. 132–55).

6 Jean Ziegler, *Wie kommt der Hunger in die Welt? Ein Gespräch mit meinem Sohn* (München: Bertelsmann, 2000, p. 136).

7 It is also a moral challenge to grant rights to poor people and to recognize poor people as our teachers:

> It will be necessary above all to abandon a mentality in which the poor – as individuals and as peoples – are considered a burden, as irksome intruders trying to consume what others have produced. The poor ask for the right to share in enjoying material goods and to make good use of their capacity for work, thus creating a world that is more just and prosperous for all. The advancement of the poor constitutes a great opportunity for the

moral, cultural and even economic growth of all humanity. (John Paul II, *Centesimus Annus*, p. 28)

8   This is obviously a version of Frank Jackson's thought experiment 'What Mary did not know' – cf. Frank Jackson, 'What Mary Didn't Know', *The Journal of Philosophy* 83:5 (1986, pp. 291– 5).

9   Pedro Arrupe, *The Social Commitment of the Society of Jesus* (1971), in Pedro Arrupe, *Essential Writings* (Maryknoll/New York: Orbis, 2004). A similar observation has been made by Amartya Sen about starvation as the most telling aspect of poverty (Sen, *Poverty and Famines*; Oxford: Oxford University Press, 1981, p. 12).

10 See David Arnold, *Famine: Social Crisis and Historical Change* (Oxford: Blackwell 1988, p. 18). For observations on famine in China in 1942 by White and Jacoby, see Theodore White and Annalee Jacoby, *Thunder out of China* (New York: Sloane Associates, repr. 1980).

11 Cf. Charles Taylor, *Sources of the Self* (Cambridge, MA: Harvard University Press, 1989).

12 Cf. Hans Joas, *Die Entstehung der Werte* (Frankfurt/Main: Suhrkamp, 1997).

13 Haruki Murakami, *Untergrundkrieg* (Cologne: Du Mont, 2002).

14 Cf. Karin Knorr-Cetina, *Wissenskulturen* (Frankfurt/Main: Suhrkamp, 2002); Karin Knorr-Cetina, *Die Fabrikation von Erkenntnis* (Frankfurt/Main: Suhrkamp, 2002; Klaus Amann, 'Menschen, Mäuse und Fliegen: Eine wissenschaftssoziologische Analyse der Transformation von Organismen in epistemische Objekte', *Zeitschrift für Soziologie* 23:1 (1994), pp. 22–40.

15 We could also ask the painful question whether scholarship contributes to the production of world hunger by the discourse it generates – by generating a discourse on world hunger the phenomenon increases, especially if the discourse does not add to the causal dynamics of the problem, but simply adds a vast conceptual 'world'. With the production of a discourse, we have experts working on the problem, securing a livelihood on the basis of the problem, with a professional interest in keeping the problem part of the debate. A discourse seems to offer possibilities to control the problem and at the same time a conceptual framework pointing to the complexities of the social problem to be tackled weakens the possibilities for focused change. A discourse provides a conceptual 'home' for a problem, possibly at the expense of causal interventions, and it transfers the culture of accountability to the conceptual level. One could argue that poverty research contributes to poverty production through the research industry with its vested interests around that problem – see e.g. Lakshman Yapa, 'How the Discipline of Geography Exacerbates Poverty in the World', *Futures* 34:1 (2002, pp. 33–46). This suspicion has also been uttered for the case of hunger – Mary Tiles, 'Science and the Politics of Hunger', *Philosophy of Science* 64 (1997, pp. 161–74). Similarly, we could ask whether ethics contributes to the persistence of immorality or whether theology with its discourse on redemption does not contribute to the persistence of experiences of hell on earth. Ethical reflection has served as a justification for atrocities (e.g. 'logic of the minor evil') in a way similar to the contribution of theology to the persistence of injustice by too strongly painting a picture of the world as a transitory stage of tests.

16 Jenny Edkins, *Whose Hunger? Concepts of Famine, Practices of Aid* (Minnesota: University of Minnesota Press, 2000, pp. 49ff).

17 Ludwig Wittgenstein, *Philosophical Investigations* (Oxford: Blackwell, 1967, pp. 217).

18 cf. Judith Shklar, *The Faces of Injustice* (New Haven: Yale University Press, 1990); Jonathan Glover, *Humanity: A Moral History of the Twentieth Century* (London: Pimlico, 2001 [1999]); Susan Neiman, *Evil in Modern Thought* (Princeton University Press, 2002).

19 Statements on 'over-population' are ethically relevant: 'The argument "too many people" too often means in the author's inner judgement too many of the *wrong sort* of people. It expresses a deeper repugnance and incomprehension, a failure to understand, even to accept the right to exist, of people of another race and culture' (Arnold, *Famine*, p. 40ff; see also E. F. Mettrick, 'Population, Poverty and Ethical Competence', *International Journal of Ethics* 29:4 (1929, pp. 445–55). A critical point about 'over-population' has been made by Nobel Peace Prize winner Muhammad Yunus, the founder of the Grameen Bank, in his Commonwealth Lecture 2003

(Commonwealth Institute, London, 11 March 2003). Let me quote a very important statement from Yunus' introduction which says a lot about the potential of 'raw revelation' and 'messy theology in the world':

> I don't see the possibility of a human being becoming a 'problem' when it comes to his or her own well-being. All the ingredients for ending the poverty of a person always comes neatly packaged with the person himself. A human being is born in this world fully equipped not only to take care of himself (which all other life-forms can do too), but also to contribute in enlarging the well-being of the world as a whole (that's where the special role of a human being lies).

20 Cf. Harry Frankfurt, *The Reasons of Love* (Princeton: Princeton University Press, 2004, Ch. 1).
21 It can even be argued that droughts are not to be interpreted as 'natural disasters' – cf. Nicole Ball, 'Understanding the Causes of African Famine', *Journal of Modern African Studies*, 1976. Ball claims that a drought should properly be viewed as resulting from a combination of social, political, economic and environmental factors (p. 520).
22 George Steiner, 'Ten (Possible) Reasons for the Sadness of Thoughts', #1 – see http://laughingbone.blogspot.com/2005/07/george-steiner-ten-possible-reasons.html.
23 Steiner, ibid.
24 William James, 'Pragmatism's Conception of Truth', Lecture 6 in William James, *Pragmatism: A New Name for Some Old Ways of Thinking* (New York: Longman, Green and Co. 1907, pp. 76–9, 80).
25 Cf. Charles S. Peirce's pragmatist criterion of meaning – Charles Peirce, *Collected Works*, 6 vols, ed. C. Hartshorne and P. Weiss (Cambridge, MA: Harvard University Press, 1931–35, 5.9).
26 Bernhard Bolzano, *Lehrbuch der Religionswissenschaft. Teil I* (Stuttgart: F. Frommann, 1994, §16, pp. 86ff.).
27 Self-transformation not only as a conscious effort but also as a process of being moulded is a sign of recognizing revelation: 'The transfiguring of the world in Christ can seem partial or marginal if we have not learned, by speaking and hearing parables, a willingness to lose the identities and perceptions we make for ourselves: all good stories change us if we hear them attentively; the most serious stories change us radically' (Rowan Williams, *On Christian Theology* p. 42). Ethics with a disruptive force takes itself seriously and is thus a reply to the challenge of dikedicy.
28 Aristotle, *Metaphysics* VII, 3, 1029a19–21.
29 cf. Hilary Putnam, 'How Not to Solve Ethical Problems', in Hilary Putnam, *Realism with a Human Face* (Cambridge, MA: Harvard University Press, 1990, pp. 179–92, esp. 181ff).
30 By the same token, Thomas Nagel reminded us that the fact that we can reflect upon the absurdity of our lives, placing them in a bigger and bigger context, is in fact not a shame but a sign of our abilities to ask questions and thus a sign of our human dignity; cf. Thomas Nagel, 'The Absurd'. *The Journal of Philosophy* 68:20 (1971, pp. 716–27).
31 Arnold, *Famine*, p. 7.
32 Talking about 'the world' may evoke in us a sense of helplessness and confusion. Where should we begin to talk about the world? Where does it commence and where does it end? This frustration could be compared with the frustration of the language philosopher trying to think about language as such or again it could be compared with the frustration of the sociologist who is to talk about a vast region or a whole nation. It has been observed that particular villages – if they are carefully chosen – turn out to serve as 'windows into a region' helping us to understand the structure of a whole region by way of example. The method of 'windows into regions' has been proposed by sociologist S. Seneratne in Sri Lanka (cf. Robert Chambers, *Rural Development* (London: Intermediate Publications, 1983, p. 66f). Similarly, we can understand language by analysing particular language games in order to understand the dynamics of rules and rule following or the embeddedness of language within a form of

life. Because of the connections between various language games and because of the link between linguistic and extra-linguistic activities, we can gain important insights into the way language works and the purposes it fulfils (cf. Wittgenstein, *Philosophical Investigations*, p. 65ff.).

33 Kirsten Hastrup, 'Hunger and the Hardness of Facts', *Man* 28:4 (1993, pp. 727–39, esp. 727).

34 Wittgenstein, *Philosophical Investigations*, p. 109.

35 Cf. Philip McMichael, 'Global Food Politics', in Fred Magdoff, John Bellamy Foster and Frederick Buttel (eds), *Hungry for Profit: The Agribusiness Threat to Farmers,Food, and the Environment* (New York: Monthly Review Press, 2000, pp. 125–43); H. Friedmann, 'The Political Economy of Food: The Rise and Fall of the Potwar International Food Order', *The American Journal of Sociology* 88 (1982, pp. 248–86).

36 J. Edkins, *Whose Hunger?*, p. 23. Food is a cultural concept: 'Cooking is a moral process, transferring raw matter from "nature" to the state of "culture", and thereby taming and domesticating it ... Food is therefore "civilised" by cooking, not simply at the level of practice, but at the level of the imagination' (Deborah Lupton, *Food, the Body and the Self* (London: Sage, 1996, p. 2).

37 Sen, *Poverty and Famines*, p. 43.

38 A key concept to understanding world hunger will be the concept of 'vulnerability': 'Perhaps the most helpful general conceptual framework on hunger is that suggested by Watts and Bohle (1993). They have produced a method for the causal analysis of hunger and famine, through what they call the "space of vulnerability". This gives some theoretical substance to the investigation of individual famines. They argue that the three dimensions of entitlement, political economy and empowerment are the most important for understanding the various manifestations of vulnerability in social and geographical space' (Peter Atkins and Ian Bowler, *Food in Society: Economy, Culture, Geography*; London: Arnold and New York: Oxford University Press, 2001, p. 123). By selecting basic dimensions of a conceptual grid to understand world hunger one has made an important step in the direction of possible strategies.

39 Atkins and Bowler, *Food in Society*, Ch. 23. That is why it is useful to talk about 'food regimes' to grasp the problem of food in society conceptually (ibid., Ch. 3).

40 A. Sen, *Poverty and Famines*, esp. Chs 4 and 10.

41 Jean Drèze and Amartya Sen, *Hunger and Public Action* (Oxford: Clarendon, 1989, p. 118). The fact that we are confronted with a network of decisions points to the fact that there is a lot that can be changed about the conditions that bring about world hunger.

42 See e.g., Janet Poppendieck, 'Want Amid Plenty: From Hunger to Inequality', in F. Magdoff, J. Bellamy Foster and F. Buttel, eds, *Hungry for Profit: The Agrobusiness Threat to Farmers, Food, and the Environment* (pp. 189–202, 198):

> As we institutionalize and expand the response, of course, we also institutionalize and reinforce the problem definition that underlies it. Sociologists have long argued that the definitional stage is the crucial period in the career of a social problem. Competing definitions vie for attention, and the winners shape the solutions and garner the resources. It is important, therefore, to understand the competing definitions of the situation that 'hunger' crowds out. What is lost from public view, from our operant consciousness, as we work to end hunger? In short, defining the problem, as hunger contributes to the obfuscation of the underlying problems of hunger and inequality. Many more people are indeed hungry, but hunger, like homelessness and a host of other problems, is a symptom, not a cause, of poverty. And poverty, in turn, in an affluent society like our own, is fundamentally a product of inequality ... Defining the problem as hunger ignores a whole host of other needs. Poor people need food, but they also need housing, transportation, clothing, medical care, meaningful work, opportunities for civic and political participation, and recreation. By focusing on hunger, we imply that the food portion of this

complex web of human needs can be met independently of the rest, can be exempted or protected from the overall household budget deficit.

43 Herbert Gans had already discussed the positive function of poverty – with the underlying assumption that a persistent phenomenon like poverty must serve some interests and satisfy needs – in an influential paper in the 1970s; see Herbert Gans, 'The Positive Functions of World Poverty', *American Journal of Sociology* 78:2 (1973, pp. 275–89). His insights can be applied to the tragedy of world hunger as well.

44 Pontifical Council Cor Unum, *World Hunger – a Challenge for All* (Vatican, 1996, 10c).

45 Cf. Onora O'Neill, *Faces of Hunger: An Essay on Poverty, Justice and Development* (London: Allen and Unwin, 1986, p. 18ff).

46 O. O'Neill, *Faces of Hunger*, p. 3.

47 cf. P. Atkins and I. Bowler, *Food in Society*, p. 134ff; Arnold, *Famine*, Ch. 4.

48 cf. Peter Unger, *Living High and Letting Die: Our Illusion of Innocence* (New York: Oxford University Press, 1996).

49 Cor Unum, *World Hunger*, p. 64. World hunger points very forcefully to sinful conditions: hunger is connected with cooperative conflicts within societies (cf. Drèze and Sen, *Hunger and Public Action*, p. 47ff.). William Wilde, for example, reports from Ireland: 'There was a famine in the summer of this year; called for a long time afterwards "samhra na mearaithne" (the summer of slight acquaintance) because no one used to recognise friend or relative, in consequence of the greatness of the famine' (J. Edkins, *Whose Hunger?*, p. 20).

50 Susan James, 'The Duty to Relieve Suffering', *Ethics* 93:1 (1982, pp. 4–21).

51 F. M. Lappé and J. Collins, *World Hunger: Twelve Myths* (London: Earthscan Publications, 1986, p. 131).

52 Karl Popper, *Vermutungen und Widerlegungen* (Tübingen: Mohr, 2000, pp. 51, 286); Karl Popper, *Logik der Forschung* (Tübingen: Mohr, 1984, p. 15).

53 Garrett Hardin, 'Lifeboat Ethics: The Case Against Helping the Poor', *Psychology Today*, September 1974.

54 O'Neill, *Faces of Hunger*, p. 26.

55 According to MacIntyre an epistemological crisis arises when a person has to acknowledge 'the possibility of systematically different possibilities of interpretation, or the existence of alternative and rival schemata which yield mutually incompatible accounts of what is going on around him' (Alasdair MacIntyre, 'Epistemological Crises', in Stanley Hauerwas and L. Gregory Jones, eds, *Why Narrative?* (Grand Rapids, MI: Eerdmans, 1989, pp. 138–57, esp. 139). A disruption is more than that. First, because we are confronted with a sense of urgency and the necessity to make judgements and a decision; secondly, because it is not about different possibilities of interpretation, not even different possibilities of interpreting one's Self, but about the question of the righteousness of 'being in the world' and the insight that tragical circumstances make it impossible.

56 Cf. Dan Diner, *Beyond the Conceivable* (Berkeley, CA: University of California Press, 2000); S. Neiman, *Evil in Modern Thought*, Ch. 4.

57 Cf. Susannah Ticciati, *Job and the Disruption of Identity: Reading Beyond Barth* (London: T&T Clark, 2005).

58 Gustavo Gutiérrez, *On Job: God-Talk and the Suffering of the Innocent* (Maryknoll: Orbis, 1987.)

59 Jean Drèze and Amartya Sen have listed several factors that constitute differences between 'hunger then' and 'hunger now': health problems in relation to food stem today often from having too much; the persistence of hunger linked to substantial inequality; the dependence of one's group's ability to command food on its relative position and comparative economic power *vis-à-vis* other groups can be especially important in market economies; the recognition of the importance of the institution of wage labour; changes in production and the problem of environmental degradation; recognition of the role of the state in combating hunger (Drèze and Sen, *Hunger and Public Action*, pp. 4–7). Furthermore, in a global village the ethical dimension of the challenge of world hunger and famines is changing, as Onora O'Neill wisely

remarked: '*Any* famine raises pressing problems for those immediately affected; modern famines raise questions for the far wider range of individuals, institutions and collectivities who *could* affect the course of famine' (O'Neill, *Faces of Hunger*, p. 16).

60 Arnold, *Famine*, p. 6. There are many ways of 'reading' the concepts that constitute the conceptual framework to understand world hunger. We can think again and again about the challenge of world hunger and in the pain of thinking about world hunger our established categories may lose some of their plausibility. There are many decisions involved, as we have seen, as there are paradoxes and mechanisms of great complexity. There is, to give an illustration:

> a fundamental tension between the goal of reducing hunger as quickly and as permanently as possible and the desire to make at most marginal changes in consumption and production patterns. Leaving very unequal levels of consumption untouched while trying to relieve hunger through market mechanisms, will require much more food than the hungry themselves will consume. Leaving very unequal asset patterns unchanged increases the need for 'supplementary' nutrition programmes and increases the risk that they will become relatively permanent subsidies for people. (C. Christensen, 'World Hunger: A Structural Approach', *International Organizations* 32:3 (1978), pp. 745–74, 773).

A deeper look at world hunger will unveil many decisions concerning one particular point with effects on other areas.

61 C. S. Lewis, *A Grief Observed* (London: Faber & Faber, 1966 [1961], p. 8). In analogy to the three levels of theodicy we could distinguish three levels of dikedicy – a theoretical reflection, a practical reflection with a clear position and practical interests, and a personal reflection that acknowledges self-involvement. Facing world hunger forces us to engage in a personal reflection that considers the fact that we are involved as non-innocent actors. This concession allows for the disruptive power of world hunger to unfold.

62 Cf. Frithjof Bergmann, *On Being Free* (University of Notre Dame Press, 1979).

63 Liam O'Flaherty, *Famine* (FF) (Dublin: Wolfhound Press, 1991 [1984]).

64 Onora O'Neill, 'Lifeboat Earth', *Philosophy and Public Affairs* 4:3 (1975, pp. 273–92).

65 J. Edkins, *Whose Hunger?*, p. 121.

66 Friedrich Schleiermacher, *The Christian Faith*, edited by H. R. Mackintosh and J. S. Stewart (Edinburgh: T&T Clark, 1928, pp. 721–2).

67 Thomas Talbott, 'Providence, Freedom and Human Destiny', *Religious Studies* 26 (1990, pp. 227–45); cf. Eric Reitan, 'Eternal Damnation and Blessed Ignorance: Is the Damnation of Some Incompatible with the Salvation of Any? *Religious Studies* 38 (2002, pp. 429–50).

68 This is, of course, a famous motif to be found in Camus' writings.

6

The Wound of Knowledge: Epistemic Mercy and World Hunger

Clemens Sedmak

World hunger unfolds its disruptive power as a permanent 'thorn in the flesh', as a thorn in the well-protected flesh of our convictions and the body of our ethical judgements. We may feel tempted to ask that this thorn would be taken away and we might receive the reply that God's grace is enough (2 Cor. 12.8ff). A thorn in the flesh is a constant reminder of our weakness. This weakness is an emptiness that invites silence and surrender; it creates a space where words cannot console us, where human actions cannot create a comfort zone where we can come to the rest of self-righteousness. In other words: disruptions create deserts. The disruptive power of world hunger creates the desert of emptiness – we do not have the language, we do not have the epistemic tools and we do not have the practical means to fill the space in a way that the void can be taken away. Acknowledging the disruptive power of world hunger means to accept the permanency of the desert as part of the human condition. The desert is a place where we can seek God rather than the consolations of God. Knowing about world hunger brings us out into a desert of knowledge, into an epistemic void. The epistemic desert is a place where the painful quest for truth is not distracted by a clear structure of the epistemic landscape or the possibility to come to a rest in the urban dwellings of safe theories. Living in an epistemic desert means 'knowing rough'. It means accepting a state of epistemic home-lessness. Epistemic homelessness is a lack of safe solutions and obvious roads to travel. It means both facing the challenge to stay (and endure the pain of staying) and the challenge to wander around. There is always, as we have seen, the temptation to reduce world hunger to a technical or to a moral 'problem'. There is the temptation to give up staying as well as the temptation to give up wandering around. There is the temptation to minimize the pain by developing theories, generating terminologies, initiating some course of action. And this is fair and just. You have to get orientation even if you are knowing rough. But this orientation will not allow you to come to a rest, to give up the painful quest for truth, to mollify the hardships of rough knowing by nurturing the illusion of 'solutions'.

Temptations arise in moments of hunger (see Mt. 4.2), in moments where you feel a void, an emptiness. People who sleep rough are tempted to flee into alcohol as a means of comfort; people who know rough are tempted to flee into recipes for change or a spiritualization of the situation as a means of comfort. There is always the temptation to read the desert as a friendly place, to turn away from the world if not literally then epistemically by looking for the general and not the particular, by looking for the metaphorical and not the real, by looking for the invisible and not the visible. Transformation Theology as developed in this book is an attempt to accept the pressing difficulty of situations without using protective metaphors or strategies of spiritualization too quickly. Basically, transformation theology is about the fact that encountering the world can be painful, and that this pain is a source for theological and ethical reflection.

1. Epistemic Vulnerability

Transformation Theology talks about epistemic vulnerability. This is one of the lessons of world hunger. The disruptive power of world hunger erodes our epistemic systems and creates a desert of knowledge, a vast emptiness that needs to be filled with things known, things hoped for, things done, things believed in. Knowing about world hunger creates a wound that does not allow us to say that the world is good as it is, that does not allow us to say that it is possible to live in the world without pain and suffering. World hunger strikes a wound of knowledge. It is the wound of knowing something and at the same time the wound of not knowing enough.[1] We know that 24,000 people die from hunger each and every day. And yet we do not know what to do about it, how to cope with this knowledge without diminishing or denying it, how to fight against the tragedy of world hunger with the means that are at our disposal. There is the wound of knowledge grounded in coping with something we know and there is the wound of knowledge based on ignorance and the pain of not-knowing or not knowing enough. In the case of world hunger it is one and the same wound. It is the wound of not knowing enough and it is the wound of knowing too much. It is the wound of 'docta ignorantia', of informed ignorance. The price we have to pay for disruption consists in creating this wound of informed ignorance, since it disrupts our categories and forces us to understand this process as a disruption.

The kind of epistemic vulnerability stripped bare by the wound of knowing about world hunger is not simply the possibility of making a wrong turn, a mode of fallibility. It goes deeper than that. It is the expression and result of the fact that epistemic justice is beyond reach in the face of world hunger. Epistemic justice is a quality of systems of orientation by which they are able to do justice to the facts, or to consider all relevant perspectives and then achieve epistemic equilibrium.[2] Epistemic justice reflects a process of reflection and deliberation that arrives at a point of epistemic satisfaction where efforts of knowing and understanding can come to rest. Epistemic justice is a way of settling within a particular position and system of orientation. It is a condition where an epistemic home has been built. This is obviously an important aim in the treatment of ethical questions. Problems here can be answered in a way that a solution gives shelter to a problem. But this is not always the case. There are situations where we have to live with knowing rough.

A classical example where epistemic justice cannot be reached is the tragic structure of an ethical dilemma such as 'Sophie's choice': if a mother is in a position where she has to choose which one of her children should survive, she will in any case make a bad choice. Whatever she does, she will have to live with guilt and shame and remorse and the wound of knowing that she did something that led to terrible consequences.[3] The epistemic wound of knowing about the tragic does not heal. It is the wound of knowing too much and at the same time knowing too little. An epistemic wound takes on a disruptive structure with at least three effects:

(1) It is unpredictable when and where this wound breaks open. It is comparable to a situation of bereavement where the pain of loss can sink to the bottom of our lives for a while, and all of a sudden, without any identifiable external reason, come back to the surface and torment us again. The disruptive effect of an epistemic wound is not a constant and calculable pain, but an unpredictable way of suffering that does not take 'its course' or offer patterns of regularity. If you have lost your child, you may be at peace in one moment, and then an encounter with a child on the street, a reminder of something your child has done or said, or simply an inner movement of the soul, may trigger the source of pain and the wound of knowledge starts to hurt again, and this pain may be so strong that your peace of mind is lost.

(2) A second effect of an epistemic wound is its life-shaping character – it is part of the human condition of the knower. It constitutes a new way of being in the world as a vulnerable being that cannot control the cognitive contents by a 'grammar of knowledge' or by rules of epistemic hygiene. A person with an epistemic wound is transformed in her heart, in her very being, by the burden of knowledge she has to carry. We may think of the story of Robert A. Jonas, the father of Rebecca.[4] Rebecca was born prematurely in July 1992. She was too weak to survive; she lived for less than four hours and died in the arms of her father. Knowing about Rebecca during the months of pregnancy and expectation transformed her parents' lives. Knowing about Rebecca's birth and death created a wound of knowledge that has become a defining part of their identity, a constitutive dimension of their being in the world. The knowledge about Rebecca's life and death is a source of pain that shapes the view of virtues such as gratitude and solidarity, that shapes the pillars of a human form of life such as an ethics of memory or an ethics of the courage to go on living in spite of pain.

(3) Thirdly, an epistemic wound gives reasons to act. Referring to this wound

offers both the motivational strength and the justificatory potential to act. Let us come back to the story of Rebecca: the father weeping about the death of his daughter does not have to offer reasons for his tears beyond saying 'My daughter was born and died'. The father trying to cope with the loss will not have to offer reasons why he visits the tomb of his child and why he would perform a special ritual on 29 July, the day of Rebecca's birth and death. The wound of knowledge gives reasons to act. If a parish is involved in fasting in order to contribute to the fight against world hunger, and you ask the reason for their actions, it is enough for the people to say: There is so much hunger in the world. An epistemic wound gives reasons to act.

Epistemic vulnerability consists in accepting wounds of knowledge. Living in the world means living within structures of the tragic, structures of a finality of non-resolution that cannot be controlled by conceptual means nor eradicated by causal mechanisms. The world is a place where we are reminded of our epistemic vulnerability, the fact that there is so much tragic knowledge, knowledge that carries with it the potential to harm us. An ethically sensitive person will acknowledge that ethical dilemmas are part of our everyday life. Should I have a birthday party for my daughter or give money to a relief agency? Should I finish writing an inspirational book or visit friends who need my company? Should I turn down a job offer from a dubious company or risk financial hardships for my family? Should I engage in political struggle and risk the well-being of family members or support oppressive structures by my silence? Should I get out of my comfortable living with all its responsibilities or carry on with a constantly bad conscience?[5] An ethical knower is a person living under conditions of epistemic vulnerability. There are tragedies that keep unfolding their disruptive power the more we know about them: world hunger, homelessness, migration and refugees, HIV/Aids. Living with epistemic vulnerability is part of being a person in the world, a person with relationships, a person who allows the world to shape herself. In other words: a person who is not aware of her epistemic vulnerability has lived a sheltered life. In his novel *Ah, but Your Land is Beautiful*, South African writer Alan Paton describes the courage a young black South African displays by becoming involved in the political struggle against apartheid. He is well aware of the risk he takes and the possible wounds that might be inflicted on him, but he says: 'I don't worry about the wounds. When I go up there, which is my intention, the Big Judge will say to me, Where are your wounds? and if I say I haven't any, he will say, Was there nothing to fight for? I couldn't face that question.'[6] Being in the world and facing the human condition does not leave people uninjured. We live under conditions that render epistemic justice impossible. We have to learn to live with open wounds and contradictions. The disruptive power of world hunger does not allow 'processed theories'; we are left with raw thinking and rough knowing. Epistemic justice is not attainable. We cannot afford a view from nowhere in the midst of suffering; we cannot hide behind a veil of ignorance. The scenario of the above-mentioned gathering of victims made very clear that we have to face the wounds of knowledge and live with these wounds. In fact, knowing about our epistemic vulnerability is a first step of understanding what it means to live in the world. It is also a step towards self-transformation and the bread value of ethical reflection as a response to the challenge of dikedicy. Europe carries the wound of knowing about Auschwitz. It is this wound that makes people sensitive to current developments; it is this wound that makes people humble when thinking about being human and the human condition; it is this wound that allows for a true conversation that cannot come to an end. As a wound it does not simply disappear. Auschwitz is a strong reminder that epistemic justice about what happened in Europe in the twentieth century is not attainable. World hunger with its own force is a reminder with a similar message: that there is something deeply wrong with us and the world, and that we cannot arrive at a point where we can claim that 'this is *the* solution'.[7] Living with this wound means having to live a life of 'knowing rough' without the consolations of epistemic justice.

If epistemic justice is not attainable, what is the alternative? The alternative is mercy, not justice. Let us explore this answer. How could we approach a concept of *epistemic mercy* and what does that mean?[8] The structure of epistemic mercy as a response to epistemic vulnerability can be outlined in four points:

(1) Epistemic justice consists in the construction of general concepts; epistemic mercy is the plea for the particular. Living with wounds of knowledge makes epistemology as 'messy' as local theologies since the imperative to respect the particular transforms epistemology into a set of local epistemologies. To have epistemic mercy means not to fit objects into general categories, transforming them into 'epistemic objects', a dynamics that has been sketched in the fifth chapter. Epistemic mercy is the quality of a knower who accepts the particularity and irreducibility of the individual and the particular. It is the quality of a knower who knows about the limits of the general. Rowan Williams has mentioned at some point that authenticity means not to go too far away from the concrete and the particular.[9] Transformation theology is ready to face the particular, the concrete, the sensible; in short, the entry points for disruption. Epistemic mercy is about respecting the particular dynamics of a situation, the particular response that a situation calls for. We cannot face world hunger in terms of 'how to deal with this problem in general terms'. We will hardly arrive at a bread value of our ethical reflections unless we are willing to face the question: 'What does the tragedy of world hunger mean for me? In other words: How am I to respond to it, how does world hunger disrupt my life, and how far do I make space for this disruptive power to unfold?' The plea for the concrete, sensible and particular is especially forceful in the presence of the tragic: you cannot respond to the tragedies of 7 July 2005 in London in a general way. Donald MacKinnon has reminded us that it is 'a grave mistake to generalize about tragedy as if there were an "essence" of

the tragic'.[10] Faced with the tragic we have to search for an adequate response, however stumbling and tentative, exposing our insecurity and loss of epistemic consolations. Epistemic mercy is a commitment to the particular and concrete, the sensible and unique.[11] It is a commitment to keep the wound of knowledge with its disruptive power open.[12]

(2) Epistemic mercy means to be able to live with the contradictions and the challenges of the tragic. It is an attitude of humility that acknowledges that the way things are in the world cannot be transformed into a smooth (however complex) epistemic situation without disrespecting the particular demands of situations. Epistemic justice is about reaching equilibrium. The concept of epistemic mercy reminds us of the invitation to accept disruptions and the disruptive power of the tragic. If we accept the disruptive power of world hunger we cannot attain reflective equilibrium, we have to acknowledge the non-solvable, the non-reducible. Epistemic mercy means to be humble and accept the force of the causal that cannot be fitted into neat, conceptual categories.

(3) Epistemic mercy means to accept that 'ideas' cannot be forced. There is a moment of grace in the process of understanding. In his famous talk on *Wissenschaft als Beruf* Max Weber pointed out that scholarship and scientific study are in need of inspirations and idea.[13] A good scholar is a creative person. In fact, the idea of a gathering of victims would force us to give a justification for the topics we deal with, the questions we treat, the issues we face.[14] Epistemic mercy acknowledges the importance of ideas when confronted with the faces of world hunger or poverty. Poverty is not a technical problem where we need as much money as possible; it is a challenge that calls for ideas. Powerful strategies like microcredits or street newspapers have been triggered by ideas. And ideas cannot be constructed. Epistemic mercy accepts that there is a moment of 'Unverfügbarkeit' in the knowledge process, a moment of non-accessibility. From a theological perspective, of course, we could ask ourselves whether there is a causal connection between prayers and ideas.[15] There is a moment of the gift-like in the process of knowing, a moment of grace. Epistemic mercy is an attitude that accepts the limits of planning and predicting in the construction of theories by acknowledging the importance of ideas that emerge through inspiration.

(4) Epistemic mercy, finally, is about the recognition of limits. It is a humbling insight that the process of getting to know something or someone does not come to an end. It is a reminder of limits and the wounds of knowledge that we know that there is so much that we do not know. It is humbling to realize that we do not control the aspects of our ethical sphere. Purposeful action takes place within contexts of purposelessness.[16] It is in this sense that epistemic mercy is an invitation to live with limits. A special kind of limitedness that needs to be considered is shown in the wounds of knowledge and the knowledge about the structurally tragic that is part of our living in the world.

Epistemic mercy with its emphasis on the particular is open to disruptions. Only a view that takes into account particulars can be disrupted. Epistemic mercy is an attitude of the knower who is ready to live with disruptions. It is at the same time a commitment to living under conditions of epistemic vulnerability. Epistemic vulnerability makes us see certain acts of ethical cognition as tragic acts. As a tragic act it is in a certain sense the opposite of a speech act. The basic idea of a speech act is to say something and by doing so to perform a particular action. A tragic act is an epistemic structure where a person says something and by saying makes what she says implausible or impossible. If we say that world hunger is an ethical problem we can go on talking calmly and in a matter-of-fact way about world hunger, and in a way that treats it as a problem that can be solved. By approaching the issue in this way we do not do justice to the tragedies involved. There has to be a certain hesitation, a certain honest stumbling. It is this attitude of hesitation as an expression of love, respect and concern that makes fluency and literacy in ethical tragedies impossible.[17] Speech acts about ethical dilemmas and tragic situations seem implausible since the mode of silence and hesitation seems more adequate than eloquence and epistemic self-assurance. And the knowledge process we engage in forces us to recognize the tragic structures of the world. Understanding world hunger means to recognize the tragedies involved, the tragic reality of human lives ruined and shortened, the tragic reality of structural connections between wealth and poverty. And these insights render our ethical discourses in themselves tragic, since we are caught in performative contradictions. You cannot have a fluent discourse in the modes of hesitance, silence and disruption. In this sense, epistemic vulnerability disrupts the logic of our speech acts. For doing ethics in the face of the victims and the challenge of dikedicy forces us to acknowledge that in the light (darkness) of world hunger, talking and analysing and more talking and more analysing produces negative outcomes, produces semantic emptiness and a pragmatic void.[18] This is the fundamental tragedy of ethical discourse that produces a wound of knowledge of its own.

There is another important element here: the temptation to cover the tragic by vast amounts of knowledge. We are tempted to cover the wound of knowledge with insights and expertise. We are tempted to fall into some kind of epistemic activism, trying to collect as much knowledge as possible to soothe the pressure of not knowing enough. We may get so immersed in this process of theory construction that the wound of knowledge loses its painfulness. The more we know the more we might lose the sense of urgency and the sense that there is something that has to be done, that has to be changed and transformed, even within ourselves. There is the temptation to evade the sense of the tragic in our condition of epistemic vulnerability by honouring knowledge in its ascribed intrinsic value. We could introduce the term 'epistemic threshold hypothesis'. There is in ethical discourse a threshold which dictates that when we have attained a certain degree of knowledge, we do not gain more understanding when we acquire new pieces of information, but actually lose understanding. There seems to be a point where we could say: the more we know, the less we understand – if we take 'understanding' to be a sapiential skill that translates into ordering and judging in a way that bridges the gap between the conceptual and the causal. It is at the point of this epistemic threshold that the wound of knowledge breaks open, the wound of not knowing enough and at the same time knowing too much. To put it in simple words: we can read a hundred books on the challenge of world hunger and after that we are (depending on the books) pretty well informed about the phenomenon of world hunger. And being confronted with the complexity of the issue we lose the sense that there is anything that can be done at all, and might feel inclined to take refuge in a state of cynicism or scepticism analysing the shortcomings of concrete action. Cynicism is an attitude that is convinced of the ultimate fruitlessness of human life and acting. This trap cannot lightly be dismissed, especially since intellectuals are able to embed events into a larger context. If we embed a certain event E into a context K, then E usually loses importance if extending K. This is the danger of moving too far away from the concrete and the particular. It is this cynical attitude that made intellectuals criticize Mother Theresa's work 'from the outside'. It is this attitude that invites forms of sophism, forms of creating 'grey areas' and thus blurring the differences between 'right' and 'wrong', forming complexity, producing insecurity of action and finally justifying any position – an approach that can be justified by pointing out the complexity of the issues. We must not forget that the tragedy of world hunger is very simple: people are starving and we live lives of abundance. Ethically speaking, it seems to be more difficult to come up with justifying dozens of qualifications than to justify that a concrete course of action needs to be taken.

Epistemic vulnerability is a condition that tells us that we carry wounds of knowledge as part of our being in the world. These wounds present themselves with an authority of non-resolution. We need epistemic mercy to be able to recognize these wounds and live in the world at the same time. The finality reached is not a Cartesian finality of a *fundamentum inconcussum* that presents itself as an epistemic authority but is a finality of non-resolution.[19] This authority, however, can be seen not as an arrival point, where our mind can come to rest as in Descartes' case, but as a point of departure that demands action and motivates us to act. Epistemic vulnerability can make us say: it is in our weakness that we are strong. It is our weakness that reminds us of the task of transformation. Epistemic mercy is the attitude that prevents the wound of knowledge from losing its openness, its painfulness, its disruptive power. And this disruptive power is the power to change and transform, a transformation which is demanded as the only possible response to the tragedy of world hunger, whenever hunger is viewed as more than merely a 'problem'. The task of transformation can be read as a Christian imperative to renew the face of the earth. In the words of Oliver Davies: 'Central to Christian tradition is the conviction that the transformation which takes place in Jesus according to the Easter narrative is one which brings about a changed state with respect to our own humanity, which is to say our redemption from sin and death into newness of life.'

2. The Fundamental Praxis of Feeding the Hungry

Where should we get the strength for transformation? And what is the power to transform? The will to transform has to be guided and informed by imagination, narrative and example. And the wound of knowledge can gain special force in this task by appealing to the authority of 'fundamental praxis'. Fundamental praxis can be defined only by citing examples. More exactly, it receives its explanation in the examples of people who have shown by the testimony of their lives what it means to give hope in the midst of tragedy. For instance, it is impressive (meaning it makes an impression, it leaves a mark, it transforms one's life) to see Dietrich Bonhoeffer's struggle with the pressure of being exposed to forces beyond his control in prison.[20] It is impressive to see the power to forgive displayed by Nelson Mandela or Desmond Tutu. Fundamental praxis is not a praxis without wounds or mistakes, failures and scars. On the contrary: fundamental praxis gives us an example of how to live a full human life including the dimensions of human growth in the midst of pain and suffering and be able to come to terms with limits. Fundamental praxis teaches us what it means to be a loving person in the world which is a place of intractabilities. By looking at the power of such examples, ethical considerations can become deep, thick and fresh.

Examples bridge the gap between the general and the particular. Examples 'indicate' something. Examples are especially necessary in situations where we do not have general rules.[21] There are no 'general rules' of how to live the human life. We need examples, models, testimonies. Such models can be called models of 'fundamental praxis'. Fundamental praxis is a way of being in the world that makes us see the world in a new light. Fundamental praxis is a kind of paradigmatic life that serves as a model for a full life, that creates opportunities for disruption by making people see new possibilities of being human. A fundamental praxis gives a thick, deep and fresh example of what it means to be in the world. A fundamental praxis serves as a point of reference that gives us a sense of priorities and urgencies. Especially in the confrontation with world hunger, where we easily feel lost and confused, models of human life give orientation and a sense of direction. When we accept a person's life as a paradigmatic model, as a form of fundamental praxis, we have reached a foundation, again not in the Cartesian sense with its moment of 'arrival and end', but in the sense of having gained access to a motivation to act, to a model of life that helps us come to terms with the sadness of thoughts. Looking at examples of fundamental praxis helps us go beyond the conceptual and to enter the sphere of the causal, of transformation. Models of fundamental praxis provide narratives of identity that go beyond the people living the paradigmatic life; their lives are a source of identity for us. In this sense, the promise of a fundamental praxis is the promise that the force of love can shape a person's life. Love as a 'concept' has lost much of its promise of renewal. It seems flat and weak, worn out and withered, too good to be true and too unrealistic to be causally relevant; and its causal weakness as such has threatened its integrity. The reality of love stripped bare, without the veils of kitsch, empty promises, sentimental feelings and moments of affective fundamentalism, is about the force that gives identity to a human person – the force to love, the force to care about something. The right to care about something is the above-mentioned right to act morally. World hunger denies people the right to act morally. It not only brings about a deprivation of commitments and relationships, but it also makes acts of giving and caring difficult, if not impossible. In confronting the tragedy of world hunger and the wound of knowledge we have to admit that we are lost. We have lost universal standards for living a righteous life in the world and we have abandoned the hope that there is one right course of action. But by turning to examples of fundamental praxis, and by acknowledging the always surprising power of love, we can gain grounds for hope once again. The disruptive power of world hunger can act as the thorn in our flesh that makes us struggle to become people of love. People like Dom Helder Camara, the legendary Brazilian bishop, or Peter Benenson, the founder of Amnesty International, show that one single person can make a difference. The most important 'fundamental praxis' of all is – from a Christian point of view – the life of Jesus, the Christ. And this life teaches us vitally what it means to love, to live a life of love, to be a loving person. In order to understand the fundamental character of Jesus' life therefore it is helpful to read what is said about Jesus in the New Testament as a revelation about love. The incarnation of God is the culmination of divine causality. God is love and divine actions are love. In his discussions of revelation as divine causality above, Paul Janz has shown that the 'content' of revelation, as a divinely causal self-communication, is declared by the scriptures to be most fundamentally 'a righteousness which comes from God'. But something further must now be added to this. For while the divine righteousness is indeed the 'content' of the divinely causal self-communication, the form in which this righteousness is communicated is love. The essential form of the divine causality in Jesus Christ is therefore always love. That is why it seems helpful to interpret the scriptures based on the heuristic assumption that whatever is said about Jesus (his words, his deeds) reveals something about God in the praxis of love. We could call this an *agapeistic interpretation* of the sacred texts. Jesus' life shows what it means to love.

Let us look at this love in the light of hunger. Jesus feeds the hungry on various occasions. What do we learn about love, for example, from the feeding of the 5,000 as described in Mt. 14.13–21? An agapeistic reading of this text will tell us that Jesus was praying in a lonely place, nourishing his soul through encounter with his divine Father (Mt. 14.13). God is the fountain of love. Love is not an energy that is generated by human means. It stems from a divine source. In fact, love is the very way or the form in which divine causality is at work. Jesus retreats from the world to a deserted and not very hospitable place, expressing his love for God and seeking a sacred place and hour where he can deepen the presence of God's love within him. Being in the world in a loving way, we could learn from this, means retreating from the busy-ness of the world in order to receive the courage and strength to love. We have to be at home in the desert in order to be able to face the marketplace.[22] The desert is the place of silence and the painful quest for truth. It exposes our failures and does not allow for any long-term nourishment of illusions. The desert is a place of disruptions of our images of our selves and of the world. It is the place where we can least control the access to God, where we have to open ourselves to divine causality.[23] Silence is the place where the wound of knowledge can break open. It is the place of attentiveness, also attentiveness to pain. Without silence, we cannot 'get any closer to knowing who we are before God'.[24] The desert is the place where we have to live with the wound of self-knowledge as well as with the wound of knowledge and yet have an identity. It is in this sense that we can say – a response to dikedicy – that the difficult task is not self-accusation, but self-justification,[25] self-justification without self-righteousness, which means the impossibility of self-justification and therefore a necessary turn to divine causality. Living with the wounds of (self)-knowledge makes sin a costly enterprise, rather than a cheap illusion. This happens in the desert. A person can only live with the tragedy of world hunger calmly and at peace if she drinks from the well of the desert, if she is nourished by the emptiness of the desert. It is only there that trust in the power of love can arise (cf. 1 Jn 4.18).

Jesus disrupts his own being in the world by seeking the encounter with his Father. By doing this, Jesus is generating grounds for divine disruption, space for divine causality. The passage also tells us that the people set out after Jesus. They try to disrupt him in what he does. They are making claims because they have seen the power within him. The lesson to be learned here is that love does not remain within itself. It is not hidden. Love is a force that goes beyond itself, reaches out, touches and transforms people, has an impact on its environment. A loving person can make all the difference in the world. And there seems to be a tremendous hunger for loving people, for the fundamental praxis of loving people. We can see this phenomenon of the causal dynamics of love that attracts and transforms people throughout history, in people like Francis of Assisi, George Washington Carver, Martin Luther King, Mother Teresa, Mahatma Gandhi. Fundamental praxis shows that *'otro mundo es possibile'*: that there is the possibility of and the opportunity for difference. And this 'window into new-ness' attracts people. They follow Jesus, walking many miles, accepting hardships and making an effort to be with a man of love. Why? Because they are hungry. Because their lives do not give them the nourishment they need.

When Jesus saw the crowd, he took pity on them and healed the sick (Mt. 14.14). Love is about attentiveness. Love is not blind. On the contrary,[26] love opens the eyes, since love takes an interest in the world and in what is happening there, in other persons and in what is happening to them. Love is eye-opening. A person who opens herself up to love is invited to see the world with new eyes, to take a fresh look at things. Love rests on an attitude of awareness and attentiveness. And it leads to compassion. Jesus took pity on the people he saw, because he saw not only people, but hungry people. He saw their hunger and their plight. Compassion is a dynamic where the boundaries of the self are continually renegotiated.[27] In compassion, one becomes willing to extend the boundaries of what belongs to oneself, and to count as part of the self the life of other people. Compassion is about entering commitments that include other lives. Jesus accepts and invites the interweaving of his life with the lives of others. A striking feature of this dynamic is its vastness. Jesus does not take pity on one particular person but extends his compassion to a whole crowd. This is only possible if the love-based attitude of compassion has shifted from an emotional state of being affected by another person's plight into a firm commitment, a commitment to serve. Moved by his compassion, Jesus heals the sick. Love transforms, love heals, love touches, love seeks the encounter and the union. Love is an expression of a robust concern that is expressed in active care.[28] And this robust concern can be expressed not only vis-à-vis an individual person, but also vis-à-vis a crowd. Doesn't this teach us something about the way we are invited to face the challenge of world hunger? The fact that millions of people are affected does not mean that we would not be invited to extend the boundaries of our self in order to include them. Facing world hunger in a loving way does not mean to be paralyzed by emotions. It means rather that we can show a strong commitment and a robust concern by being active, one step at a time, with the extent of the challenge in mind – facing the truth about world hunger in the same way that Jesus faced the crowd, saw it, did not avoid and evade it, and showed his commitment to serve by ministering to the crowd – one by one.

In the next verse we find the realism of human causal reasoning in conflict with divine love. The disciples approach Jesus in the evening to tell him that he should send the people to the nearby villages so that they can buy bread (Mt. 14.15). Again, there is a lot we can learn about love: love creates a new order of space and time. A new order of space since love makes people feel at home and their geography of belonging is changed; a new order of time since love transforms '*chronos*' into '*kairos*' and makes people forget how time passes. So, evening has come. And it is only then that people realize what time it is and that they are hungry. The disciples are thinking in human terms – and understandably so. There are limits to responsibility. We can calculate our responses. To translate this attitude into the context of the challenge of world hunger – we can make the decision to donate a certain amount each month to the cause of world hunger, and with this decision to see this chapter in the book of how to live ethically to be closed. This is a very sensible approach. And yet Jesus teaches us that love is disruptive, striving for the '*magis*', striving for extending the boundaries of the self in a kenotic move, since divine causality can enter the individual person in a situation of self-emptying. Jesus tells his disciples that the people do not have to go away. Give them something to eat (Mt. 14.16). What a strong imperative, especially in the light of world hunger! A philosopher would immediately spot that this imperative cannot be universalized in a Kantian sense. It is a call to the disciples and a reminder of their specific responsibility. If this was the foundation of a general law, our communities would break down. You cannot ask people to feed other people beyond the limits of reasonable and limited responsibility. We touch the frontiers of the rational, if we understand the rational as the prudential. Love rewrites the boundaries between duties and supererogatory actions. Love rewrites the boundaries of what is ethically relevant, as witnessed for example in the new areas of ethical concern identified in the sermon on the mount (Mt. 5.28). Love can take the form of an imperative with a clear vision of where to go and an equally clear exhortation to do it. Shouldn't we accept the power of the imperative 'Give them something to eat' facing the challenge of world hunger? It seems that (reasonable and well-justified) answers of the kind 'This is unrealistic', 'This goes beyond our means', 'This violates the sense of self-responsibility of the hungry' are discounted by Jesus. Love goes beyond reason in the same way that turning the other cheek goes beyond justice. If the boundaries of the self are truly extended beyond one's autonomy,[29] loving beyond the calculus of well-defined rules becomes the norm. In other words: disrupting the rules of reason and the prudential considerations of rule-following makes room for divine causality to enter our human plans.

The disciples' reply to that far-reaching exhortation is as reasonable as the advice they gave Jesus just before. They count the stock, they calculate people and available food, they translate the situation into measurable terms, and measure what can be measured. They remind Jesus that there is nothing available but five loaves and two fishes (Mt. 14.17). Again, this is a very reasonable approach well known from strategies for coping with world hunger. Let us concentrate on the quantifiable dimensions of the social situation involving world hunger and let us calculate the available means. Jesus does not comment on the quantity. By the way he acts, he teaches us that love translates situations into terms beyond measurement and calculation. We do see clearly that the virtue of temperance is not applicable to love, since love is striving for the *magis*, since love is disruptive and surprising. Jesus disrupts the plans and self-understanding of his disciples. They do not see themselves as bearers of a sustainable and encompassing responsibility. They do not plan to feed the people. Jesus disrupts both identities and ideas. He teaches us something about love by simply telling them to bring the available food to the centre of the situation. All of a sudden the food becomes food on a 'common ground', food for all, food in the midst of a situation of scarcity. We have been told that scarcity is the basic factor that determines economic thinking. An agapeistic reading of the passage will tell us that love undermines the idea of scarcity. Love is not a scarce good in the sense that the fountain could go dry. The spring of love is divine. Love is the expression and form of divine causality. This source cannot be exhausted. As much as God's grace disrupts our ideas of human causality (chains of cause as merits and effect as reward), God's love (which is also expressed in grace, of course) disrupts our ideas of scarcity. Jesus takes the little food available. And he acts on that. He does not wait for more food to come. He does not send them out to buy or produce more food. He takes the available resources and acts on these grounds. And he acts lovingly – inviting, saying grace, blessing, sharing. The lesson could be this: in any given situation it is possible to act lovingly. Even in situations of scarcity. It actually means that love goes beyond the right to act morally, it could open doors to act morally in situations where a person is denied the right to act morally.

The dynamics of the 'wounded healer', powerful examples like Dietrich Bonhoeffer or Walter Ciszek,[30] remind us of the door love opens in the midst of a situation where people are denied the right to act morally. Jesus teaches us to act on limited resources based on an attitude of and a commitment to love – and the fruits will show. Again, the fountain of this love is God who is the one whom we thank, who is the one to whom we turn to bless our loving efforts and to fill us with love. Facing world hunger, the message is clear: Go ahead. Make a start. Make a new beginning on the basis of limited resources. Many initiatives like 'Terre des Hommes' or 'Bread for the World' witness to this dynamic – love triggers new causal chains and they bring about unexpected newness and sustainable transformation. It seems worthwhile to point out that Jesus invited his disciples to an attitude of selflessness, of going beyond self-centredness. It is not mentioned that they themselves ate; they are described as those who distribute the food and collect what is left over. We can assume that they are part of 'all' who ate (Mt. 14.19) but it is not explicitly stated. An agapeistic reading of the text will tell us that the fact that this is not mentioned says something about what it means to love. By acting lovingly, Jesus transforms and creates community – love transforms a crowd into a table community with no one excluded. As romantic as this may sound, the message is clear and bold: extend the boundaries of your self, take a first step and if you are acting on love, you make yourself vulnerable to the divine causality that goes beyond any worldly power. To make the point clearer: Jesus was not only feeding people, he was also teaching them, inviting them to reflect, honouring common sense and human rationality. But he gave a clear primacy to praxis. In order to get to know God (i.e., in order to get to know love), you have to do God's will (i.e., you have to live a life of love). The praxis of love is a fountain of knowledge, rather than the other way round. Many scholars have criticized Mother Teresa for being naïve and for not changing the structures that bring about world hunger. But it can hardly be denied that Mother Teresa changed the face of the earth much more sustainably than the wise who criticized her – as much as Frère Roger has changed the reality of ecumenical dialogue much more than those writing documents or books – the wise who remain within conceptual securities without entering boldly the sphere of causal resistance and even the disruptive power of divine causality brought about and expressed by love.

The fundamental praxis of Jesus has shown us that divine causality presents itself often in the mode of Damascus, it does not come 'cheap', without self-transformation, self-renewal, repentance and the commitment to new beginnings, however small. In the face of world hunger the praxis of Jesus teaches us that love expresses itself on the individual level, and on the basis of that – through people of self-renewal – love can become causally relevant on a structural level. There is no sustainable structural change without reform of the human heart. Love is not a power to be introduced into the world by structural means, let alone a legal apparatus. Love goes beyond a language of rights that invites us to see human coexistence and social coordination in legal terms.[31] This is the constant struggle of the Church: how to be a loving institution.

An agapeistic reading of the scriptures will make us understand ever more deeply the living reality of love, and the divine causality expressing the transformative and disruptive power of love. If we accept that love is the form of divine causality and that love is disruptive, then we will accept that revelation is of a disruptive nature. 'The most fundamental way in which God relates to creation is in such disruption and transformation. And this would mean that there are no structures of reality that are not subject to disruption.'[32] Accepting divine causality within the Christian perspective means to accept the promise that all things will be new, that love has the power to transform everything – everything, including world hunger, the situation of the hungry and the situation of those who witness the starvation of others without being transformed by this knowledge. The challenge of world hunger has to be faced on the basis of love, expressed in robust concern, self-transformation, clear commitments, an openness to disruption and a striving for the *magis*. For an ethics in the world, love will become the key category. It is the category that helps us to cope with the ongoing challenge of dikedicy. It helps us to bridge the gap between the two kinds of accountability laid out by Paul Janz, and to understand the embodied praxis of our human existence sketched by Oliver Davies.

3. Love, Commitment and Disruption

World hunger places us in a situation of guilt, and quite often frustration and despair. This is the price we pay for our epistemic vulnerability. The wound of knowledge teaches us that we do not live innocent lives. It is a situation similar to the one found in South Africa after the end of the apartheid regime. There were people with blood on their hands, people who committed atrocities not only as individuals, but as a whole people who were structurally encouraged to do so. This is a point where the category of 'structural sin' is filled with depth and thickness. Desmond Tutu and Nelson Mandela made it clear that there is only one way forward as a nation. And this was the way of truth and forgiveness. In other words: the way of love. We are well aware that the realities of this way have been idealized and that this way has caused distress and frustration, conflicts and new dangers to the social balance. But from an ethical point of view which emphasizes the key role of love, there is no alternative to the basic idea being expressed here: we are sitting in the same boat. If we want to have a future as a community, it has to be a future for all members of the community.[33]

From a Christian point of view, a loving person has become a means of divine causality. It is in this sense that ethics in the world will be kenotic: the old self dies in order to allow the divine power of love to enter the human person, to transform the self and, through the person, the whole world.

Before we get lost singing the praises of love in general terms, it may be worthwhile taking a deeper look at what we must mean by love. It seems fruitful to develop an understanding of love using the terms 'commitment' and 'disruption'. Love is basically divine power, causal power, but it is at the same time an attitude, a cluster of capabilities and a cluster of strong commitments and robust concerns. As a commitment, love has the structure of a promise. The promise for the future that lives are intertwined, that the boundaries of the self are extended, that the other person is seen as the new person. It is in this sense that we can understand Margaret Farley's words: 'When I make a commitment to another person, I dwell in the other by means of my word.'[34] Love as a commitment can safeguard us from our own inconsistencies, for it commits to the whole future and the whole way of being in the world. 'The remedy for unpredictability, for the chaotic uncertainty of the future, is contained in the faculty to make and keep promises' (H. Arendt). As a commitment, love works like a promise that gives identity to the person who makes the promise and to the person who receives the promise. Love creates these identities by making commitments. Every act of love is a commitment. Robert Brandom developed the theory of discursive commitments that are generated with every utterance.[35] A person who says something binds herself to what she says and is from then on identified with this commitment. Similarly, a person who loves makes a promise, enters an identity commitment that will shape the identity of all the persons involved. Jesus healing one person makes a 'statement' about himself, about the divine source of his power, about the identity of the person he healed and about our human way of being in the world. Love as care and concern is about creating a thicker and thicker pattern of identity-building commitments, of 'commitments to newness' as we could call them, since love is, as we have seen, about transformation and self-transformation. In the face of world hunger, love as commitment means the concern for the hungry that is expressed in ever-new creative ways of transforming the hunger in the world. Initiatives like 'Menschen für Menschen' (Karl Heinz Böhm) or 'Mary's Meals' or 'Care' – all of which have come into existence as very small initiatives, borne by individual people – have shown that the power of love is a commitment to newness, to creativity and to transformation.

A second useful tool to help us gain a deeper understanding of love is that of disruption, which has already been identified as central to the kind of ethics outlined in this chapter. To love a person means to allow this person to disrupt you. A person is allowed to disrupt you if you do not only have concern for this person but if you recognize the resisting reality of this person that cannot be 'treated' in any way. If we turn the hungry into epistemic objects and, in this sense, abstract entities, they lose their disruptive power and we cannot claim that we love them. They are then 'processed', reduced into epistemic objects that fit neatly into categories. To love a person means to acknowledge the resistant force and disruptive power of this person. I do accept that we cannot be disrupted by the millions of starving people in the same way that we can allow ourselves to be disrupted by the death of a child or a partner. But in any case we cannot justify from a humanitarian let alone Christian point of view, an attitude of indifference vis-à-vis world hunger, an attitude that does not leave space for emotions such as anger and shame and that would not allow us to take clear steps in the right direction. The bread value for any way of doing ethics is essentially committed to a self-transformation which must take place. Love is a power that transforms the loving person. It has the power to make people new. Love means to encounter the world in a new way and to transform the world by doing so. In this sense, we can say with Oliver Davies: we are more in the world when we are in love.

Let me illustrate this point that love is the power to disrupt and transform. In his book *A Grief Observed* Clive Staples Lewis struggles with the loss of his beloved wife.[36] He is wrestling with God, trying to cope with life in the darkness of this difficult experience. There is much to learn about love from these reflections. Lewis tells us that through the experience of loss an 'invisible blanket' seems to separate himself from the world (ibid., p. 5). This blanket comes along with a sense of inertness and laziness. To love a person gives 'reasons to act'. Losing a loved one renders a person powerless and diminished. The world becomes smaller, the self is diminished, the world becomes flat, the self is rendered empty. The world, we could say, has lost its 'freshness', seems 'flat, shabby, worn-out looking' (ibid., p. 31). The world has lost its capacity to provoke fresh perspectives, an attitude of discovery and a sense of unpredictable newness. The loss of freshness and newness and the loss of a reference point fills Lewis with a 'permanently provisional feeling' (ibid., p. 29). The world has lost structures and contours since the loved one, whose presence gave us a sense of value criteria and ethical 'weight', is gone. To love a person means to have criteria by which to distinguish the important from the less important. To love a person fills the world with depth and thickness and freshness. That is why we need the capacity to love in order to develop thick, deep and fresh concepts. To love a person means to see the world in a specific and special way, which is not compatible with a disengaged view from nowhere. To love a person instils a sense of preferences and priorities and provides an orientation for our actions. To love a person renders this person irreplaceable. To love a person means to give this person a special place, to win a particular perspective. Love is about generating the particular as particular, not as an application of something general. It is, we could say, the strongest impediment to constructing epistemic objects (representing general categories). We do not love a particular person as a 'case of something general', but rather we employ general categories with a thickness, depth and freshness in light of the particular experiences of love. It is this unpredictable particularity that brings about the resistance accredited to a loved one. Lewis worries about this loss of resistance. The deepest experience of his conjugal love was the experience of resistance: 'The most precious gift that marriage gave me was this constant impact of something very close and intimate all the time unmistakably other, resistant – in a word, real' (ibid., p. 17). Lewis also uses the expression 'obstinately real' (ibid., p. 44). The transformative power of love touches all dimensions of human life, especially the body. To love a person tells you something about the world and your place in the world. It gives you a sense of self, also in one's perception of one's own body. Lewis finds clear words to describe this new emptiness. His body has become a place where the absence of his wife 'comes locally home to me, and it's a place I can't avoid. I mean my own body. It had such a different importance while it was the body of H's lover. Now it's like an empty house' (ibid., p. 12). To love a person means to offer oneself to the loved one, and to be loved is to be an open house where the loved one can dwell, a home in the physical, the intellectual and the spiritual dimension. The sphere where people can touch one another and have an impact on each other's life is the sphere of the sensible. 'Time and space and body were the very things that brought us together; the telephone wires by which we communicated' (ibid., p. 14). It is this aspect of being in the world, the aspect of a *hic et nunc* that allows people to inter-act and to inter-judge. George Herbert Mead has underlined the role of 'the other' in building our own identities.[37] But the insights we gain into the causality of love go deeper: our identity is both shaped and sustained by structures of disruption, of newness rather than mere otherness, of transformation rather than provocation.

Love is about resistance and disruption. The acknowledgement of resistance shows that the loved person has been recognized as real, as a source of newness, as a fountain of disruption. The resistance of a loved person shows that what I do and how I do it does make a difference. There are limits to the arbitrariness of acting. 'The image has the ... disadvantage that it will do whatever you want' (ibid., p. 20). Similar to the rules of grammar limiting the arbitrariness of the use and development of our linguistic devices, love structures the world, constitutes a 'grammar' of the world in the sense that structures of preferences and priorities and criteria of judgement are established. But again, these structures of priorities and criteria of judgement do not determine a kind of reliability that does not allow for newness and surprise. On the contrary: to love a person means to open up possibilities for surprise. 'Reality never repeats' (ibid., p. 23). This makes the loved person irreplaceable. To love a person opens a depth and freshness of the world, even through grief. Lewis mentions that the emptiness he felt after the death of his wife astonished him time and again, 'like a complete novelty' (ibid., p. 49). To love a person means to love in the way of newness. Turning a loved person into an epistemic object closes the lid on the box of surprises and opportunities for newness. Encountering a concept is not the same as exposing oneself to unpredictable causal dynamics in the relationship with another person. Lewis complains that a cemetery is not a source of resistance. He remembers 'being rather horrified' when a man announced in the churchyard that he would 'visit Mum' (ibid., p. 19). There is no loving resistance from the six-by-three-foot flowerbed. The resistant force and disruptive power of a loved one is more than a momentary event; it has transformative effects. To love a person structures the world, structures the landscape of meanings and values. To love a person transforms the way of being in the world which does not only affect the present and the future, but affects also the past. It is in this sense that Lewis can write: 'Did you ever know, dear, how much you took away with you when you left? You have stripped me even of my past, even of the things we never shared' (ibid., p. 52). Love does not open a new chapter in the book of life; it calls for rereading and rewriting of the whole book. It changes what the book is about; it changes the author. The disruption of love is not a single event like a temporary interruption, it is a transformation towards newness. This transformation is ongoing. One of the miracles of love is 'a power of seeing through its own enchantments and yet not being disenchanted' (ibid., p. 60). Love makes us see more clearly, makes us see more without turning us into cynics who have lost trust in the transformative power of love. Love does not give way to helplessness and hopelessness: since it goes beyond the conceptual framework, it allows disruptive causality to take place – another insight we find in Lewis' book: 'All reality is iconoclastic. The earthly beloved, even in this life, incessantly triumphs over your mere idea of her' (ibid., p. 56).

What does that mean for our ethical challenge of world hunger? It is basically a message about disruption. Can we really love all the people in the world suffering from hunger? Jesus taught us in the passage we examined that love is about extending the boundaries of self. Jesus teaches us that love is not so much about holding propositions or about performing specific actions, but rather about being a loving person – a person who is touched by God's love, a person who allows divine causality to be brought to expression through himself or herself. Love cannot be narrowed down to a set of beliefs to be embraced or a set of actions to be carried out. Love strives for the *magis*, reaches out to the unexpected, allows the spirit of God to work. Jean Vanier, to give one example, did not intend to found a worldwide community called 'L'Arche'. When he bought a little house in Trosly near Paris and invited two people with severe mental handicaps to live with him, he did what he felt he had to do. And all the unexpected and unforeseeable developments followed. To love a person is revelatory. To love a person is to make room for divine causality. To love a person is to see God's face. For the challenge of world hunger, this means that the main point is not a set of convictions (however important) or a set of actions (however necessary) – the main point in the face of atrocities and tragedies is to be a loving person. And the life of a loving person is compatible with many different ways of encountering the hungry, engaging in the fight against poverty, slavery, exploitation, world hunger. Love does not think in terms of problems and solutions. Love thinks in terms of cries and responses.

4. World Hunger and the Politics of Love

It is in this sense that a loving person would work towards an ethics that is not only disruptive of established beliefs and practices, but also open to its own disruptions. This is part of the wound of knowledge that we carry. A loving person is open to the disruptions that take place in the world: 'You never know how much you really believe anything until its truth or falsehood becomes a matter of life and death to you' (*A Grief Observed*, p. 20f). Love brings you to a point where attachment and commitment have entered this stage. Attention through love to the tragedy of world hunger tells us in clear terms what is at stake in our human lives. And love as such can also come to have an educational dimension,[38] as both an epistemological and a political force. The epistemic force of love is expressed in the attentiveness it brings to the world, in the interests expressed in robust concern and active care. We can learn from Jewish thought that to know a person is only possible if you love this person. And here love goes beyond a use of reason that puts distance between itself and the object.[39] If you do not love a country, it is impossible to understand the depth of the country. If you do not love those who suffer, it is impossible to understand the depth of suffering. Love is 'partial' and this partiality is part of being in the world. This partiality, as we have seen, will lead us to struggle with the depths of human suffering, and by understanding some aspects of this depth, we will feel like strangers in the world. Paradoxically, the partiality of love brings about an effect of alienation from the world. Love is about respecting the dimension of the mysterious and accepting the resistance of the unresolved. However, the authority of non-resolution is an invitation to act rather than an authority that makes you quiet, silent, inert and passive. Understanding the depths of the tragedies of the human condition will tell us what a wisely reasonable way of acting may look like; for our cognitive faculties, as we have seen, are shaped by tragedies. We have to live with our wounds and we have to be willing to keep the wounds open in their disruptive power and we have to be willing to endure wounds in the process of knowing.

Ethical questions must therefore be asked in a way that disrupts how we see the world. As such, reading the world is somewhat similar to what Franz Kafka has prominently said about the reading of books. In an often cited letter, Franz Kafka wrote:

> I think one should only read books that bite and sting. If the book we read does not wake us up with a thump to the head, why do we then read this book? So that it makes us happy, as you write? My God, we would also be happy without books, and those books that made us happy could also be written by ourselves if necessary. However, we need these books that affect us like misfortune and that very much hurt us, like the death of someone we loved more than ourselves, as when we are banished to the woods, far from any people, like suicide; a book has to be the axe for the frozen sea within ourselves.[40]

It is similar with ethical questions which, when posed genuinely, should shock, make us feel insecure, irritate and stir up. Ethics is not about making answers easier, but about rendering questions more difficult; it is about raising the stakes. The scholars at the gathering of victims 'are radically brought into question: not just their acts but themselves. The secure place from which they observe and judge the world is threatened, disturbed and uprooted.'[41] Ethics is about self-transformation. Ethicists are invited to be people of self-renewal. And this is a sign of wisdom.

Wisdom is a kind of incarnational knowledge, a set of skills that allow us to connect our knowledge deeply with our identity. The wise person can accept limits and the openness of the world. Accepting limits and openness means being open to disruptions. It can be a sign of a narrow and closed mind if a person does not allow anything to disrupt his or her worldview.[42] Wisdom generates knowledge that has been called 'personal knowledge', both in the sense that this is knowledge based on personal ways of being in the world, and also in the sense that this knowledge has become part of the personality, part of the identity of the knower. Knowledge about world hunger as personal knowledge in the second dimension (knowledge as an integral part of the personality) means to integrate the challenge into one's life by looking at one's life as such. The ethicist is called to look at his life as such and think about questions of the full and fulfilling life, about questions of the way a human life should be. Janusz Korczak, the Polish paediatrician, has written a prayer asking God that his life may be difficult, yet happy and useful. Similarly, Jean Vanier has reminded us that he does not think that Jesus has emphasized happiness as a key value – nowhere in the New Testament do we find the beatitude: blessed are those who are happy. These are statements about life, statements we can more easily understand after the confrontation with world hunger. Speaking concretely, perhaps the best way to deepen one's personal knowledge about hunger in our contexts of secure livelihood is fasting. Fasting contributes to self-discipline, compassion and a sense of gratitude. Mahatma Gandhi considered fasting one of the most powerful means to make spiritual progress.[43] Having had the experience of fasting, personal knowledge of world hunger can lead to a greater sense of the urgency of the problem, to a depth, thickness and freshness of concepts – not only of concepts concerning famines and starvation, but also to concepts like 'the Eucharist' or 'table fellowship'. As personal knowledge, knowledge about world hunger transforms the person and leads to action.

Finally, let me say something about the main responsibility of ethics facing the challenge of dikedicy, facing victims who suffer indescribable pain. The gathering of victims will ask for the bread value of ethics, and by doing so they will ask for the grounds of hope. Bread value only transcends a Jamesian cash value if the difference ethical work makes creates grounds for hope. It is only in this sense that we can come to face the challenge of dikedicy in the full intractability of its reality. Ethics can be 'justified' only on the grounds of the hope that it produces. It is in these moments of deprivation that ethics suffers the litmus test of dikedicy. Why ethics? The answer to hopelessness is obviously not to be found on the conceptual level of epistemic goods such as propositions or statements. Much more important than the good one can provide is the relationship with that good. Ethical wisdom is not about 'owning epistemic goods' ('knowing propositions') but about being able to work with epistemic goods. It is about epistemic skills rather than epistemic goods. Ethics in the face of dikedicy is therefore about honouring disruptions and enabling disruptions to happen; and the bread value of ethics facing world hunger is the hope it generates in the face of these disruptions. Hope is not an epistemic good that we hold, but rather a promise, a commitment, that motivates and channels skills and capabilities. If the ethics we do in the world can provide grounds for hope in a way that establishes 'islands of integrity', or through examples of fundamental praxis against world hunger, or in models of fulfilled lives in the midst of tragedies – such an ethics will have real bread value. And this bread value translates into '*docta spes*', hope with a reason, providing reasons to act.

What is it that we can learn from the foregoing aporetic structures, from irresolvable issues, from open questions and ongoing challenges? What exactly does world hunger teach us about the world? Or as a theologian might want to ask: what does world hunger teach us about God? If we take Rahner's idea seriously that it is only as I draw closer to the real world of my own crea-turehood, or to the real world of sensible human embodiment in space and time, that I may also draw closer to God – what does that say with regard to world hunger? If every retreat from this world is a way of distancing ourselves from God, what does world hunger tell us about God? It tells us about the hungry as sources of revelation; it tells us about God's presence in the midst of suffering. Once again: accepting world hunger as a disruption means accepting Somalia and Biafra, Dafur and Ethiopia as a 'Damascus' – accepting the pain of falling to the ground, accepting the loss of autonomy in depending on com-panionship, accepting the pain of blindness and confusion, accepting also a mission. The continuing incarnation of Christ in the world 'cannot be conceived *representationally* (we do not really know what the new creation will look like, any more than we know quite what the ascended body "looks like") but it is known rather *ethically*: encountered in our moral consciousness' (Paul Janz). The world is the place where we are invited to become participants in the divine causality, the origin and end of which is the divine righteousness, but the eternal and irrepressible form of which is love.

Notes

1 It is the wound of Oedipus – he knew too much and at the same time as part of the events and actions that brought about his tragic condition he knew too little; cf. Christoph Menke, *Die Gegenwart der Tragödie* (Frankfurt/Main: Suhrkamp, 2005, p. 18ff.) The wound of knowledge that Oedipus suffered pushed him to the limits of his life. It is knowledge about the world and life, knowledge about those dearest to him and knowledge about himself, in short: knowledge about his identity that his epistemic vulnerability imposed on Oedipus: 'One is tempted to say that the self-knowledge he achieves is more than he can bear' (Douglas MacKinnon, 'Ethics and Tragedy', in *Explorations in Theology* (London: SCM, 1976, pp. 182–95, 191); see also Charles Segal, *Oedipus Tyrannus. Tragic Heroism and the Limits of Knowledge* (New York: Oxford University Press, 2001).

2 cf. Clemens Sedmak, 'Stukturen epistemischer Gerechtigkeit', in *Salzburger Philosophisches Jahrbuch* 46/47 (2001/02, pp. 139–52).

3 cf. William Styron, *Sophie's Choice* (New York: Bantam Books, 1980); cf. C. A. Durham, 'William Styron's *Sophie's Choice*: The Struggle of Oppression', *Twentieth Century Literature* 30:4 (1984, pp. 448–64). As in any tragic circumstance there is a theological disruption at work as well – cf. John Lang, 'God's Averted Face: Styron's *Sophie's Choice*', *American Literature* 55:2 (1983, pp. 215–32).

4 Robert A. Jonas, *Rebecca: A Father's Journey from Grief to Gratitude* (New York: Crossroad, 1996).

5 These are some of the issues outlined in Leo Hickman's highly recommendable book on 'living ethically': Leo Hickman, *A Life Stripped Bare: My Year Trying to Live Ethically* (London: Project Eden, 2005).

6 Alan Paton, *Ah, but Your Land is Beautiful* (New York: Simon and Schuster, 1996, p. 66ff.).

7 This seems to be one of the promises made by Jeffrey Sachs in his book *The End of Poverty* (London: Penguin, 2005). The idea that poverty can be eradicated if only enough funds are allocated seems to transform poverty into a technical problem rather than a social topic and a personal issue. From a theological point of view, there can be no solution to these burning questions without a thorough transformation of the heart. And even with this transformation of the heart we will carry our wounds, the wounds of knowing that we are ethically and spiritually deficient.

8 The well-known discussions whether mercy is part or a subset of justice can be meaningfully applied to the epistemological sphere as well – cf. H. S. Hestevold, 'Justice to Mercy', *Philosophy and Phenomenological Research* 46:2 (1985, pp. 281–91); I would feel inclined to argue for 'mercy' as a category *sui generis*. The five features outlined in the text will indicate that it is quite difficult to apply these to standard concepts of social or epistemic justice.

9 'A religious discourse with some chance of being honest will not move too far from the particular, with all its irresolution and resistance to systematizing' (Rowan Williams, *Theological Integrity*, in Rowan Williams, *On Christian Theology* (Oxford: Blackwell, 2001, pp. 1–11, 6).

10 D. MacKinnon, *Ethics and Tragedy*, p. 186. There is a danger in 'milking events ethically', in finding general terms for 'human history' and 'human tragedies'. It can turn ethics into an unpleasant business – cf. Tobin Siebers, 'Ethics ad Nauseam', *American Literary History* 6:4 (1994, pp. 756–78).

11 It is a sign and indication of humaneness to respect the singular in its uniqueness – cf. Clemens Sedmak, 'Menschlichkeit. Überlegungen zu einem Maß des Ethischen', in O. Neumaier, ed., *Ist der Mensch das Maß aller Dinge? Beiträge zur Aktualität des Protagoras* (Möhnesee: Bibliopolis, 2004, pp. 229–52). This respect for the particular and this consideration of the concrete could be called 'having epistemic mercy on a person'.

12 This is one of the main concerns of an ethics of remembering and an ethics of memory; Auschwitz must not lose its disruptive power, must not be turned from an open wound into a comfortable scar – cf. Anne Fuchs, 'Towards an Ethics of Remembering: The Walser-Bubis Debate and the Other of Discourse', *The German Quarterly* 75:3 (2002, pp. 235–46).

13 Cf. Max Weber, *Wissenschaft als Beruf* (Stuttgart: Reclam, 1995, esp. p. 12ff.).

14 There is a need for an ethics of writing – cf. Clemens Sedmak, 'Das Elend mit uns Theologen. Drei Lektionen', in K. Dethloff, R. Langthaler, L. Nagl and F. Wolfram, eds, *'Die Grenze des Menschlichen ist göttlich'. Beiträge zur Religionsphilosophie* (Berlin: Pararga, 2007, pp. 337–53).

15 The example of George Washington Carver who firmly claimed that his ideas were a response to his prayers is an important testimony in this context. Carver had offered literally hundreds of ideas concerning the application of the peanut and the sweet potato as a response to needs of the time; cf. Glenn Clark, *The Man Who Talks With The Flowers: The Intimate Life Story of Dr. George Washington* (Unknown Binding, 1939).

16 Cf. Bernard Williams, 'Voluntary Acts and Responsible Agents', in Bernard Williams, *Making Sense of Humanity* (Cambridge: Cambridge University Press, 1995, pp. 22–34).

17 Rowan Williams referred to the attitude of hesitance as an expression of reverence: 'A certain degree of hesitation in our willingness to offer the first kind of help that comes to our minds is no bad thing if it means that we end up attending to the reality of someone else' (Rowan Williams, *Silence and Honey Cakes*; London: Lion, 2003, p. 73). Williams made use of an idea of Simone Weil in this context – see Simone Weil, *Intimations of Christianity among the Ancient Greeks* (London, 1957, pp. 24–55) and Peter Winch and Simone Weil: *The Just Balance* (Cambridge: Cambridge University Press, 1989, pp. 107f, 164ff.).

18 In short: 'bullshit' – Harry Frankfurt, *On Bullshit* (Princeton: Princeton University, Press, 2005).

19 See Paul Janz's discussion of 'finality of non-resolution' above.

20 This does not mean that surrender means meek submission. We learn what it means to be human in situations where the core of our humanity, identity based on dignity and self-respect, is threatened. It is in this sense that we can understand Bonhoeffer's struggle, his earnestness and his sense of humour when he writes in November 1943: 'I'm now praying simply for freedom. There is such a thing as false composure which is quite unchristian. As Christians, we needn't be at all ashamed of some impatience, longing, opposition to what is unnatural, and our full share of desire for freedom, earthly happiness and opportunity for effective work' (Dietrich Bonhoeffer, *Letters and Papers from Prison*; London: SCM, 1971, p. 131ff).

21 cf. Matthias Kroß, 'Philosophieren in Beispielen. Wittgensteins Umdenken des Allgemeinen', in Hans Julius Schneider and Matthias Kroß (eds), *Mit Sprache spielen. Die Ordnungen und das Offene nach Wittgenstein* (Berlin: Akademie, 1999, pp. 169–87).

22 Basil Hume, *Searching for God* (London: Hodder & Stoughton, 1983 [1977], p. 38).

23 cf. R. Williams, *Silence and Honeycakes*, for a profound discussion of the topos of 'desert'.

24 Ibid., p. 45.

25 Ibid., p. 47.

26 cf. Dietrich von Hildebrand, *Marriage: The Mystery of Faithful Love* (Sophia Press Institute, 1991).

27 cf. Martha Nussbaum, *Upheavals of Thought, Part II* – see also Aquinas, *Summa Theologica II-II*, q. 118, a. 3, resp.

28 cf. Harry Frankfurt, 'Reasons to Love' and 'Autonomy, Necessity, and Love', in Harry Frankfurt, *Necessity, Volition, and Love* (Cambridge: Cambridge University Press, 1999, pp. 129–41); W. Newton-Smith, 'A Conceptual Investigation of Love', in Alan Soble, ed., *Eros, Agape, and Philia: Readings in the Philosophy of Love* (New York: Paragon House, pp. 199–217).

29 Autonomy is not a value in itself. This seems to be a message found on an agapeistic reading of the scriptures – accepting commitments of the kind Jesus invites us to accept means restricting and diminishing one's autonomy. This would also tell us that a reading of the human condition as 'dependent rational animals' (cf. Alasdair MacIntyre, *Dependent Rational Animals*; Chicago: Open Court, 1999) has to be interpreted in the sense that this dependence is not only horizontal, but also vertical (dependence from God's love in order to be able to live in the world).

30 cf. Walter Ciszek, SJ, *With God in Russia* (New York: McGraw-Hill, 1964); Walter Ciszek, SJ, *He Leadeth Me* (New York: Doubleday, 1973).

31 There may be dangers in applying the language of rights to all aspects of human life. This may be obvious for the contexts of intimacy or family, but even in the case of world hunger there are traps to be aware of:

> A world in which rights discourse is thought the appropriate idiom for ethical deliberation is one in which a powerful theoretical wedge is driven between questions of justice and matters of help and benefit. Justice is seen as consisting and assignable, claimable, and enforceable rights, which only the claimant can waive. Beneficence is seen as unassignable, unclaimable and unenforceable. This theoretical wedge is reflected in many contemporary institutional structures and ways of thought. Legal and economic forms are seen as the limits of justice; voluntary, charitable and interpersonal activities are seen as the domain of beneficence. Once the discourse of rights is established, generosity, beneficence and help are likely to seem less important, especially in public affairs. (O. O'Neill, *Faces of Hunger*, p. 102)

32 S. Ticciati, *Job and the Disruption of Identity*, p. 172. 'The most fundamental way in which God relates to creation is in its disruption and transformation' (ibid., p. 180).

33 An important aspect of love is its community-building character. It allows us to see world hunger in terms beyond individual agency and allows us to see human beings as members of

groups. Such a conceptual decision allows us to think more adequately about world hunger: 'An exclusively individualist picture of human agency is wholly inappropriate for deliberating about problems of famine and persistent hunger' (O. O'Neill, *Faces of Hunger*, p. 35). The invitation to frame the ethical obligations in the confrontation with world hunger in terms of groups and communities can also be found in a paper by Michael McKinsey who, worried about the fact that no single person can have the obligation to save all starving people, observes that the context changes if we think in terms of obligations of groups – cf. Michael McKinsey, 'Obligations to the Starving', *Nous* 15:3 (1981, pp. 309–23). World hunger and racial inequality are problems that individual persons cannot solve on their own. This is connected with the theoretical problem of 'diffuse responsibility': when faced with problems that must be resolved by collective action, people often feel no sense of personal responsibility – cf. L. May, 'Collective Inaction and Shared Responsibility', *Nous* 24:2 (1990, pp. 269–77); see also Virginia Held, 'Can a Random Collection of Individuals be Morally Reponsible?', *The Journal of Philosophy* 68:14 (1970, 471–81); Robert Goodin, *Protecting the Vulnerable* (Chicago University Press, 1985); L. May, *The Morality of Groups* (University of Notre Dame Press, 1987); Michael Zimmerman, 'Sharing Responsibility', *American Philosophical Quarterly* 22:2 (1985, pp. 115–22); John M. Darley and Bibb Latané, 'Bystander Intervention in Emergencies: Diffusion of Responsibility', *Journal of Personality and Social Psychology* 8 (1968, pp. 377–83). A solution to the problem will have to be linked with increasing the sense of personal responsibility and strengthening the idea of the responsibility of communities as mentioned above.

A concern in ethical responses to world hunger is the question of how far ethical demands can go. Peter Singer's influential paper ('Famine, Affluence, and Morality', *Philosophy and Public Affairs* 1:1 (1972, pp. 229–43) has caused a major debate about the limits of responsibility – see G. Cullity, 'International Aid and the Scope of Kindness', *Ethics* 105:1 (1994, pp. 99–127).

34 Margaret Farley, *Personal Commitments* (San Francisco: HarperCollins, 1990).

35 Robert Brandom, *Making it Explicit* (Cambridge, MA: Harvard University Press, 1994); see as well Allan Gibbard, 'Thought, Norms and Discursive Practice: Commentary on Robert Brandom, *Making it Explicit*', *Philosophy and Phenomenological Research*, 56:3 (1996, pp. 699–717).

36 C. S. Lewis, *A Grief Observed* (London: Faber & Faber, 1966 [1961]).

37 George Herbert Mead, *Mind, Self, and Society*, ed. Charles W. Morris (Chicago: Chicago University Press, 1934).

38 Suzanne Toton, *World Hunger: The Responsibility of Christian Education* (Maryknoll, NY: Orbis, 1982).

39 A central thought of Bonaventure in his 'A Mind's Journey to God' (*Itinerarium Mentis ad Deum*).

40 Franz Kafka, *Briefe 1902–24* (Frankfurt/Main: Fischer, 1958, p. 27f).

41 S. Ticciati, *Job and the Disruption of Identity*, p. 43.

42 André Glucksmann, *La betise* (Paris: Grasset, 1985).

43 Mahatma Gandhi, *An Autobiography or the Story of My Experiments with Truth* (Ahmedabad: Navajivan Press, 1966, esp. 240ff, 249f, 258f, 325ff, 349f).

Conclusion: A New Beginning

This book is unusual to the extent that it has three authors: a doctrinal theologian, a philosophical theologian and a Christian ethicist. Each author brings their own specific perspective, experience and skills to bear in this common project. That it is indeed a common project is something of which all three of us have become increasingly aware, as our work together has developed and deepened. Indeed, in each case insights and emphases from the co-authors have, over the two years or so that we have worked together, substantially enriched our own contributions and have led to a more generative and integrated discussion of the 'living body' of Christ and its demands for theology. All three contributions have converged in an awareness of the indispensable ecclesial orientations of this project, and indeed in the sense that something decisively new in respect of the real and reality is called for in Christian life and thought. We have lived long under the shadow of a certain kind of 'idealism' or 'conceptualism': a prioritization of principles, ideas and abstractions, in which Christianity has followed more general trends in society. Incarnational revelation, however, is like life itself about particularities and resistances and disruptions. Abstractions can appear to offer solutions to the human and theological problems of the particular and the disruptive, which turn out upon closer inspection to be less solutions than ways of avoiding the real problems in their fundamental intractability. With each 'answer', human life itself and human attentiveness is transposed to the level of mind and away from the particular, the embodied and the disruptive which are the marks of the sensible real. Life is 'thinned out', so that it becomes a little easier to live with. Yet with each abstraction, especially when these are allowed to become foundational, we move more deeply into the subjectivism of our own narrative community; and away from what we have most robustly in common with other communities and other individuals. Our attention is drawn away from the site of incarnational revelation, which is to say from space and time as the shared condition of embodied reality in the world.

As expressed in the first two chapters, the new theology developed in this book understands itself on a vital level to be a kind of reflection which is based upon the moment of present reference during the recital of the creed. It is on this level therefore specifically and overtly an ecclesial theological moment.

Perhaps it is the case that all theologies find in such a moment their warranting challenge; it is certainly the case that Transformation Theology sees itself as standing in the service of the reality of *ecclesia* where we make present reference to Jesus Christ in worship. Chapters 1 and 2 have dealt with the problematics, or aporia, of that reference for us today, and have suggested ways in which we can detach the doctrinal affirmation from its cosmological clothing. Transformation Theology is therefore indispensably a pointing into the world, to where the living body is. It is a pointing to that body as the life of the world as Christians experience it: which is to say, a world shaped by the Spirit of Pentecost as new creation. As mediation of that body, the Spirit of the body lays claim to Transformation Theology, mandating it to serve the divine causality which has transformed the world at its root and which continues to transform it, through active love.

Part of that mandate is the embrace of a more ascetical spirit for theology, a recognition of limit, in the face of the living reality of revelation and how it makes itself known to us. This has necessitated a reflection upon our own intellectual history and sources, laying bare the persistent though subtle transgressions of speculative reason in the face of the reality of incarnational revelation in the world. Chapters 3 and 4 have called repeatedly for the return to a 'critical' or self-limiting methodological integrity in theology, pulling it away from speculative theologies where it becomes self-referential, or self-sustaining and ultimately tautological. At every stage Chapters 3 and 4 have argued for a theology which in its conceptual or discursive exercise is oriented to the authoritative limits and resistances with which it finds itself confronted in incarnational revelation. The living Christ, who is the risen Christ *ex nihilo* and the ascended Christ, cannot be encountered 'representationally' by theology at all, cannot become part of any conceptual system. The reality of revelation, in its fundamentally causal character, comes to us rather through a primary attentiveness to sensibly embodied reality where revelation declares itself *as* a divinely causal disclosure; and also, as a consequence of this, as a demand on our practical willing: as a summons and a sending. It comes to us as new creation.

The doctrinal and methodological work of the first four chapters lays out a clear alternative to a theology in flight from the sensibly resistant and disruptive particularity of the real. Transformation Theology bends theology back to the primary place of revelation, which is the sensible reality of our ordinary living. At its causal origin, we encounter revelation theologically as 'finality of non-resolution', which means to say as divine disruption *ex nihilo*, like that of St Paul's Damascus road experience, which possesses all the authority of the real but which escapes our representational conceptuality (just as it escaped his). We ourselves do not know the living body in exactly that way; but we do know it through the divinely causal communication of its life to us, in and through Spirit, and in the command of grace, which gives new meaning to our lives.

These two forms of critical reflection then, the one doctrinal and the other methodological, combine to give significantly greater room to the power of God within our everyday reality of space and time. The theme of transformation embeds that power ineradicably in the actuality of our world, while the appeal to a divine causality recognizes that we know this power both by its transformative effects on the world and by its transforming demands as a sending back into the world. This leads in turn to a new theological directedness, which is an embrace of the spatio-temporal order and our sensible experience as being the proper place in which God comes to meet us. Such an openness to the real is distinctive however, since it is, at its foundation, a Christological realism, which is to say it is the embrace of the world as the domain of God's self-revelation and transformative power, in accordance with the transformation already irreversibly realized in the humanity of Christ, for our sake. Thus we can say that Transformation Theology seeks to be attentive to the power of God as it shapes us in our particularity, and in our ecclesial commissioning, from within the life of the senses and not to their exclusion. The new life of discipleship is one which is constantly disrupted by the divine causality, often through the transformative ethical demands brought upon us by the lives and circumstances of others, in ways which make real in the world the generative, life-giving creativity which belongs to new creation. All of this begins therefore to describe a new ecclesial existence in the world which we now discover to have been taken up into the incarnation in ways that change fundamentally our own life orientation.

On this basis, Chapters 5 and 6 then explore the further mandate of the Spirit for Transformation Theology through an attentiveness to the movement of divine love within the intractable challenges encountered in human living. World hunger is a major, if not the major, ethical challenge of our times, and it is an issue in which we are all implicated, whatever our politics or social orientation, whether we choose to acknowledge the challenge or not. Just as there is an aporia at the heart of our recitation of the creed, to do with the living body of Christ in the world, so too there is an aporia at the heart of our own social and political lives, which are challenged in their affluence by the arbitrary and terrible destruction of so many innocent lives. Chapters 5 and 6 suggest that we must think the two together. We must learn to live positively and creatively in the light of both. The living body of Christ which disrupts us in the creed, disrupts us also at the point where we allow ourselves to become aware of the immense suffering of others through acute deprivation and poverty. Both are one, in the unity of the gospel.

In sum, the Transformation Theology presented in this volume is distinctive in several ways. First, it proposes a model of Christian thought and life which points us back to the sensible real, to the actuality of space and time, as the place in which we should expect to encounter the reality of God, not as one thought but as one encountered in embodied resistance and disruption. It is a model which is best conceived of in terms of a new directionality, which is to say that it understands itself to be in the service of a divine causality which leads us more deeply *into* the world, and thus more deeply into the transformation which God has already irreversibly accomplished in the world, making us part of what is incomparably bigger than ourselves. It is an acknowledgement of the power of divine love and the directionality of that love, which is always received as the following that is discipleship. And so the directionality or the 'pointing' which defines Transformation Theology is on the one hand a pointing which knows that it has no other choice – if it is to be true to its doctrinal inheritance, stripped of its 'idealistic' illusions – but to be brought back to a Pauline reception of Spirit and body. And on the other, it knows that it has no other choice – as *theo*-logy – but to point to the living body of Christ that is in the world. For if there is no such body, and no such divine causality, then there is no need either for Christian theology of any kind, except perhaps to imagine it.

Secondly, the uniquely collaborative character of the book, which has evolved under a very different method of working from that of a multi-authored volume of essays, has entailed a particular kind of open, interconfessional sociality of common labour, critique and exchange. It therefore instantiates and initiates a theological model which itself realizes the intrinsic openness of Transformation Theology as content. It is a model moreover which shows the permeability of this theology as a new trajectory: it points to the further development of new collaborations as the principal themes of Transformation Theology are thought through in areas not yet touched upon in this book, or only provisionally engaged with. This kind of sociality, or method, will perhaps prove to be coextensive with the reach of Transformation Theology itself.

Thirdly, it is a theology which finds its focus in a fundamental area of doctrinal and philosophical theology which is prior to any confessional differentiation. This is not a failure to acknowledge the extent to which theology, like Christian life itself, is traditioned in confessional ways, but it is to assert the possibility that this new theology, by virtue of its fundamental character, can address all the mainstream Christian traditions. It will of course be necessary to develop Transformation Theology in terms of different confessional emphases at some point in the future if it is to engage more fully with the life of the Churches, as we believe that it should.

And so we are led finally to the question of what kinds of tasks fall to Transformation Theology. Whatever these tasks are, they will once again crucially involve a refocusing of Christian doctrine itself, under the referential guidance of the scriptures, back to the real world of sensible human embodiment as the indispensable site of incarnational revelation, and therefore as the generative ground for theological attentiveness. But for Systematic Theology, with all its intellectual and cultural resources, to point back to the world, means then also to become open to new vistas, challenges and debates. Its ecclesial commitments have to involve engagement with and service to the transformative power of the Spirit at work in the world. In other words, this is a theology which in addition to its central uplifting themes of comfort has to engage also with those difficult themes of human life: natural evils leading to despair or aggression (illness, ageing, famine), moral evils leading to divisiveness and conflict among individuals and peoples (conflict, poverty), as well as those which characterize contemporary public debate and seeking after the common good: multiculturalism, human rights, migration, bio-ethics. Progress here may be seen not so much in the startling resolution of such problematics as in discovering new ways of authentic living in the face of them: patiently following and fostering the Spirit's transformative work.

And then there has to be a further theological task for Transformation Theology, which reflects its own situatedness in the reference to world that is at the heart of the Church's confession. World itself has to be a theme from which this theology draws life. And there is no more fundamental problematic to have. For the Christian faith, as a Creator and creation-centred faith, lays claim to the world, of necessity. And precisely in doing so, it has to allow the world its own integrity. It is this recognition that the world has to be lived, dis-covered, explored, above all, with others (who may not share our creation-centred convictions), which makes the work of Transformation Theology such a potentially fertile one. It opens up the possibility of new kinds of engagement with other discourses, and with other religions – especially our neighbouring ones, Judaism and Islam, which share our commitment to living in world as *created*. And it means also that those who practise this kind of theology will always be both at the very centre of Christian belief, and yet also at its furthest borders: where belief meets non-belief and other belief. The self-critical role of Transformation Theology, its required humility, allows us to think both at the centre and at the borders, but requires us also to put trust in something else, something which itself attends to both particular and universal, centre and margin, and which itself incomparably makes real the vital generosity that is the ground of revelation. However diverse the tasks of Transformation Theol-ogy as such, it will always remain fundamental to the theologian's work, in the service of the Church, to point in faith to that which we have called, during the course of this book, the living and transformative body of Christ in the world.

Index